IMAGES
of America

SOUTH NORFOLK

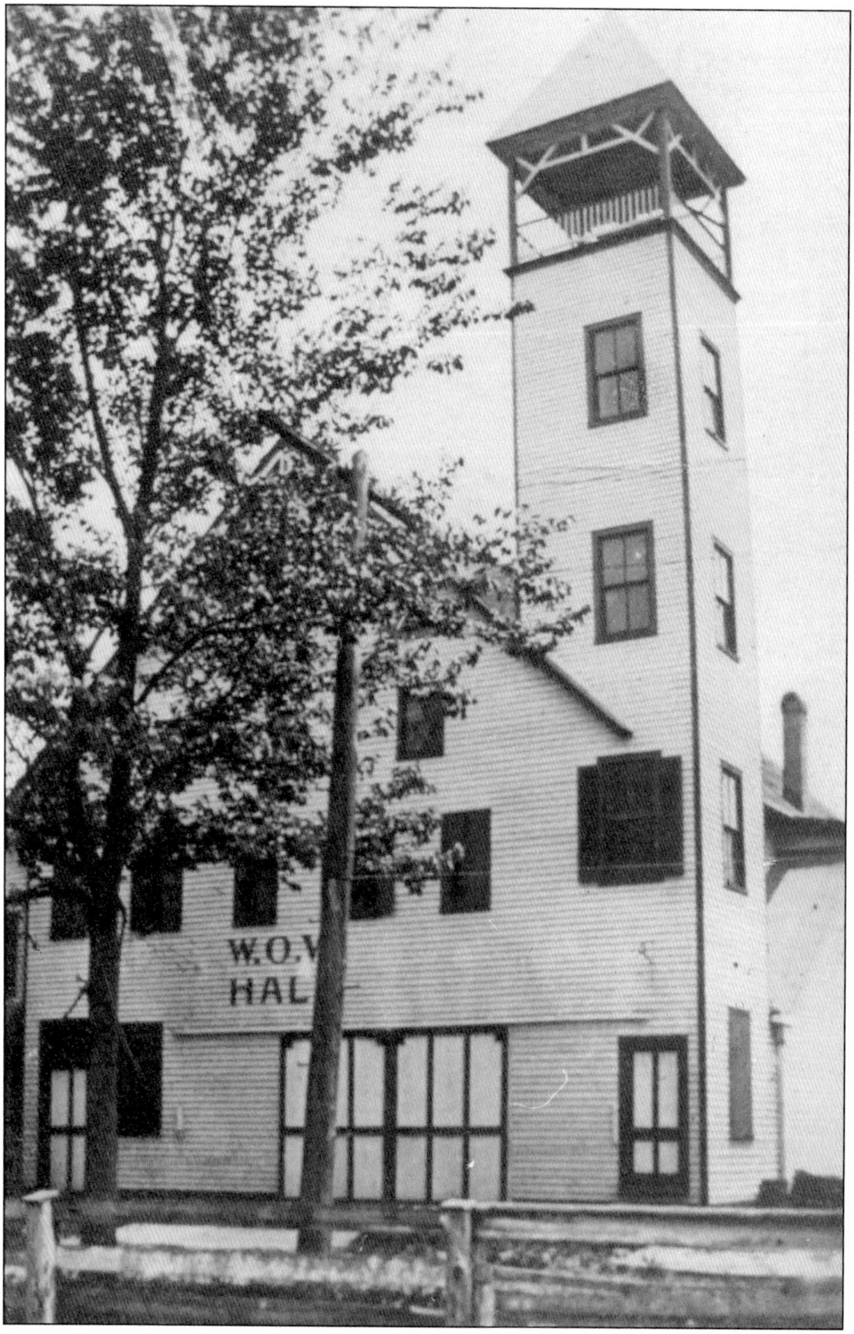

In 1915, members of the South Norfolk Volunteer Fire Department constructed this building on Twenty-second Street. It was to serve as the second fire station, but when the note came due, the department was unable to raise the necessary funds and had to sell the building. It was purchased by the Woodmen of the World (W.O.W.) lodge. On March 10, 1920, the W.O.W. Hall, as it became known, burned. When it was repaired, the bell tower was removed. During its existence, the hall served as the police station, court, town hall, election headquarters, boys club, Junior Chamber of Commerce, and possibly others.

IMAGES
of America

SOUTH NORFOLK

Raymond L. Harper

ARCADIA
PUBLISHING

Copyright © 1999 by Raymond L. Harper
ISBN 978-0-7385-0217-5

Published by Arcadia Publishing
Charleston, South Carolina

Printed in the United States of America

Library of Congress Catalog Card Number: Applied for.

For all general information contact Arcadia Publishing at:
Telephone 843-853-2070
Fax 843-853-0044
E-Mail sales@arcadiapublishing.com
For customer service and orders:
Toll-Free 1-888-313-2665

Visit us on the Internet at www.arcadiapublishing.com

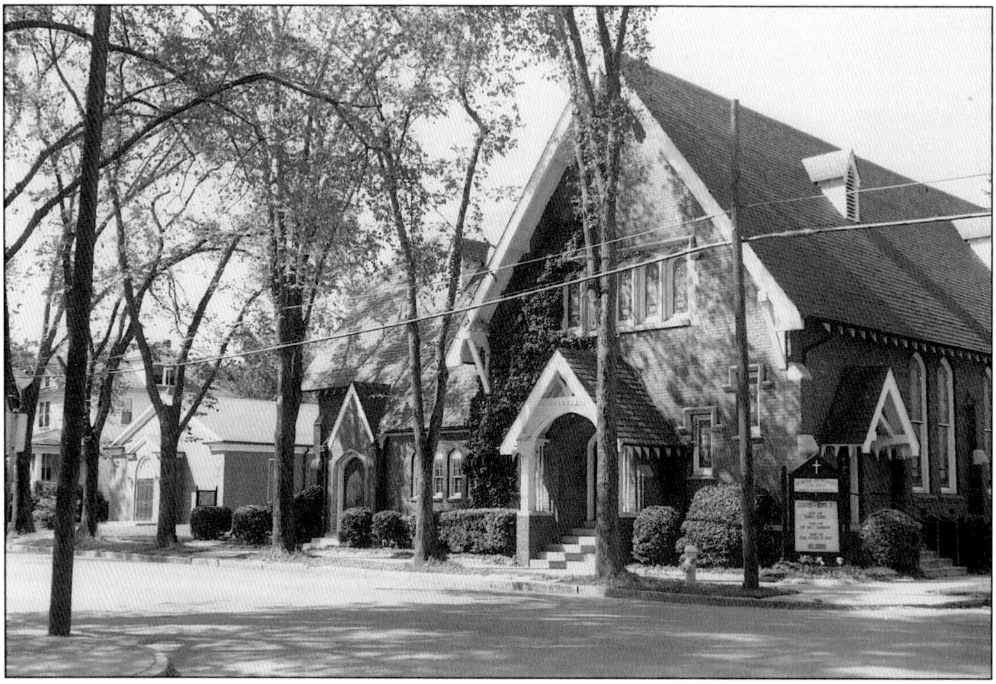

This was the Chesapeake Avenue Methodist Church as it appeared on Monday, September 8, 1958. The church, which was designed in the English parish style, was constructed on the corner of Chesapeake Avenue and Ohio Street. The cornerstone was built in 1919 and laid on Saturday, January 31, 1920. The church was built at a cost of $50,000. The new fellowship hall can be seen to the left of the main building. This structure has since been replaced by a modern sanctuary that was consecrated December 20, 1970.

Contents

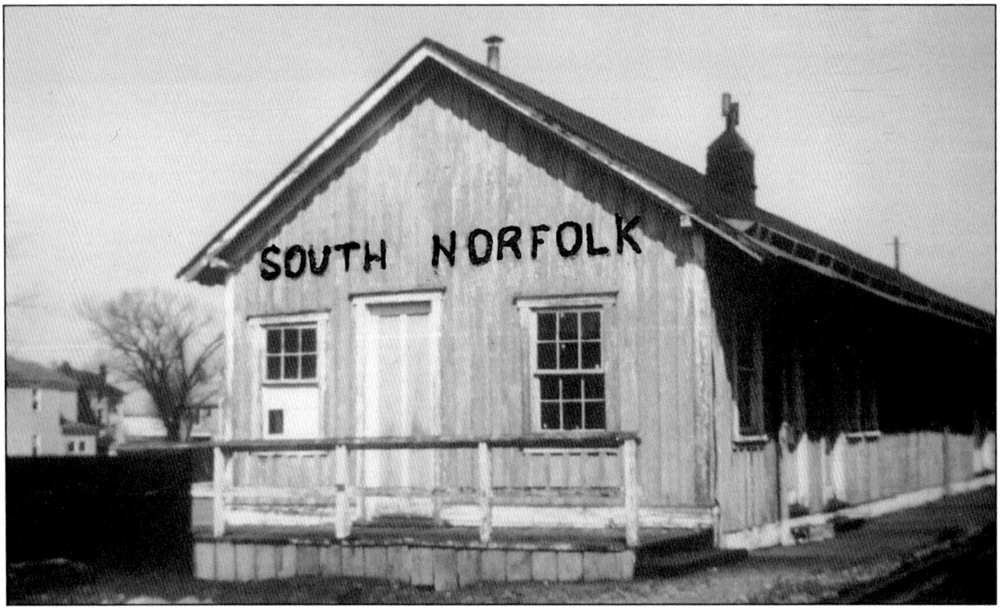

The Norfolk & Western railroad station, which was located on Seaboard Avenue at Guerriere Street, dated back to the 1880s. It was there that clothing manufactured at the Elizabeth and Chesapeake knitting mills at the turn of the century was shipped by rail to northern markets. It was also there that draftees from both World War I and II boarded the train to Richmond where they received their induction physicals. During the author's youth (1930s and early 1940s), the stationmaster was Mr. Sutherland, who resided on Ohio Street in South Norfolk. The station was torn down shortly after March 1962. The house in the left background was the home of Miss Lula Briggs, who taught in the South Norfolk Grammar School for many years.

Acknowledgments

I would like to express my sincere appreciation to the many individuals who so generously answered my never-ending line of questioning and to those who supplied many of the photographs used in *South Norfolk*. Former mayor Linwood L. Briggs Jr. and Frank L. Portlock Jr. were the largest contributors of pictures of the once thriving City of South Norfolk. Others who furnished photographs and information of equal importance were the following: former San Francisco 49ers great Ed Beard; Mrs. N.A. Blevins; Ms. Amelia Burton; Ms. Fannie Virginia Butts; Mr. Vincent Curtis; Mr. Quinton C. Davis III; Mr. Hardy Forbes; Ms. Lil Hart, clerk of the circuit court of the City of Chesapeake; Ms. Vernell Holloman; Mr. Jimmy Johnson; Dr. Raymond Jones; Mr. Kennith Kimmons; Ms. Anne Davis Kristiansen; Mr. James R. Rock; Mr. Richard Spratley; Lieutenant Paul Sutton, Chesapeake Police Department; Ms. Anne Grimes Tregembo; Ms. Belle Warden; Mr. Ray White; Ms. Kathleen Wilson; Mr. Richard Womack; and Mr. Stanley Zedd.

I dedicate this book to my wife of 50 years, Mrs. Emma Rock Harper, to our two daughters, Shari and Karen, our son-in-law, John Rudis, and our two grandchildren, Alexa Raye and Colby John Rudis.

INTRODUCTION

On November 18, 1618, the Virginia Company's London Council ordered that the Virginia Colony be divided into four large corporations. For purposes of local administration each was to be a parish of the Church of England, and was to have its own chief executive and military officer and, later, either justices or a court of law. Since each corporation was an ecclesiastical parish, it was required to have a minister, churchwardens, and vestry.

Between the years of 1632 and 1634 the Virginia Colony was divided into eight shires or counties. The eight original shires were Accawmack, Charles City, Charles River, Elizabeth City, Henrico, James City, Warrosquyoake, and Warwick River. Elizabeth City County extended on both sides of Hampton Roads. The area from which South Norfolk eventually emerged was successively part of Elizabeth City County in 1634, New Norfolk County in 1636, Lower Norfolk County in 1637, and Norfolk County in 1691. In 1639, South Norfolk was part of the Southern Shore Parish, and soon after 1643, it was included in the Elizabeth River Parish. South Norfolk as a community had its beginning in 1661 when the Southern Branch Chapel of the Church of England was built on a site between Scuffletown Creek and Jones' Creek in the vicinity of present-day Lakeside Park. There were settlers before then, but the opening of the chapel marked the beginning of the formal record keeping of events like births, deaths, and marriages. Upon division of the Elizabeth River Parish in 1761, the area became a part of the St. Brides Parish.

The area that became South Norfolk experienced some settlement during the Colonial period but remained rural until the late 19th century. The City of Norfolk, located across the Eastern Branch of the Elizabeth River, did not reach its full potential until after the post-Civil War depression, when railroads began to bring coal and produce from the west and south. The new railroads were a boon to Norfolk and also to the farms and villages of Norfolk County. Norfolk's location on the Elizabeth River gave it a prime position for shipping, but prohibited a natural expansion across the river's Eastern Branch. When the railroads came through Norfolk County, they encouraged development all along the line. New industries grew up along the Eastern and Southern Branches of the Elizabeth River, and new businesses and housing appeared near the railroad line.

Just prior to 1870, the entire southside was considered Berkley. Berkley was the village adjacent to the land that became South Norfolk and was incorporated as a town in 1890. Although several homes had already been built in the area, information indicates that developers began to make plans for development of South Norfolk as early as 1889. This land, south of Berkley and Norfolk, began to be developed by the laying out of streets and building lots. The farm comprising the land between Berkley and what is now Poindexter Street was known as the Green House tract. It was purchased by Alvah H. Martin and others for the sum of $3,500, divided into lots, and put upon the market under the name of Elmsley. Elmsley was bounded by Poindexter, Eighteenth, Liberty, and "B" Streets. The land between "B" and "D" Streets was owned by W.S. Butt. Around 1887 there was a footbridge across the creek at the south end of

Main Street which connected Berkley to the Butt plantation in South Norfolk. Some years later, a large part of Mr. Butt's land was purchased by the Greenleaf Johnson Lumber Company.

During this period, South Norfolk had grown rapidly by the development of ten different tracts, including farms of considerable acreage. Among the area's first industries were the Roanoke Railroad and Lumber Company, the J.R. Young Fertilizer Company, and Robertson Chemical Company. Prior to September 1919, South Norfolk was a flourishing community in Washington Magisterial District, Norfolk County. On September 19, 1919, the village of South Norfolk was incorporated into a town, and on January 5, 1921, it became a city of the second class. The Virginia Constitution required that a city's population reach 10,000 before that city could qualify as first class. This requirement was met in 1950 when South Norfolk annexed the town of Portlock, and shortly thereafter in 1951, South Norfolk became a city of the first class. On Tuesday, February 13, 1962, city and county voters in a merger referendum approved the consolidation of Norfolk County and the City of South Norfolk. As a result of this action, the City of Chesapeake was born on January 1, 1963.

This book contains photographs from the 1880s to the 1960s. Come along with me to the South Norfolk of long ago. It was a close-knit, very friendly community and a wonderful place to grow up. There were many activities to enjoy. There was the annual church picnic in summer, athletics of all kinds, trips to the Grand Theatre, visits to Jus Maid ice cream store or Gornto's Bakery after the movie, and the beauty of Lakeside Park. When winter came and snow blanketed the small city, an afternoon of ice-skating could sometimes be enjoyed at Lakeside Park or Johnson's Pond. Most of the local businesses used horse and wagon to make their deliveries. Many of the homes relied on kerosene lamps for light, hand pumps for water, coal or wood for heat, and the Johnny served as the necessary house. Many of the buildings and homes are just ghosts of the past, but the pleasant memories will remain forever.

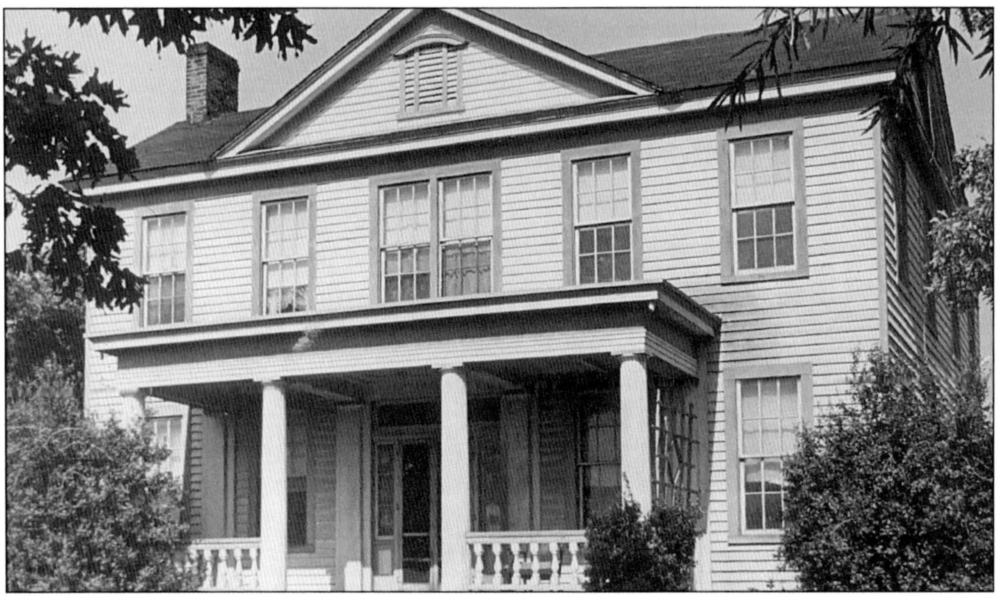

This beautiful old home was the Portlock family homestead, which was built in Norfolk County in 1854. It stood near what is now the corner of Portlock Road and Franklin Street, until 1939. At that time, the house and surrounding farm were purchased by Mr. Robert Rowland. Mr. Rowland's mother, Mrs. Mary Rowland, paid $7,000 to have the old homestead and a small brick annex moved to Mill Dam Creek. The house now faces Hamilton Street in the Portlock section of South Norfolk.

One

Downtown South Norfolk

The downtown or shopping district of early South Norfolk was centered mostly around three blocks of Liberty Street, two blocks of Poindexter Street, and one block of Chesapeake Avenue. In 1873, J.A. McCloud operated the only store in what was then known as McCloudtown. By 1888, S.W. Wilson's grocery business was situated in a small frame building on Liberty Street.

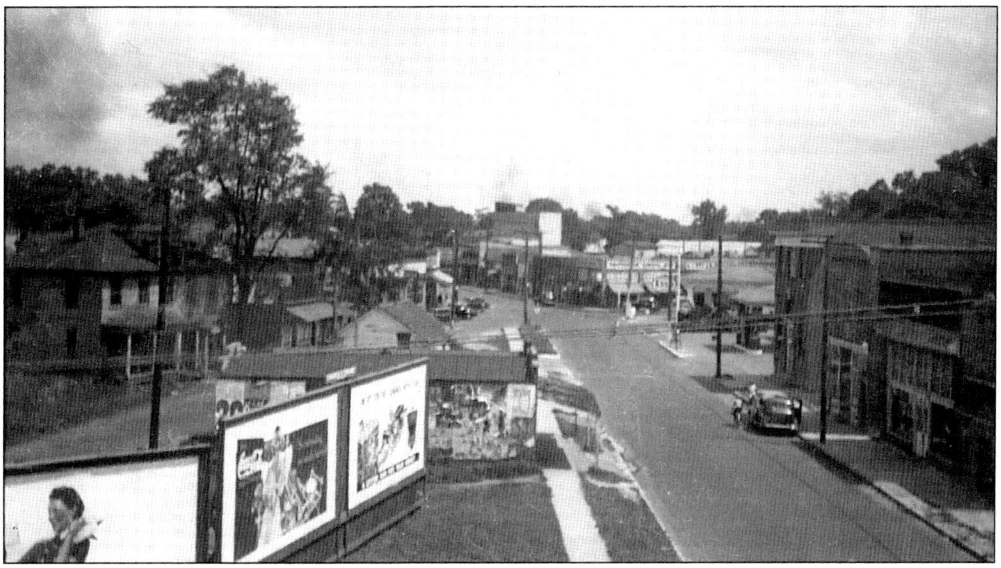

This was the intersection of St. James and Liberty Streets before the South Norfolk overpass was built. The tall building in the right foreground at the corner of Twenty-second and Liberty Streets was the Merchant and Planters Bank. The businesses near the center of the picture are Monroe's Drug Store, Waller's 5¢ to $1 store, and Burfoot's Esso station. This photograph was taken from the second floor of the old municipal building on July 5, 1937, by an unknown photographer.

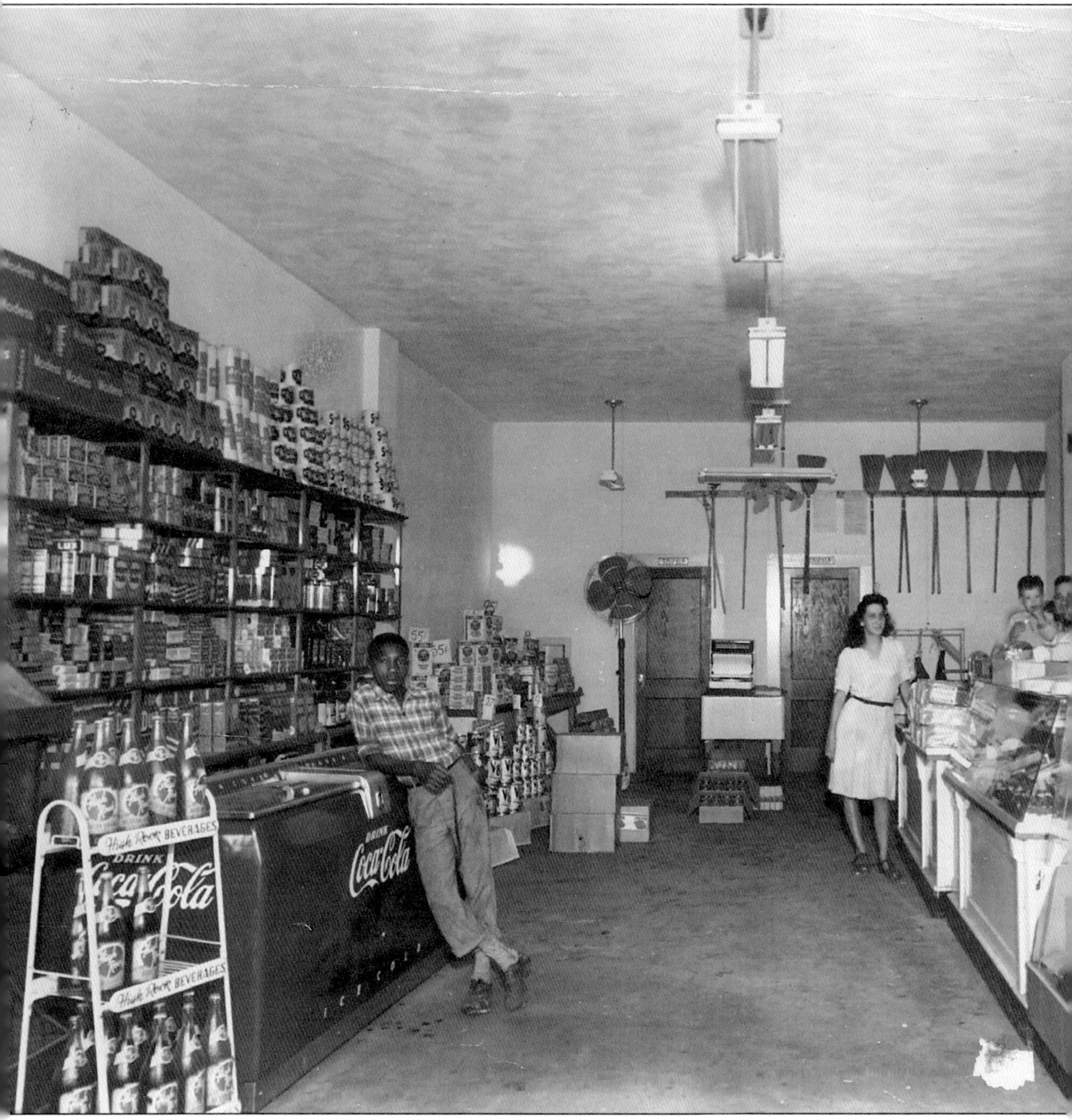

Pictured here on June 1, 1948, is the interior of Zedd's grocery store on Liberty Street near the Belt Line Railroad crossing. Many of the products that Mr. Zedd carried can not be found in present-day super markets. (Henry L. Scheuerman, photographer.)

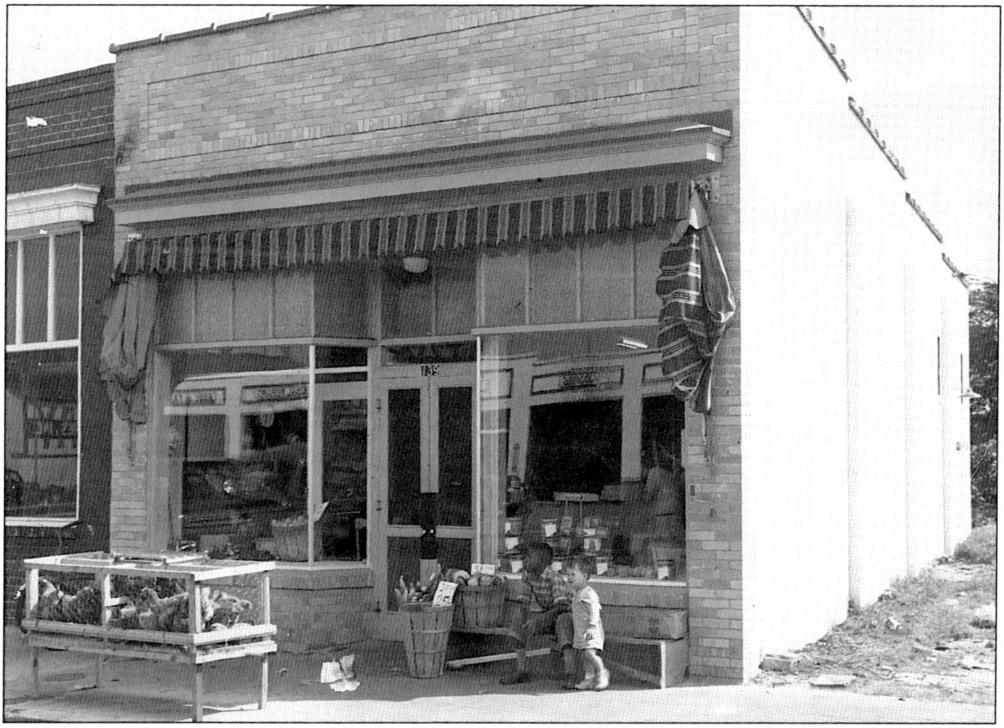

Fifty years ago, dressed chickens were not available in the local markets. As can be seen here, live birds were purchased and the customer had to kill and dress them. The store in this picture was Zedd's grocery at 139 Liberty Street on June 1, 1948. (Henry L. Scheuerman, photographer.)

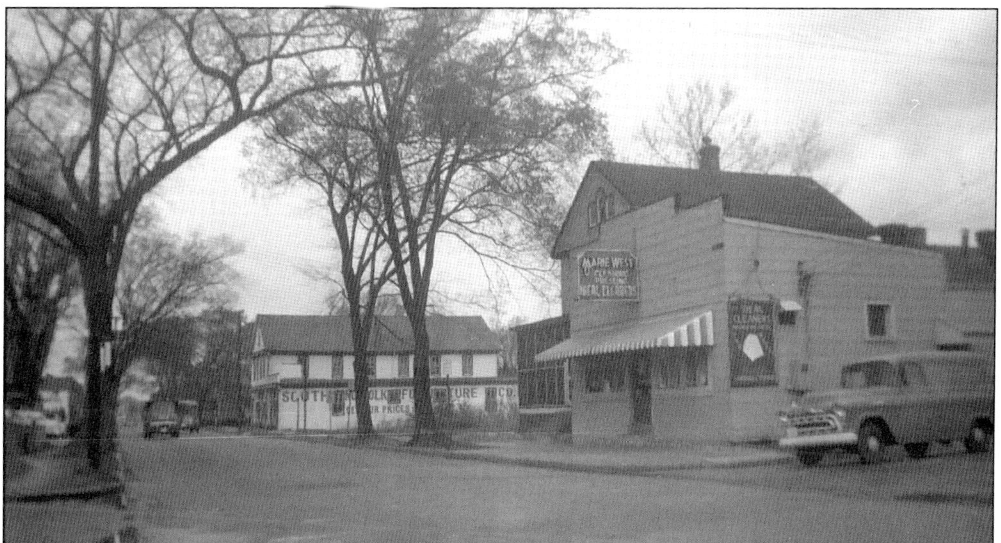

Pictured in May 1959, Marie West's Ideal Cleaners was at 615 Liberty Street on the corner of Twentieth Street. The house next to the cleaners was the home of the Greenough family for many years. There are several vacant lots between the house and Mr. Rawls' South Norfolk Furniture Company at 517–521 Liberty Street.

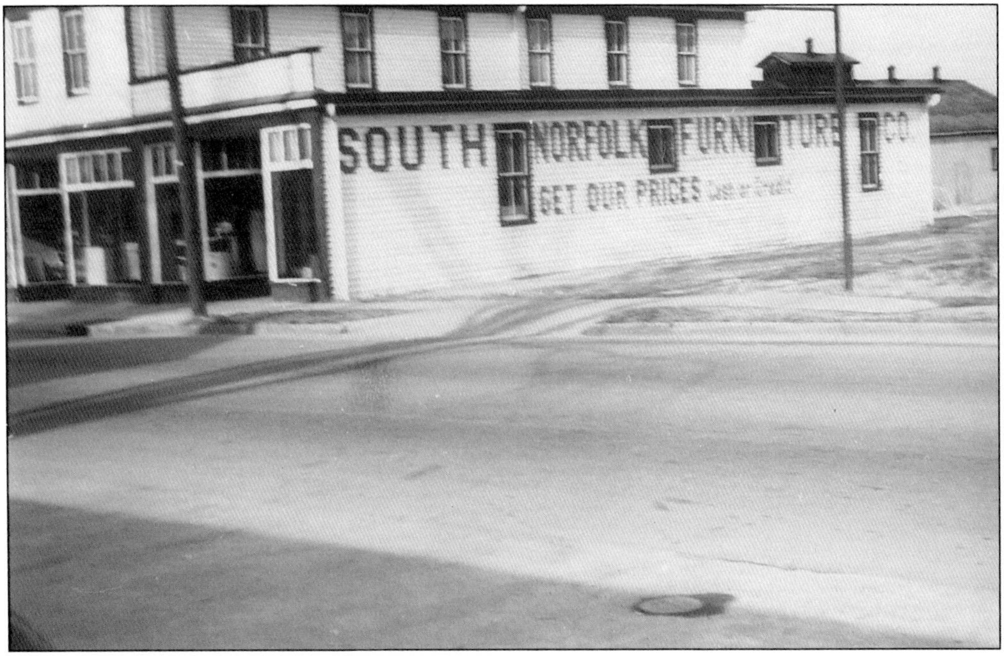

South Norfolk Furniture Company was established by Mr. L.D. Rawls in 1910, when Liberty Street was a dirt road with streetcar tracks running down the middle. This picture was taken in January 1960.

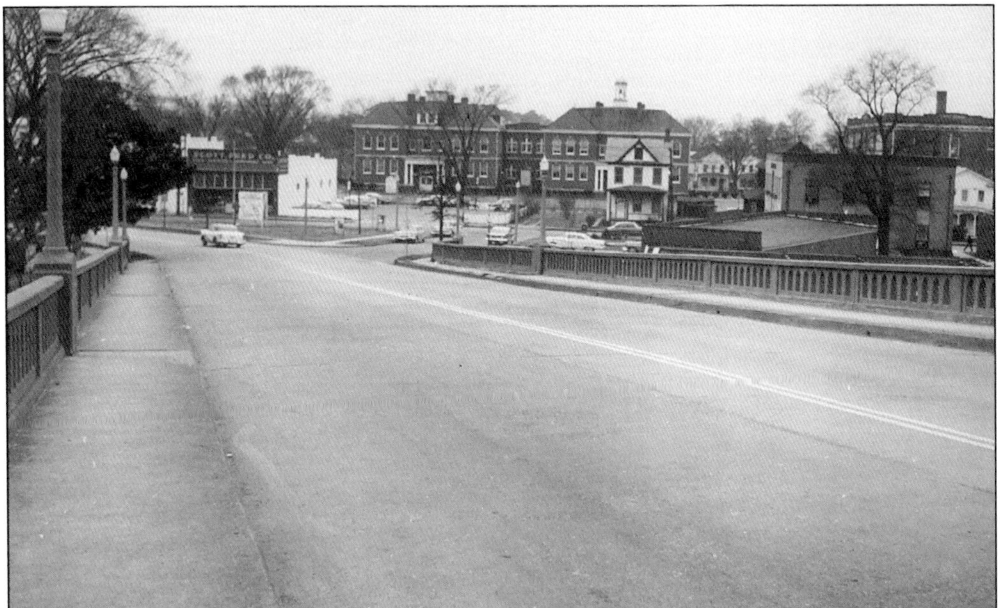

From the South Norfolk overpass, looking toward Liberty Street, one could see part of the downtown section of South Norfolk. The structures on Liberty Street are, from left to right, Scott Feed Co., the two-story house (at one time the Yavner home), the city garage, the municipal building, and the courthouse. The three tall buildings in the background are the South Norfolk Grammar School, *c.* 1959.

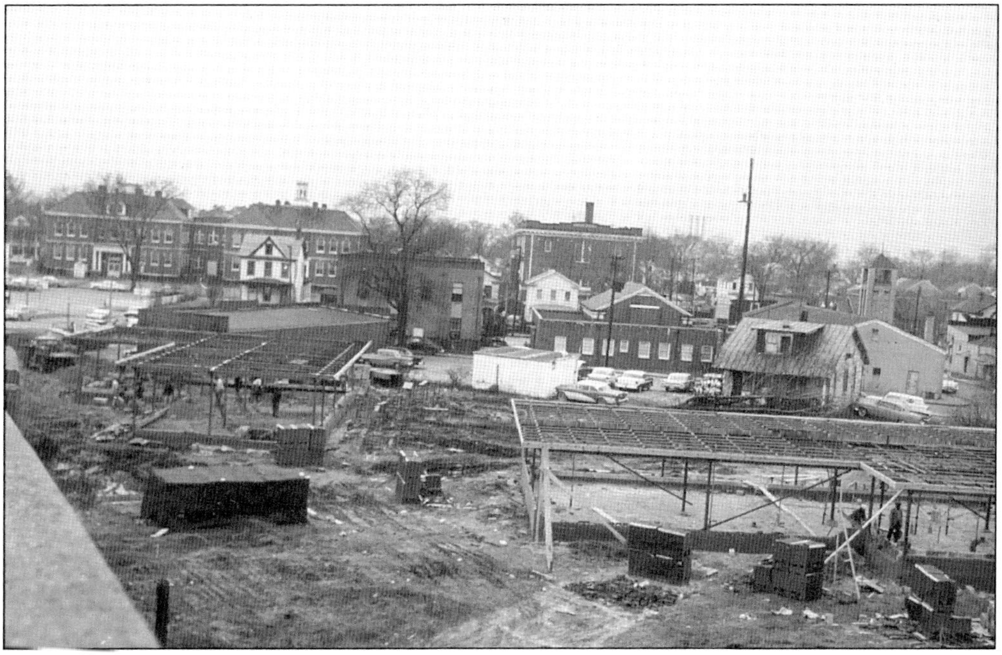

South Norfolk's new welfare and health centers were under construction in the late 1950s. Work was begun on a new police station soon after this picture was taken. When the buildings were complete, all debts had been satisfied.

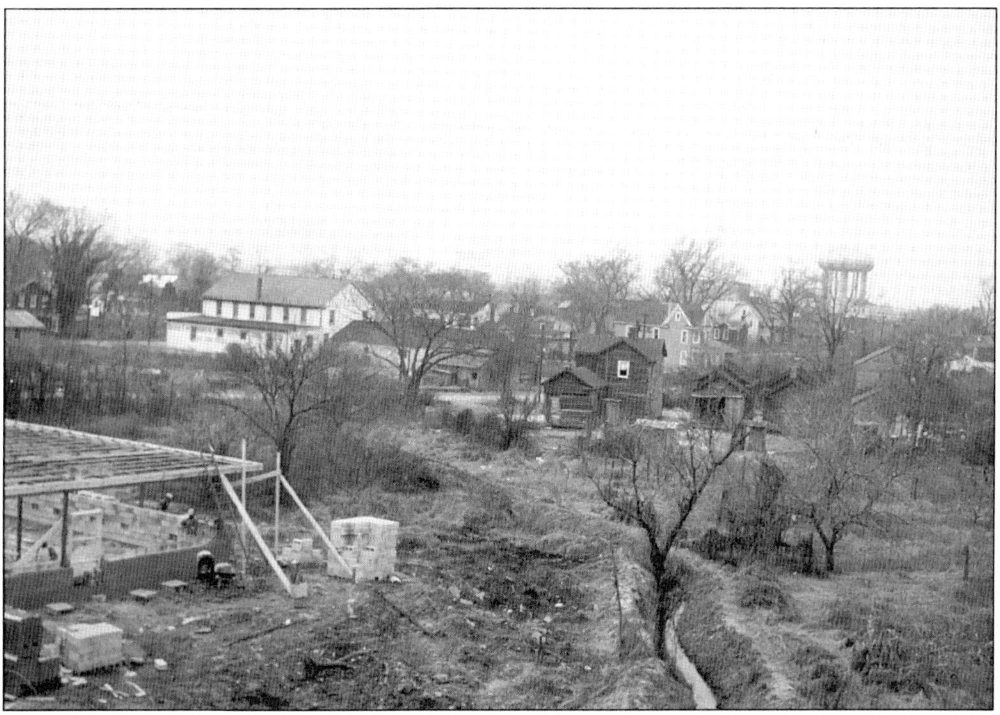

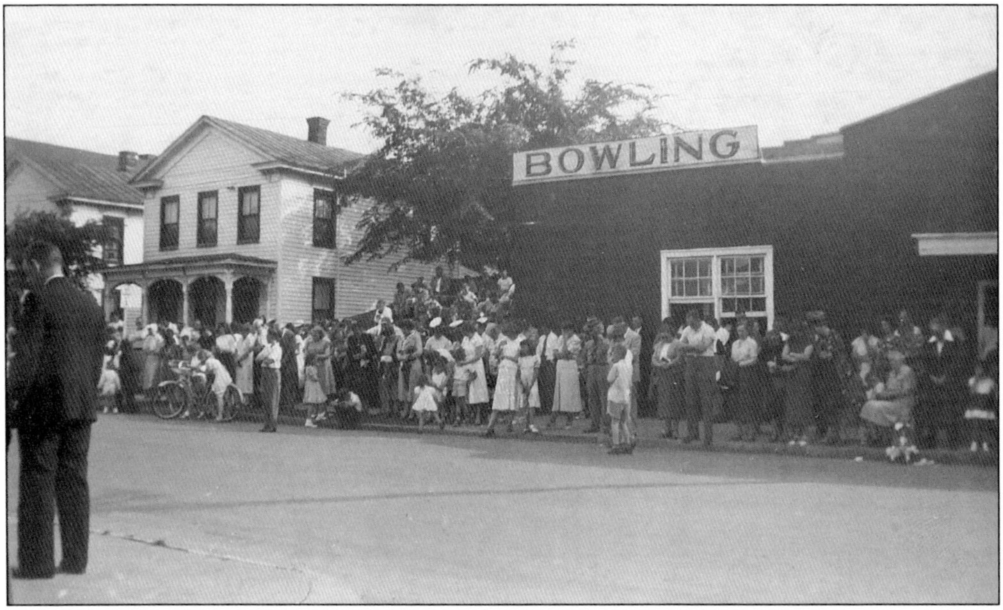

A group of citizens waiting for a parade lined Liberty Street in front of the bowling alley. The bowling alley was located at the corner of Liberty and Twentieth Streets.

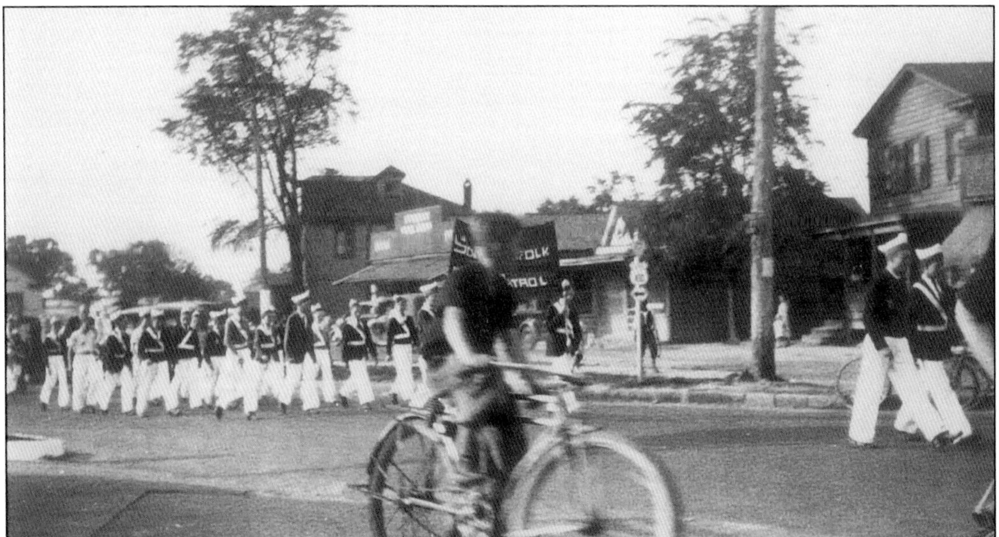

The South Norfolk Grammar School safety patrol parade is seen here passing the intersection of Liberty and St. James Streets in the early 1930s.

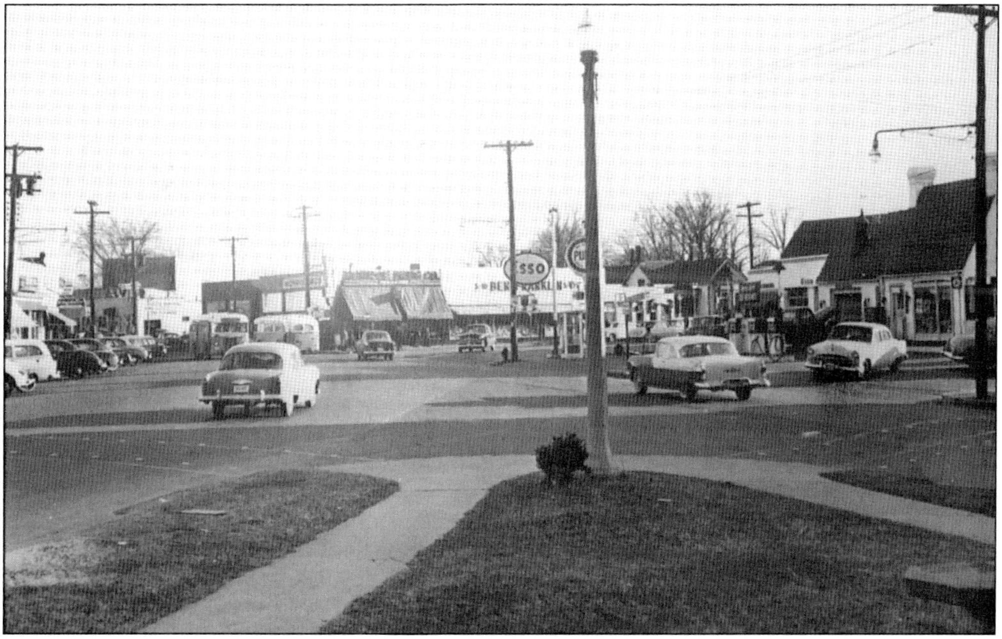

This was South Norfolk's business district as viewed from the lawn of the municipal building in the early 1950s. On the left is the group of stores referred to as Lane's Row, while in the center of the scene is Monroe's Drug Store, Ben Franklin's 5 and 10, the Funk home, Seymour's Esso Station, and, on the right at the corner of Twenty-second and Liberty Streets, is Platt's Pure Oil Station.

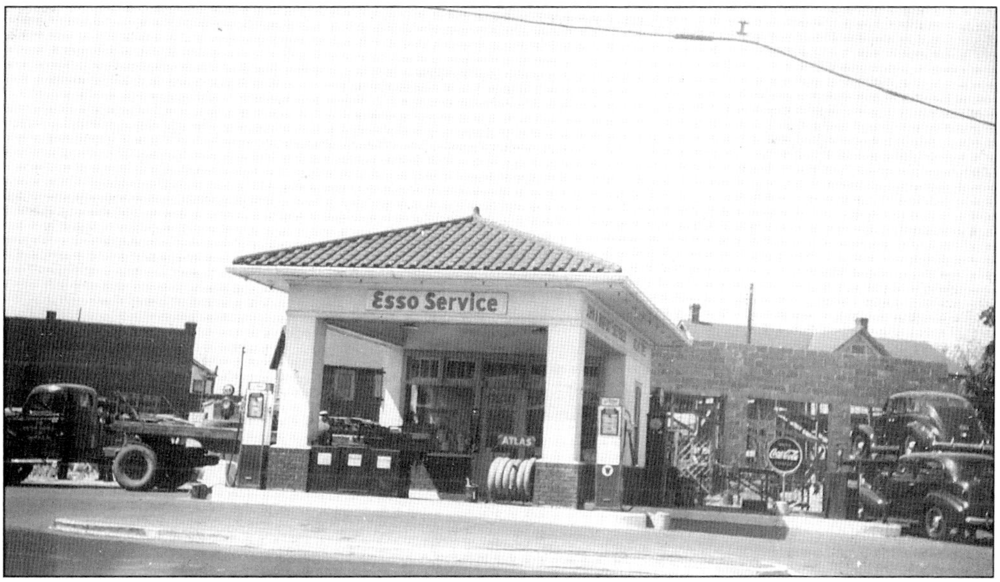

On April 6, 1940, there were three service bays under construction at John Burfoot's Esso Station on Liberty Street. At that time, a gallon of gasoline could be purchased for 18¢.

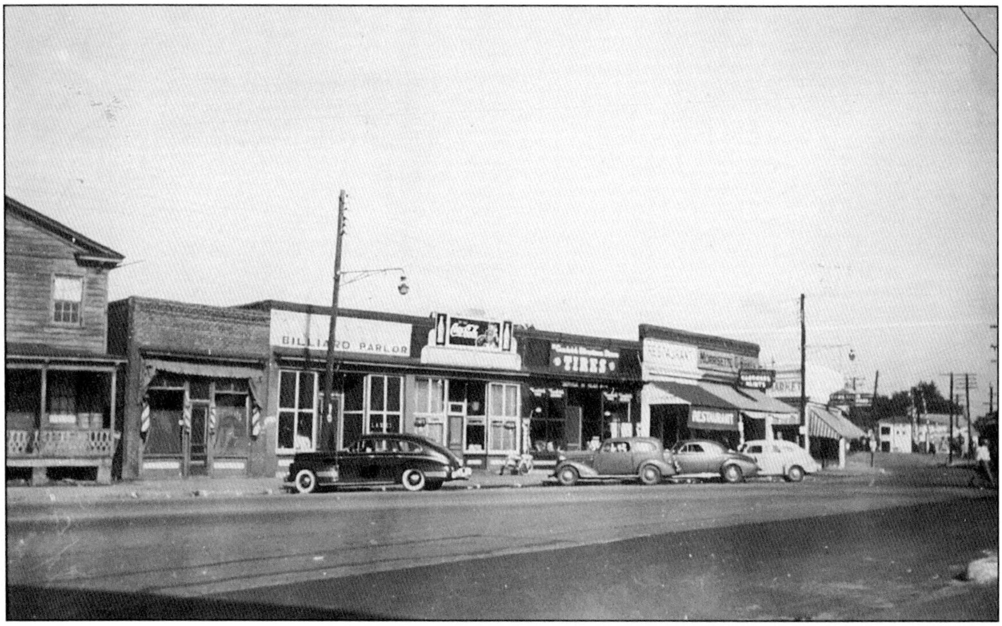

This part of the old business district was known as Lane's Row. The businesses located here in May 1942 are, from left to right, Bryant's Barber Shop, Lane's Billiard Parlor, Abbott's Tavern, the Goodrich Tire Store, McHorney's Restaurant, and Morrisette and Baker Hardware. S.W. Wilson's Market is on the corner in the next block. Around 1961, these buildings were demolished and a branch of Nations Bank was built on the site.

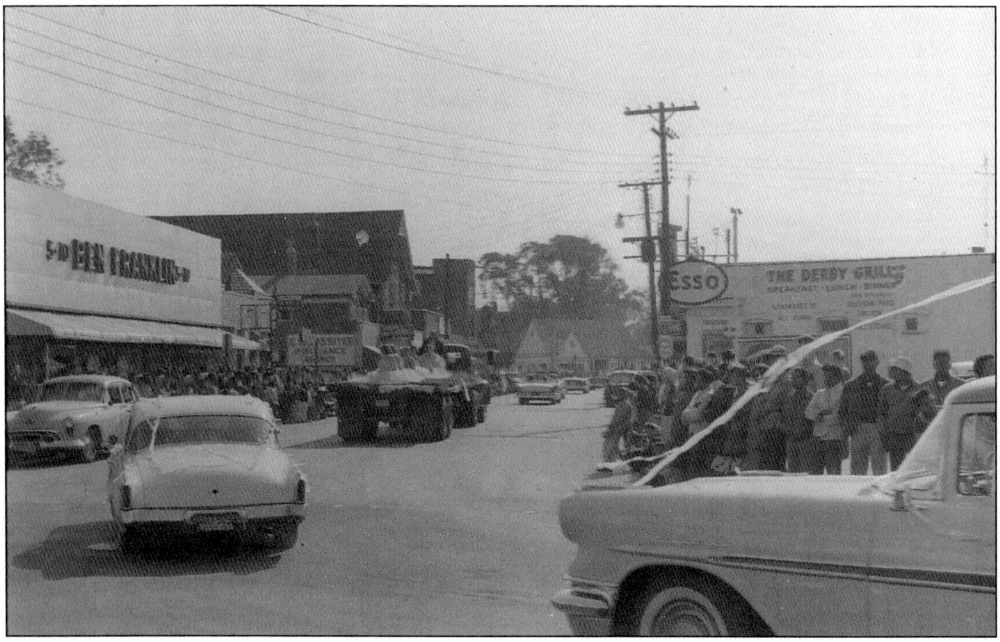

In February 1958, several crowds of people gathered at the corner of Liberty and Poindexter Streets to view a parade. From this intersection, looking toward Chesapeake Avenue, the Ben Franklin Store, Lassiter's Insurance Agency, the Odd Fellow's Hall, and Blanchard's Service Station can be seen. On the right is the Derby Grill and Mr. Seymour's Esso Station.

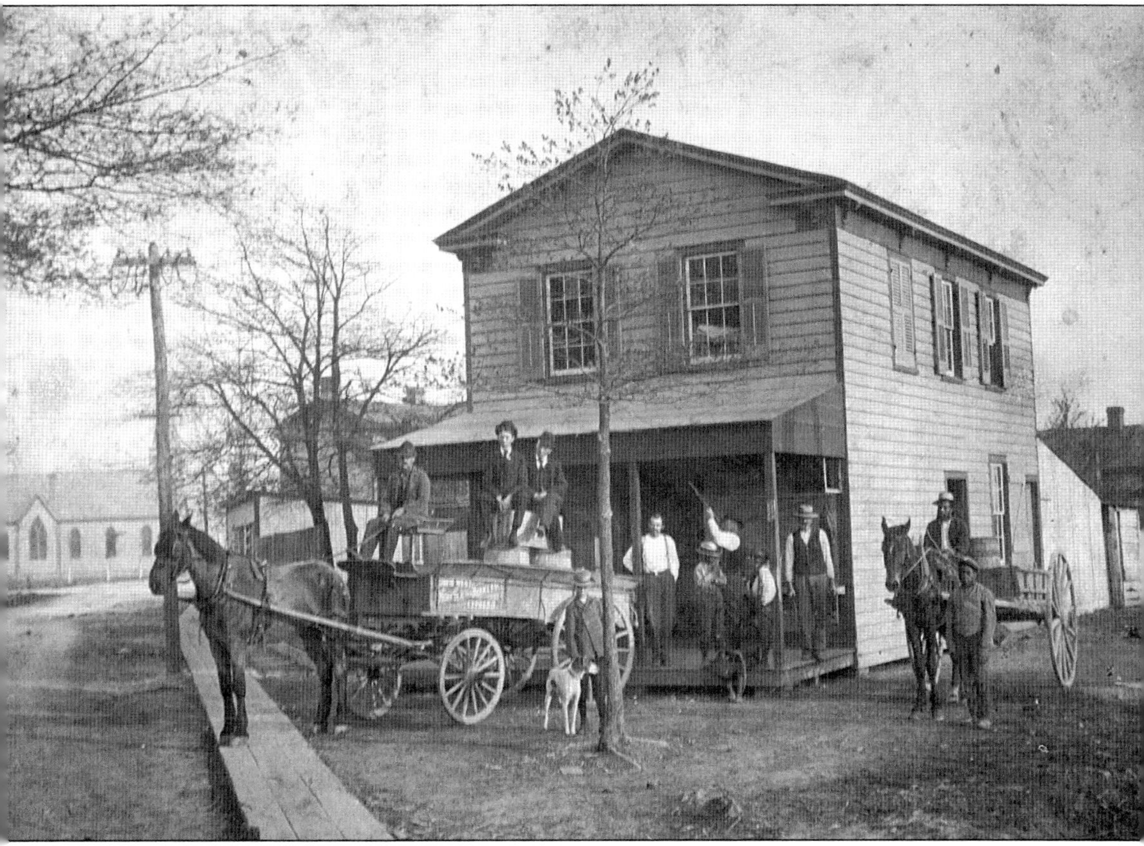

In this c. 1892 picture, we see the location of S.W. Wilson's first grocery store. The horse and wagon backed up to the porch is the Norfolk and Berkley express operated by David West. The church in the left background is the Liberty Street Methodist Episcopal Church, South.

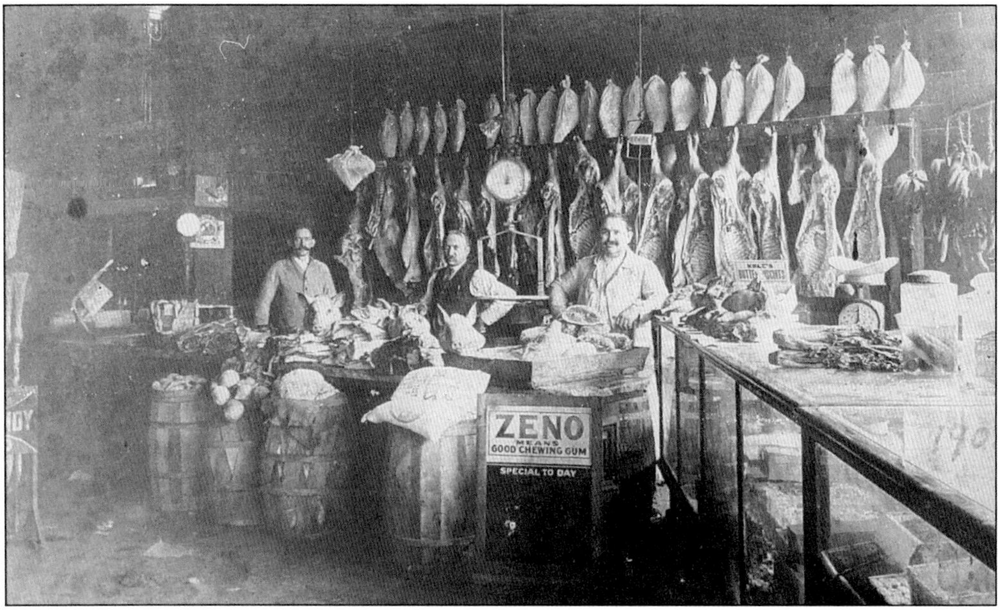

This was the interior of S.W. Wilson's early store on Liberty Street in South Norfolk. Mr. Wilson is the gentleman in the center. A close look reveals hog heads, stalks of celery, and jars of Pepsin gum on the counter tops. The barrels in front of the counters contain flour, turnips, and other vegetables. Hanging in the background are hams, hog carcasses, and stalks of bananas.

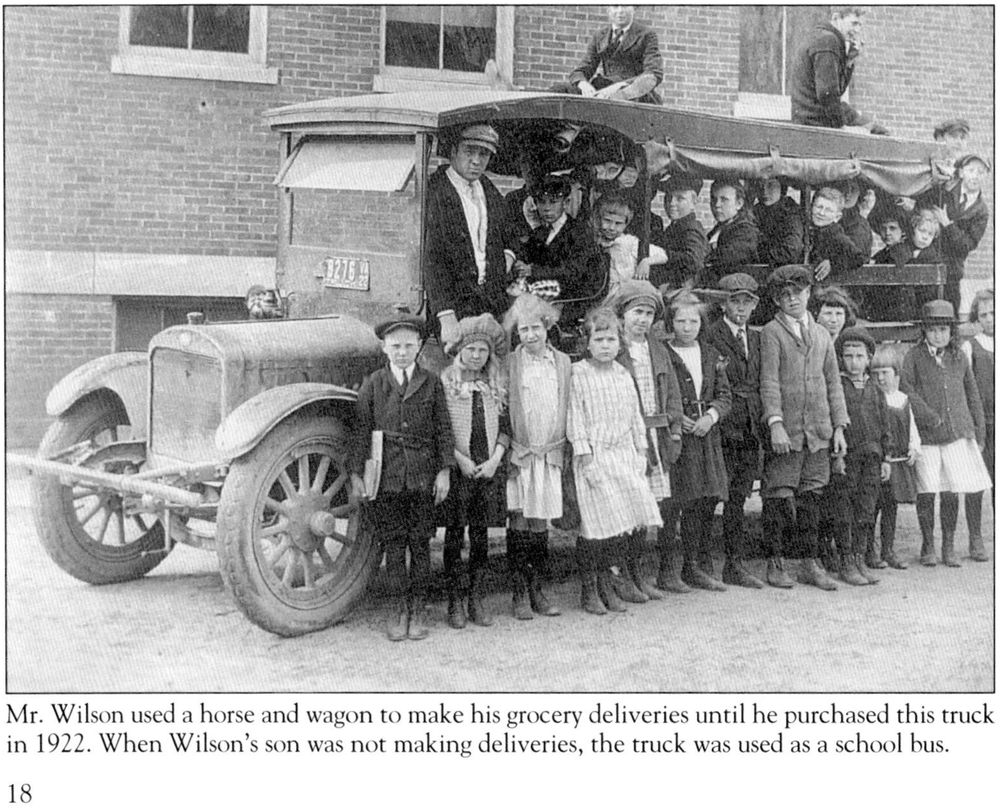

Mr. Wilson used a horse and wagon to make his grocery deliveries until he purchased this truck in 1922. When Wilson's son was not making deliveries, the truck was used as a school bus.

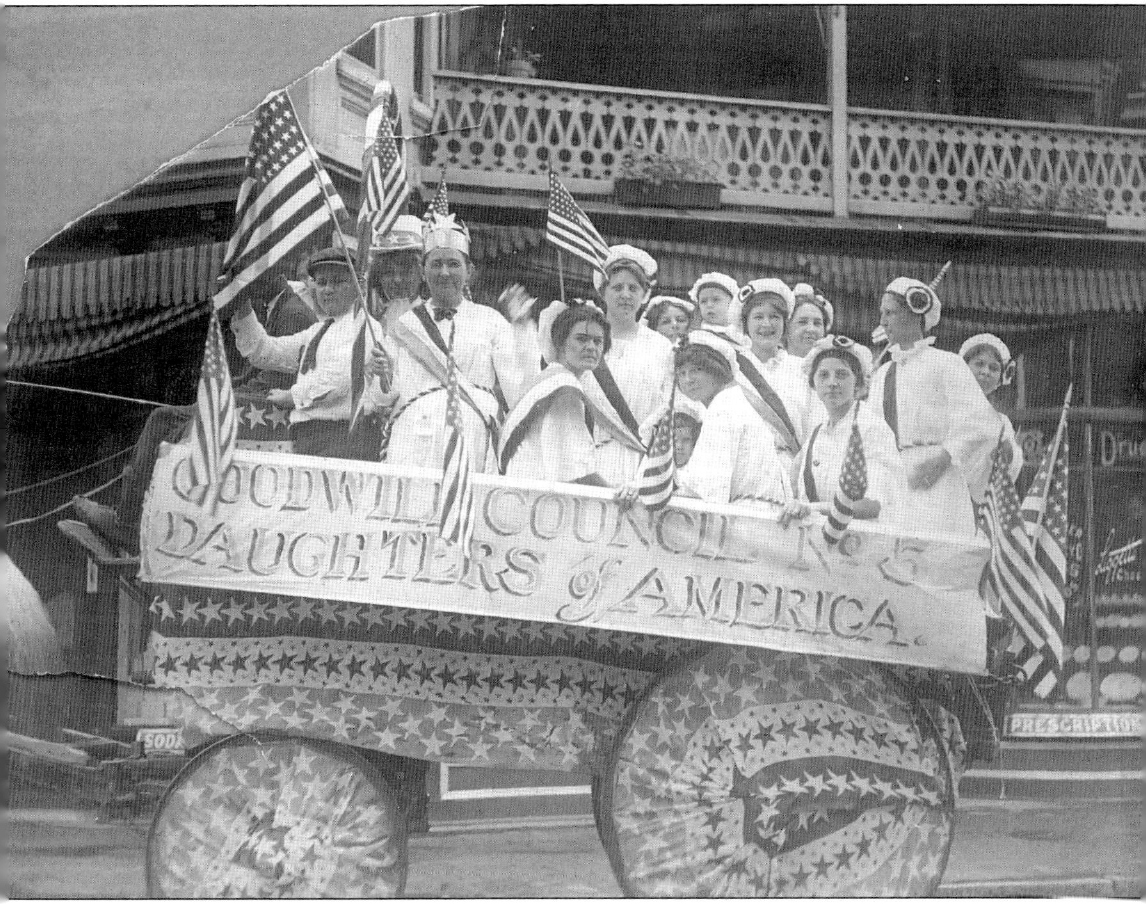

As can be seen by the sign on the wagon, these ladies were members of the Daughter's of America Goodwill Council No. 5. This photograph was most likely taken on the Fourth of July, sometime before 1920 and either on Liberty or Poindexter Street in South Norfolk. The lady seated in the middle of the wagon is Ms. Alice Pearl Morgan.

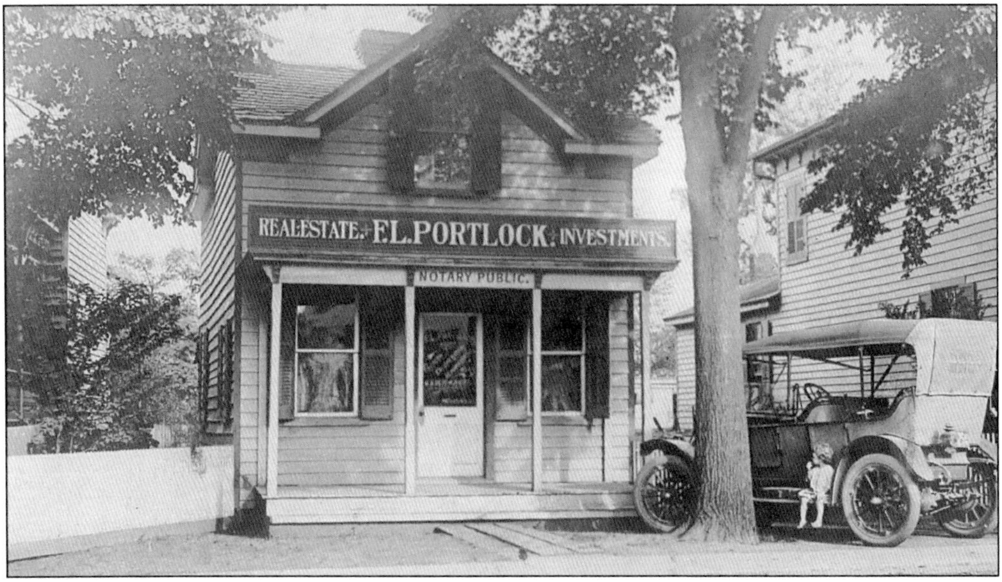

The office of F.L. Portlock was located in what became the 1400 block of Poindexter Street. The location also served as the office of D.W. Lindsey, and later as the shop of T.P. Newbern Jewler and Watch Repair. Mrs. Grace Whitehurst eventually bought the structure. It has been said that this small house once served as a tollbooth in earlier years when Poindexter Street was a toll road. The young boy eating an ice cream cone on the running board of Mr. Portlock's car in this *c.* 1913 image is Billy Morgan.

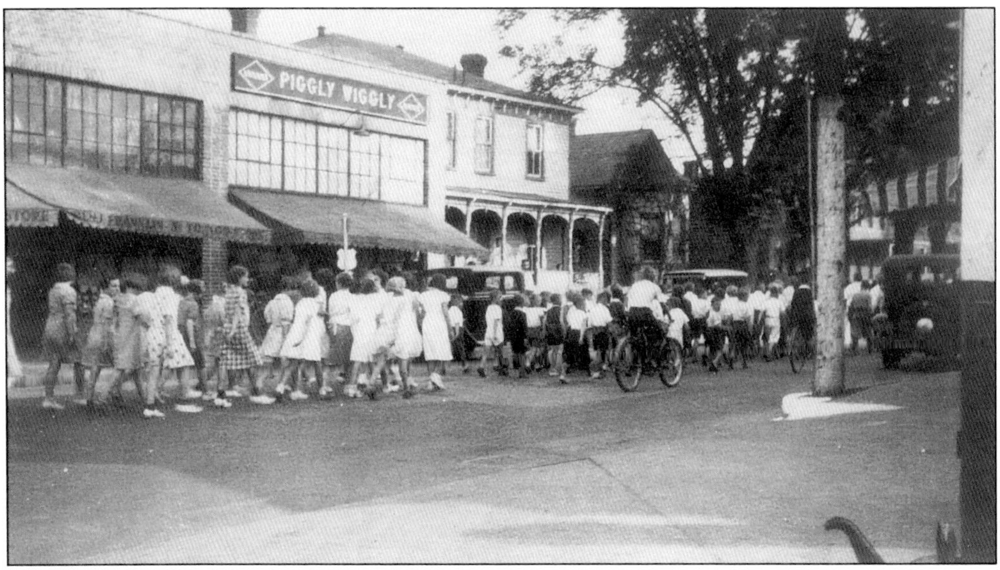

Each year schoolchildren held what was known as a Five Pointer's parade. In order to participate, a child had to pass minimum requirements for physical fitness. The five-point health standards involved weight, vision, hearing, teeth, and throat. Here the children parade down Poindexter Street in the early 1930s. On the left is Mr. W.F. Hanson's Ben Franklin Store, the Piggly Wiggly grocery, a double house, and the home of the Funk family. Captain George Funk built this house in 1894.

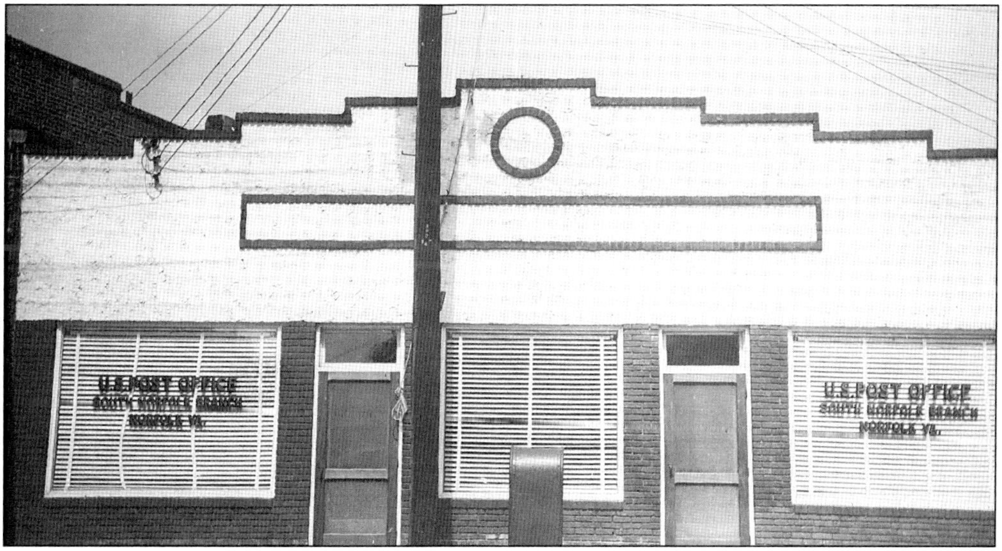

The South Norfolk branch of the Norfolk post office occupied this building constructed by John Burfoot in the 1400 block of Poindexter Street. Earlier post offices were located in J.A. McCloud's grocery store and Preston's Pharmacy.

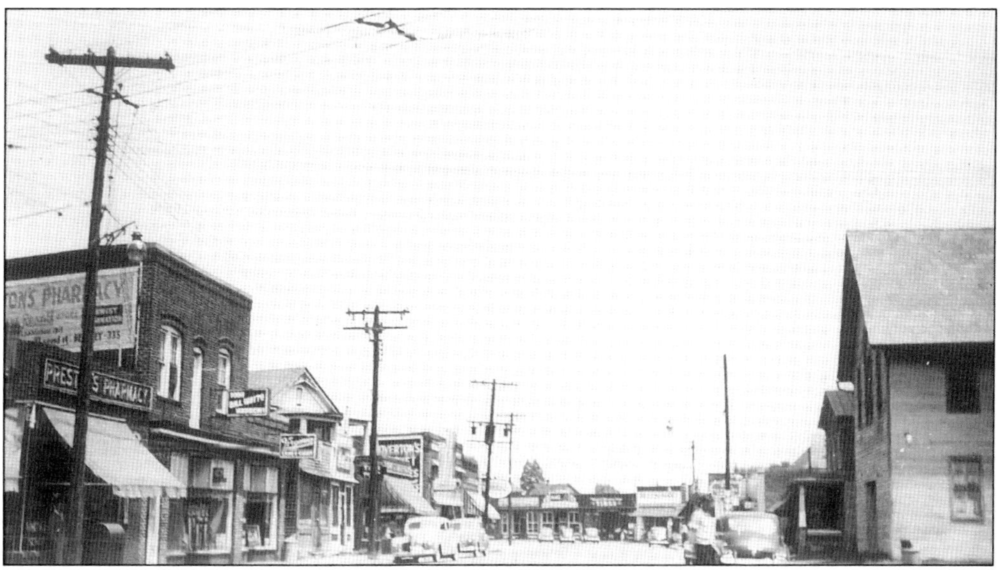

This is the 1400 block of Poindexter Street, looking east, as it appeared on May 17, 1942. The visible businesses on the left side of the street are Preston's Pharmacy, Bill White's Confectionery, Virginia Cleaners, Champion Shoe Repair Factory, Mac's Sandwich Shop, the Grand Leader 5¢ to $1 store, Overton's Market, and the Derby Grill. The large building on the right is the Odd Fellows Hall.

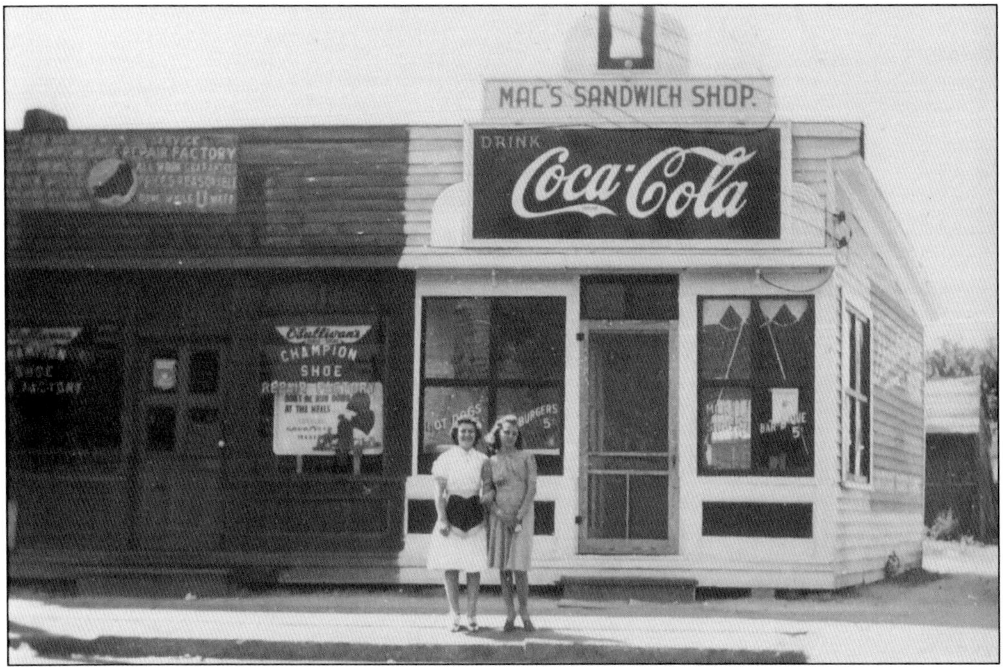

Mac's Sandwich Shop opened in September 1940 at 1411 Poindexter Street and was owned and operated by Bud and Thelma White. Hamburgers, hot dogs, bar-b-ques, and milk shakes were all 5¢ each. Thelma White is the lady on the left. Champion Shoe Repair Factory is the business next to Mac's.

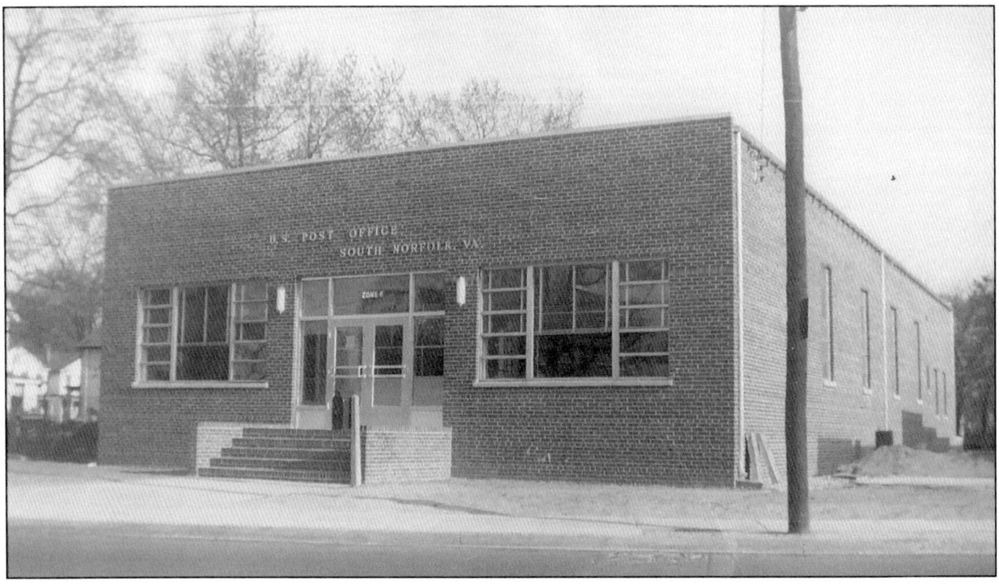

Built by Mr. Web Townsend, this building is at 1210 Poindexter Street. Upon completion, it was leased by the U.S. Postal service, and the South Norfolk Post Office relocated there from the 1400 block.

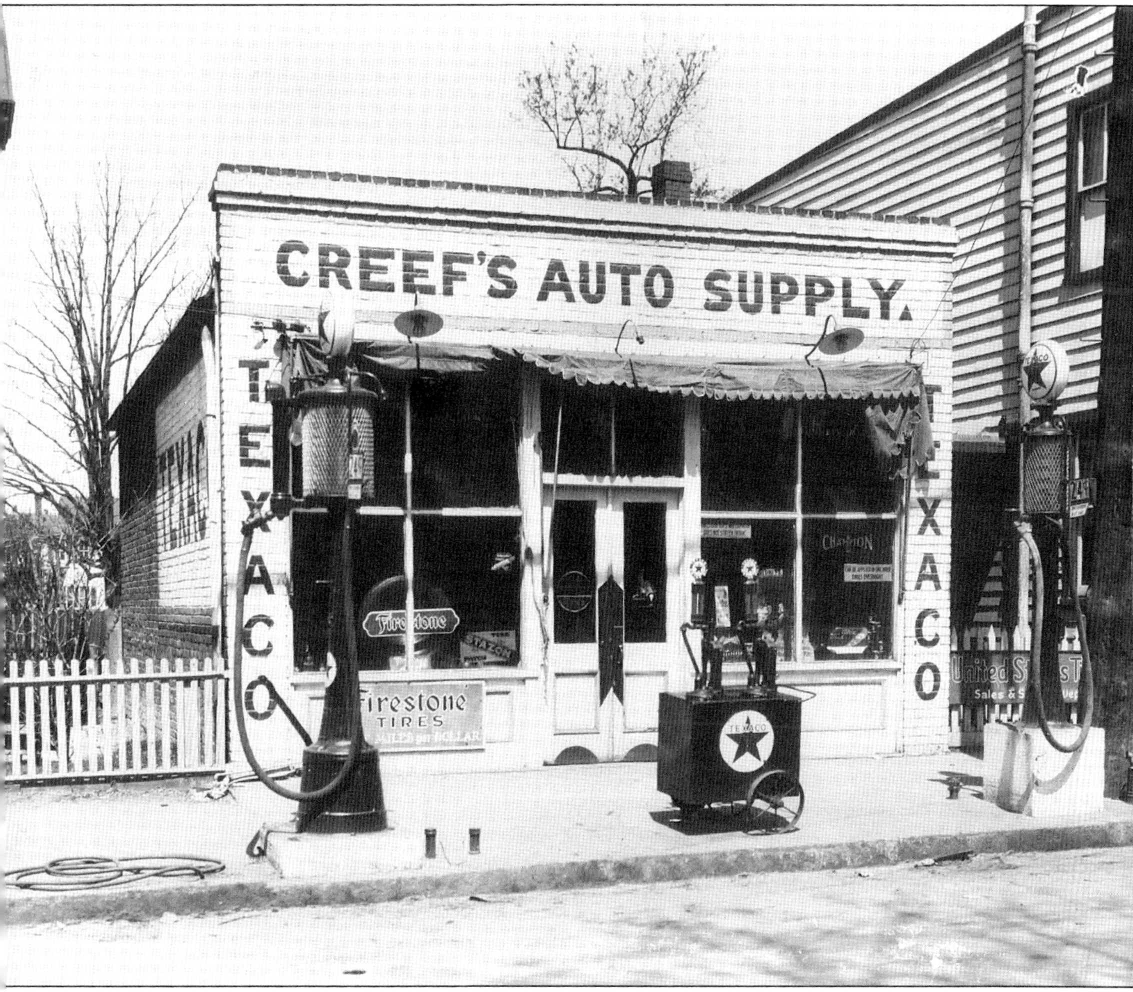

Sam Creef operated this small auto supply and gas station at 19 Poindexter Street, pictured c. 1917. Gasoline was 24¢ a gallon (a lot of money at the time). In 1930, this became the 1300 block of Poindexter Street.

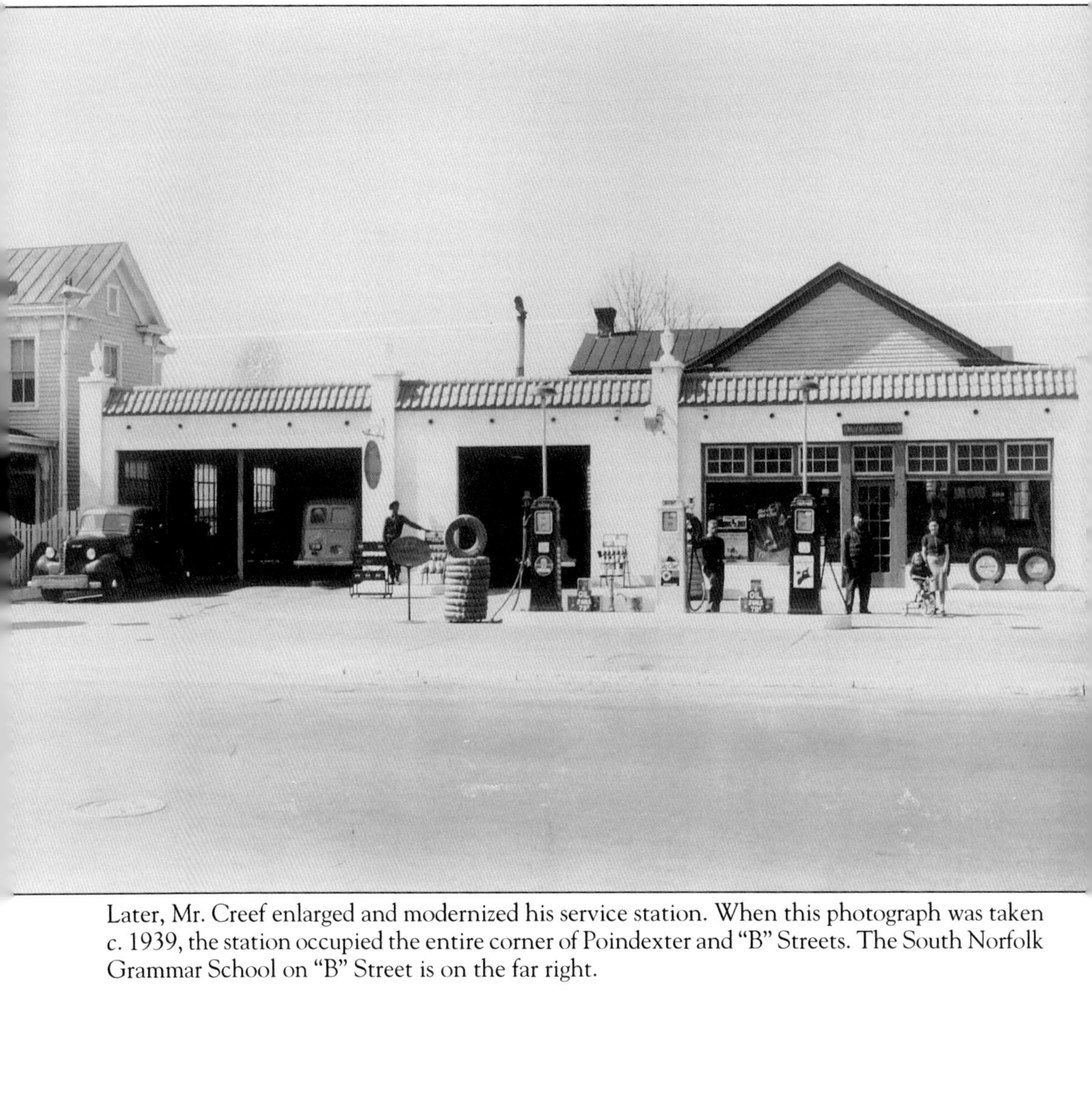

Later, Mr. Creef enlarged and modernized his service station. When this photograph was taken c. 1939, the station occupied the entire corner of Poindexter and "B" Streets. The South Norfolk Grammar School on "B" Street is on the far right.

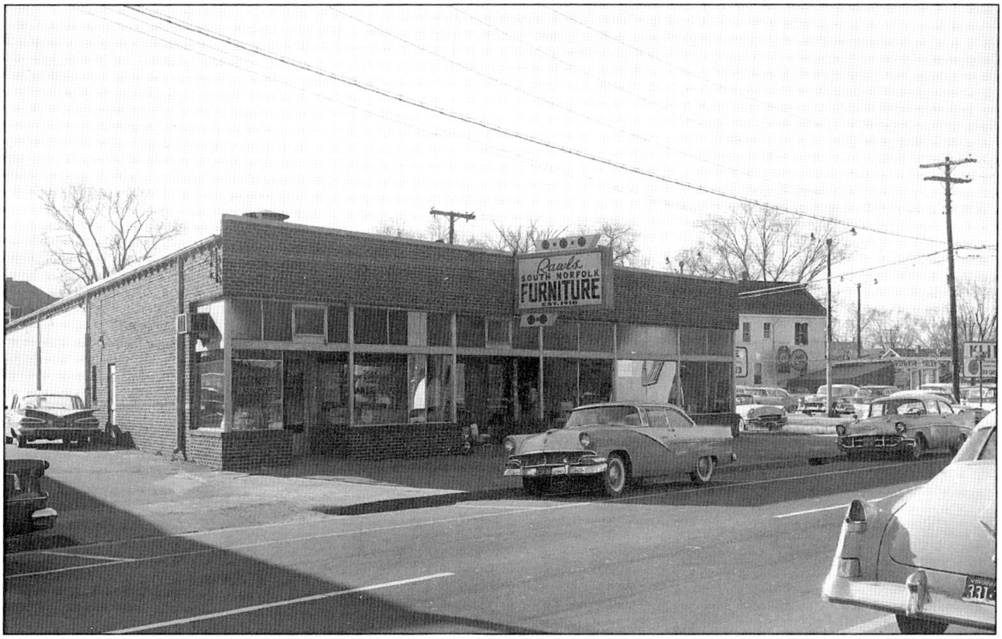

Shortly after January 1960, Mr. Rawls moved his South Norfolk Furniture Company to the corner of Poindexter and Rodgers Streets. The building was originally the location of an A&P grocery store. The left side of the building holds the office of Savage Insurance Company.

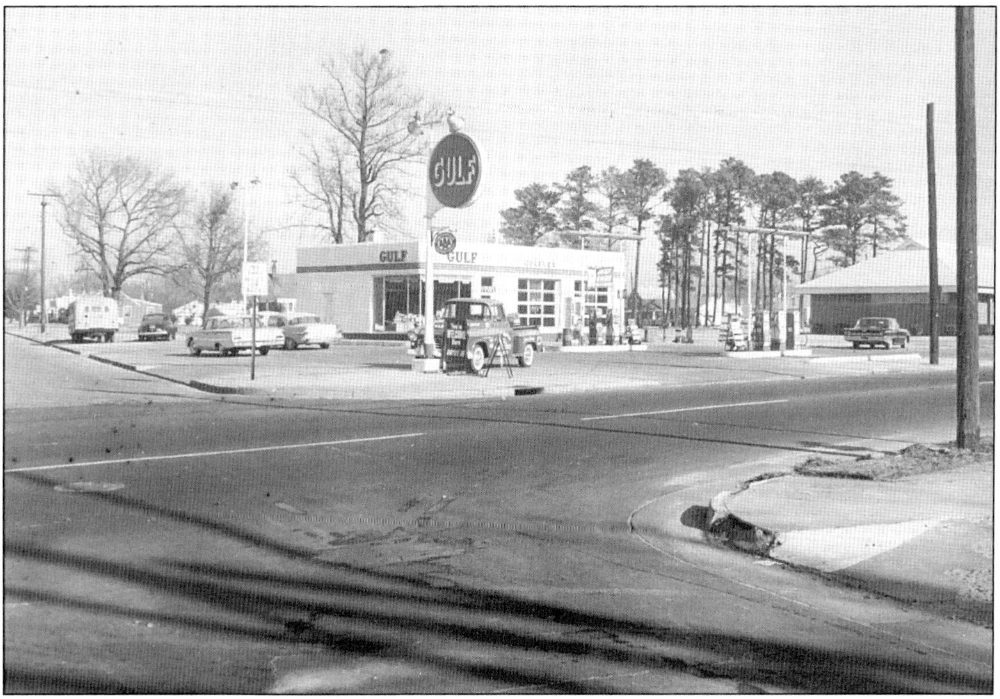

The Gulf station in this c. 1958 photograph is on the corner of Poindexter and Stewart Streets. Before the station was built, a large cement-block house was located there. The South Norfolk Memorial Library can be seen in the right background.

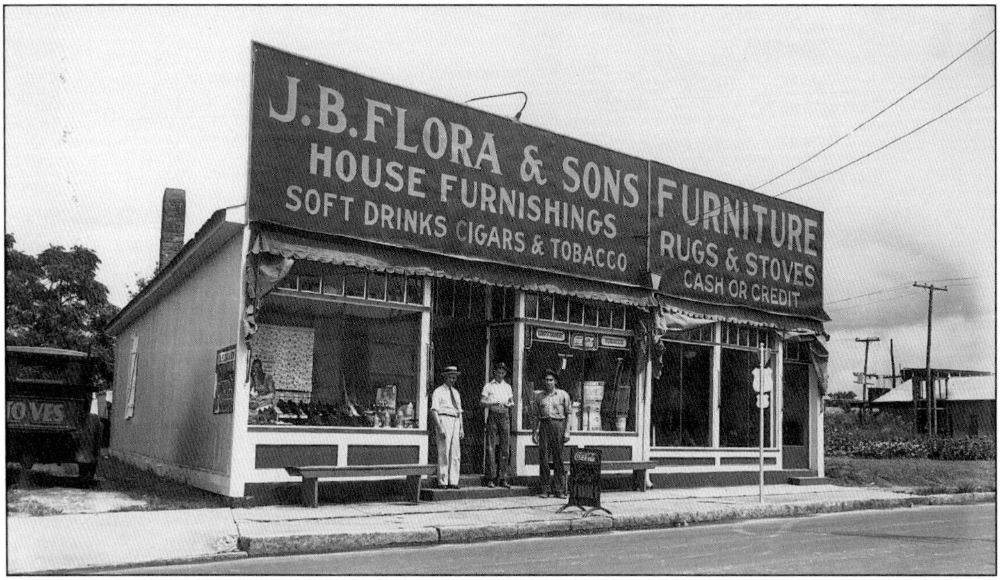

In 1927, Mr. J.B. Flora opened his House Furnishings store at 151 Poindexter Street. Flora later enlarged the store and began selling furniture, rugs, and stoves. His truck can be seen in the alley to the left of the store. The building to the right of Mr. Flora's store is Townsend's ice plant. The people in the picture are, from left to right, Mr. Flora, Duval Flora (age 12), and Mr. Frank Holbrook. When this photograph was taken in 1932, the street number had been changed from 151 to 807.

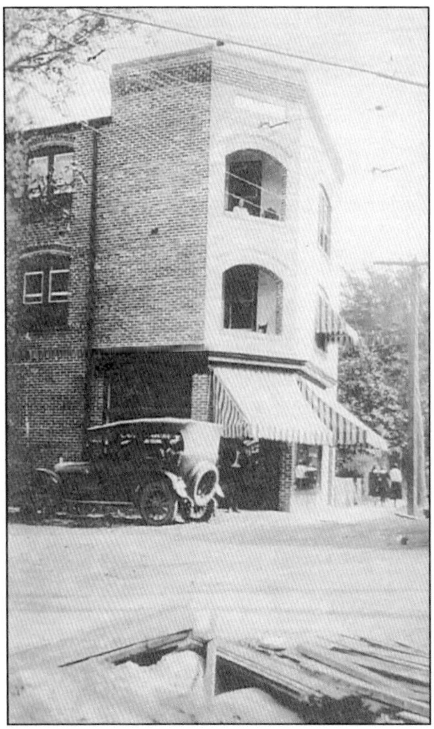

This building was constructed in 1918–1919 by Al Sawyer for Dean Preston, owner of Preston's Pharmacy. The rectangle at the top bears Preston's name and the year 1919. This photograph was taken in 1920, and at that time, the address of the building was number 1, Chesapeake Avenue. The first business at this location was a confectionery operated by a Mr. Grimstead and Mr. Lou Spencer, and there were apartments and businesses on the second and third floors. In 1922, Dr. Canada, a dentist, opened his office on the second floor. In 1930, the street number was changed from number 1 to 1001.

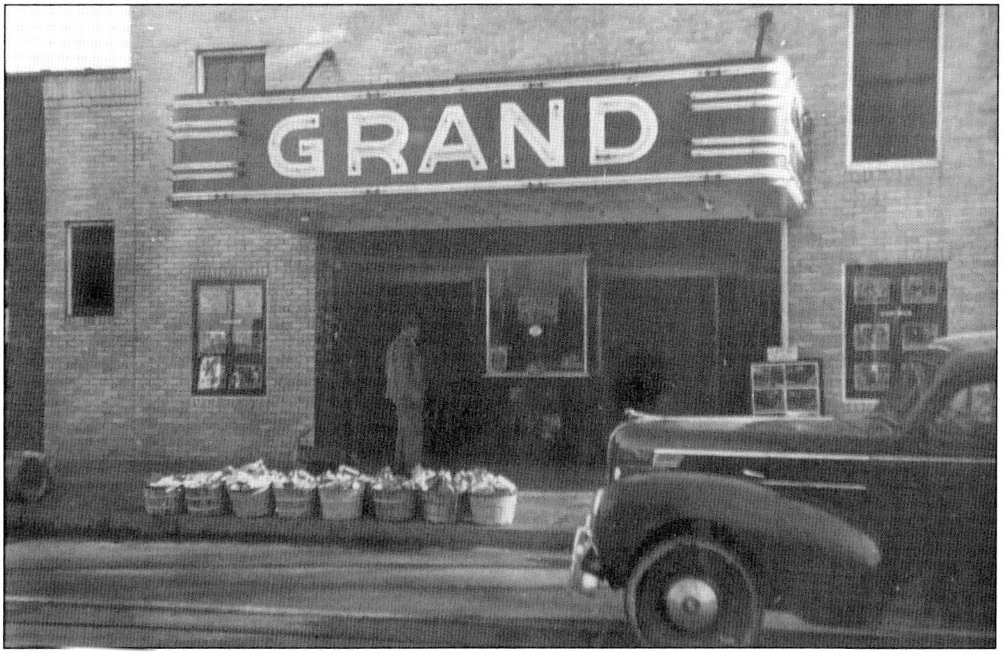

Each year in December, the Grand Theatre, in conjunction with the Joy Fund, collected can goods for the needy of South Norfolk. A special showing of cartoons or westerns took place on a Saturday morning before Christmas, and the price of admission was a can of food. This picture was taken c. 1930s.

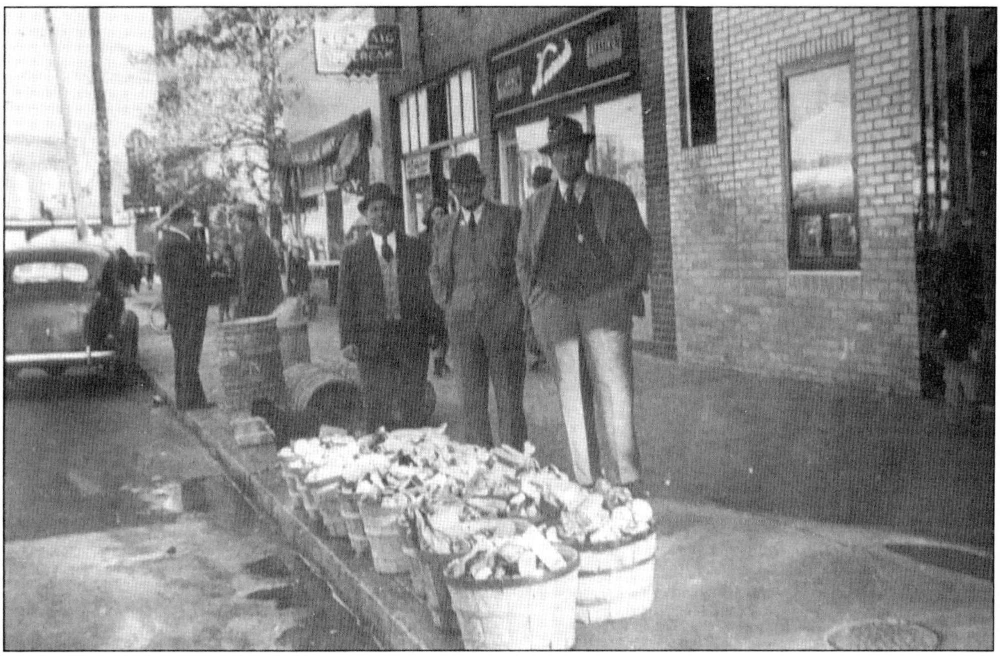

The food baskets in front of the Grand Theatre on Chesapeake Avenue were collected by the South Norfolk Joy Fund for distribution to the needy families of the city. The men donating their time and efforts are, from left to right, Jesse W. Harper Sr., A.B. "Bus" Howell, and Ed Reass.

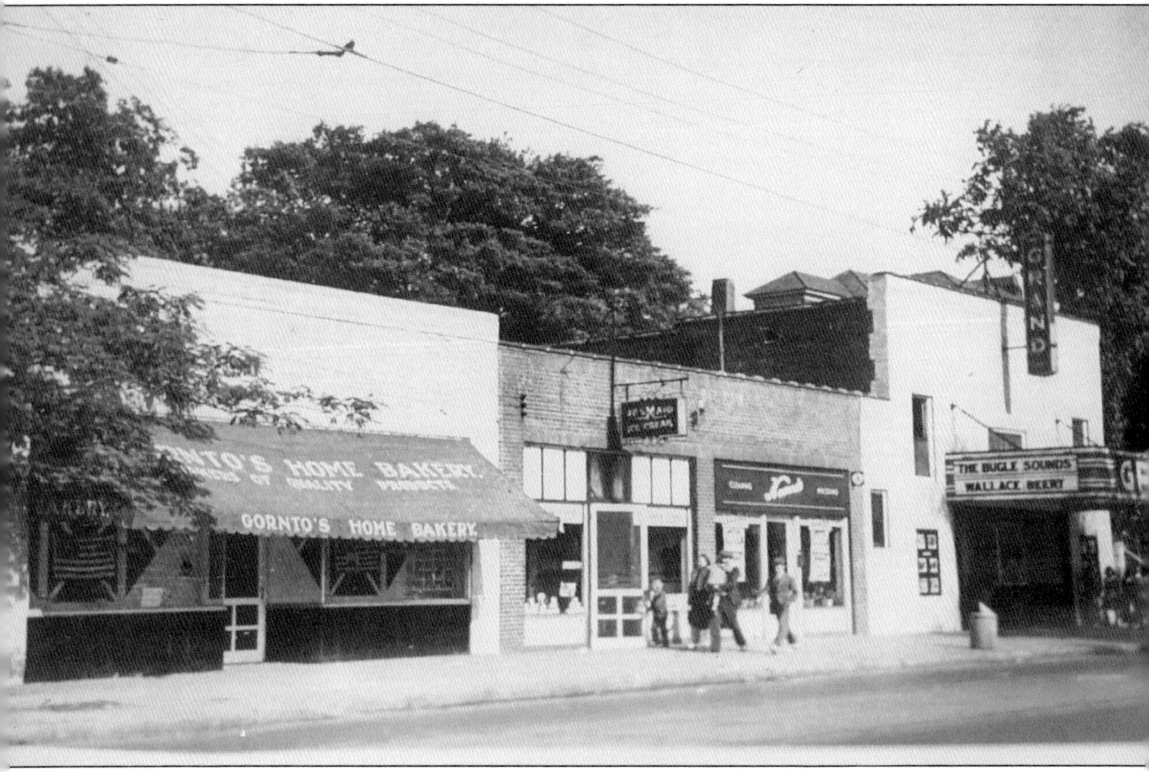

The Grand Theatre, which opened in 1919, was South Norfolk's only successful movie house. The feature usually changed five times a week. The serial was shown on Fridays, and after school, the theatre was filled with kids who wanted to see the likes of the Lone Ranger, Gene Autry, Roy Rogers, Hopalong Cassidy, and others. In the same block of Chesapeake Avenue could be found Howard Cleaners, where you could get a suit cleaned and pressed for 49¢, Jus Maid Ice Cream Store, and Gornto's Bakery. The overhead wires were for the streetcar, the primary mode of transportation at that time. This photograph was taken during World War II.

Two

BUSINESSES AND INDUSTRIES

Following the post-Civil War depression, the industrial potential of South Norfolk began to be realized through two railroad lines: the Norfolk & Western and the Virginian. With its location so close to Norfolk and its proximity to the Elizabeth River, South Norfolk was a natural site for industrial development. In the 1870s, Carter Poindexter and his son Parke established the first manufacturing plant of significance within the area. Lumber, creosoting, fertilizer, guano, and oil processing were among the early industries. The many industries drew a large number of people for employment and resulted in a need for housing and smaller businesses.

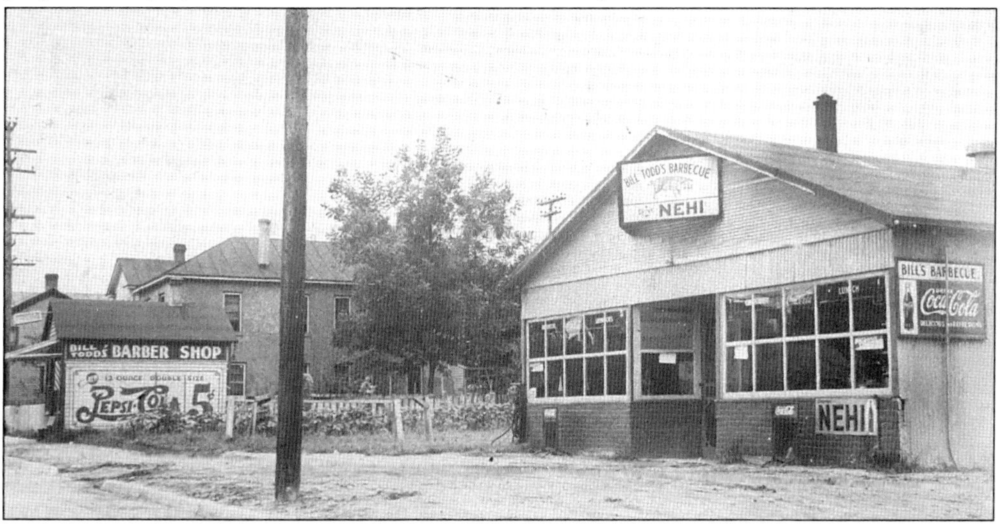

This building, which housed Bill Todd's Barbecue in the 1100 block of Bainbridge Boulevard, was originally an automobile repair garage, pictured here *c.* 1930. It then served as the home of the South Norfolk Assembly of God. Mr. Todd also operated the barbershop seen on the left. The sign advertising new Pepsi Cola, 12-ounce double size for 5¢, compares Pepsi to Coca Cola, which was sold in 6-ounce green bottles. This location is now the corner of Bainbridge Boulevard and Poindexter Street and is the entrance to the Jordan Bridge, which connects South Norfolk with Portsmouth, Virginia.

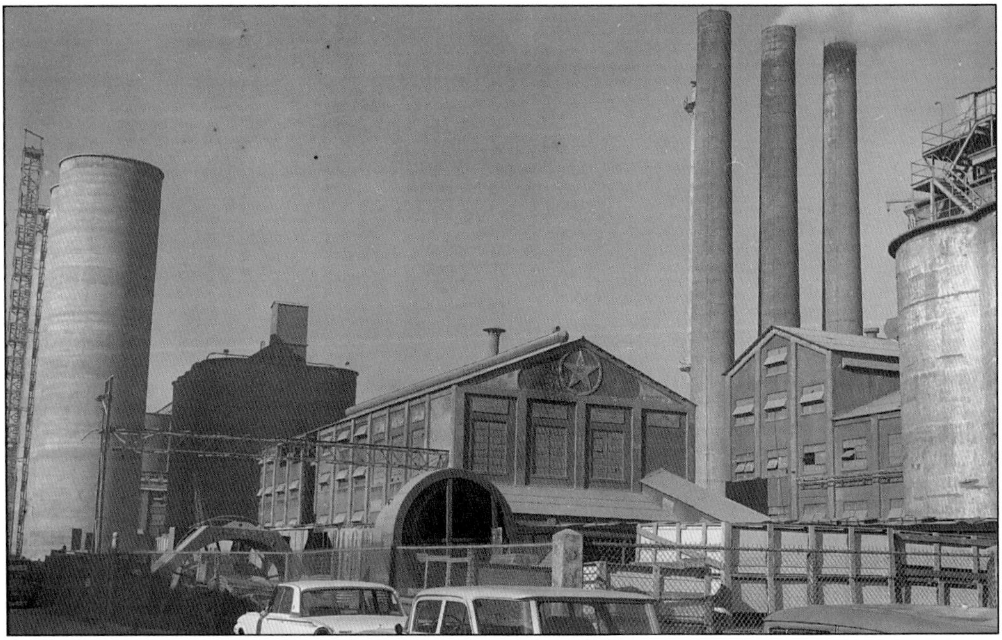

The first cement plant was completed in 1926 by the Portland Company and had a capacity of 3,600 barrels per day. The plant employed 180 day workers and a force of about ten laboratory and clerical people. The weekly payroll amounted to $1,250. A large plant expansion was accomplished in 1957.

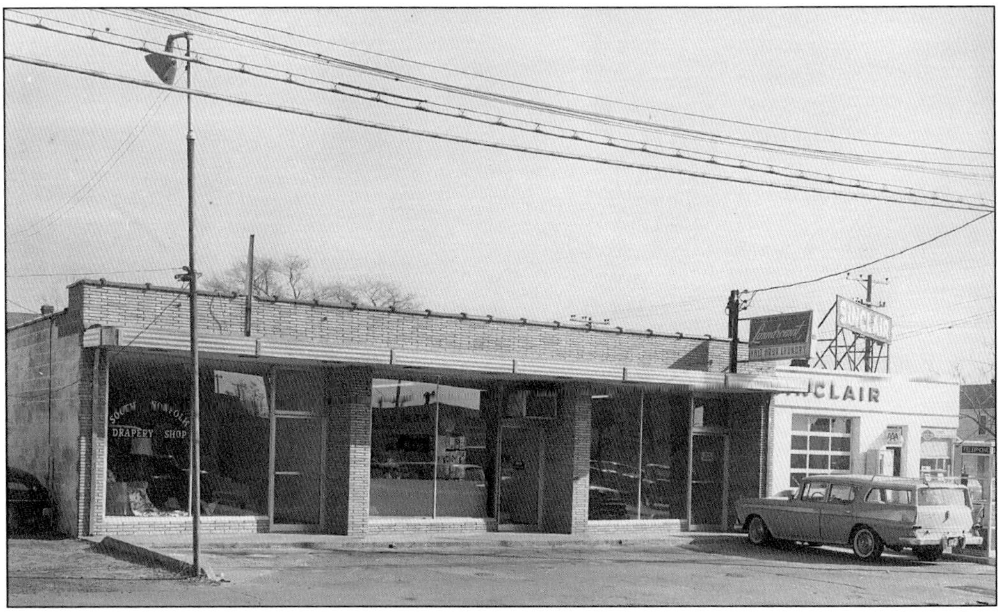

In the 1930s, Mr. Hargrove operated a neighborhood market on Bainbridge Boulevard at the corner of Park Avenue. He eventually built this group of stores that became known as the Hargrove Building. Among the occupants throughout the years were the South Norfolk Drapery Shop, Boot's Fashion Shop, and a laundromat. After Mr. Hargrove closed his market, the building was torn down and the Sinclair service station was built on that corner. This picture was taken c. 1957.

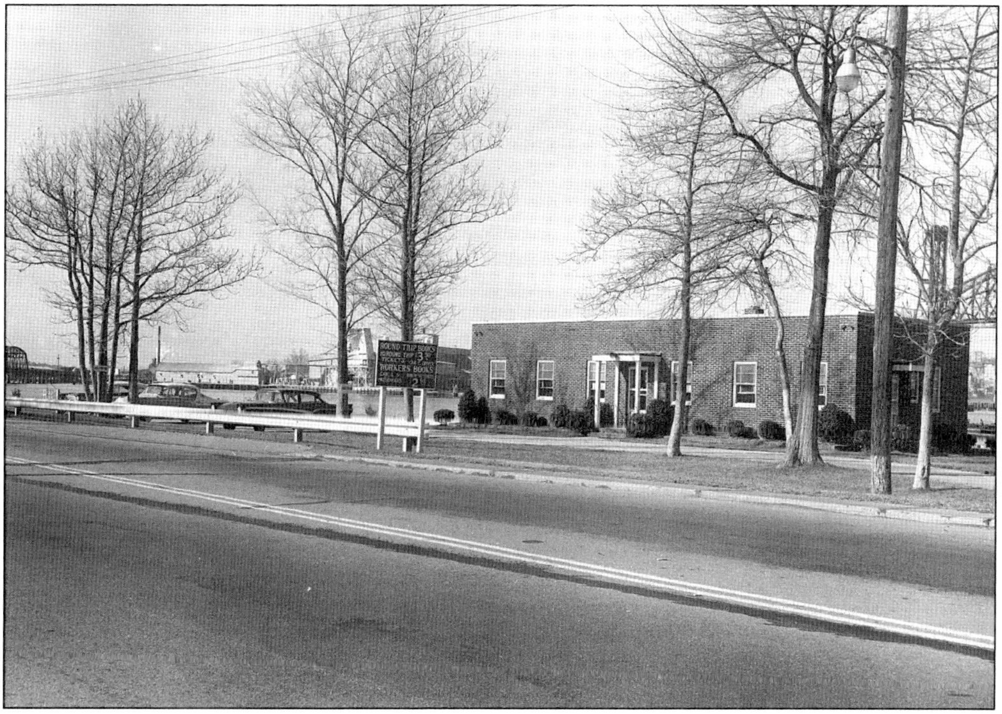

This new building on Park Avenue housed the business offices of the Jordan Bridge. It was built between 1957 and 1961.

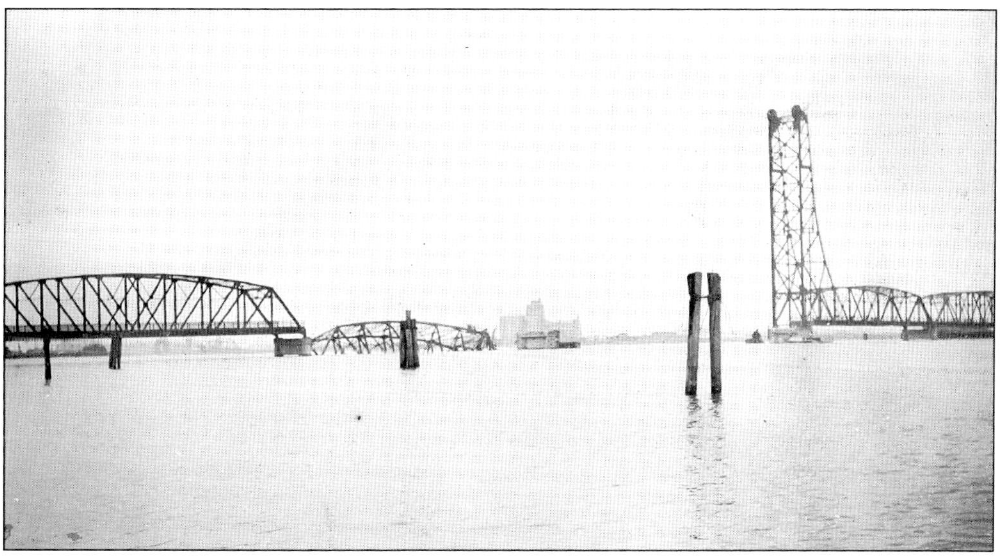

In June 1939, a tugboat towing a barge rammed the Jordan Bridge and knocked a section of the bridge into the Elizabeth River. This photograph was taken on June 2, 1939.

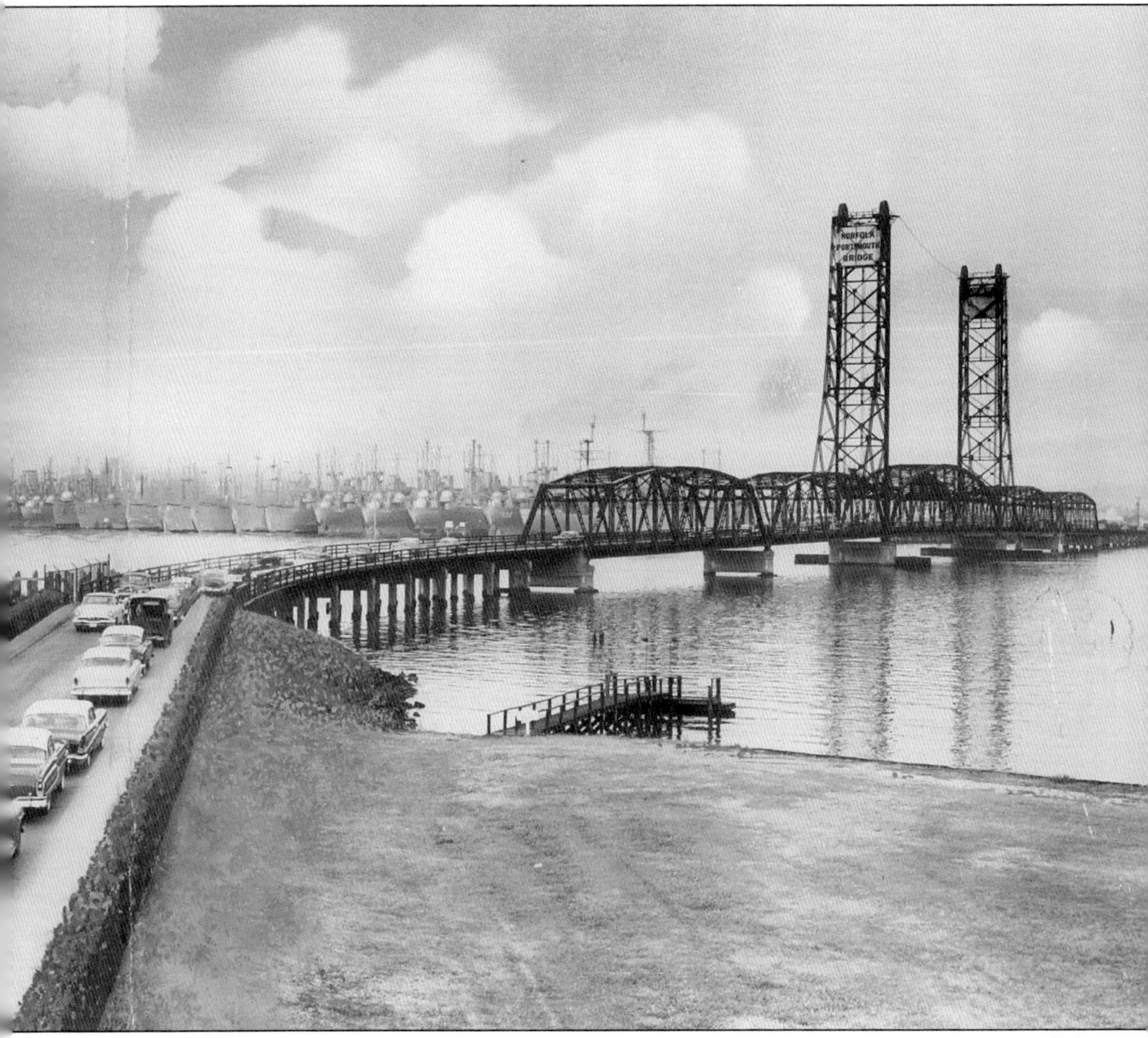

Construction of the Norfolk-Portsmouth (Jordan) Bridge began on August 15, 1927, and the bridge was opened for traffic on August 24, 1928. A very large mothball fleet was anchored near the bridge at one time.

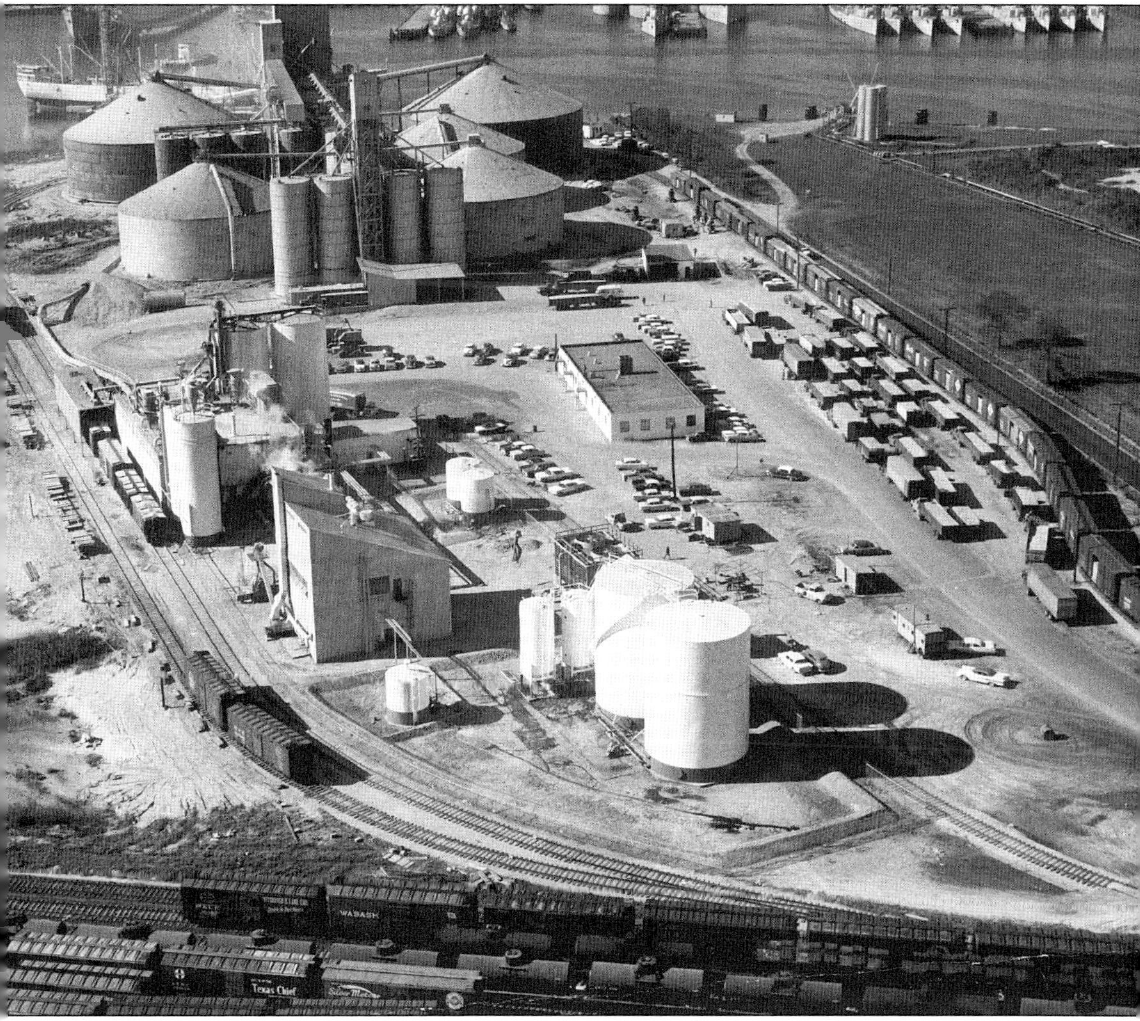

This aerial view shows the many activities carried on at Cargill Inc., located at 501 Barnes Road in South Norfolk. The trucks at the right, next to the train, are unloading grain or soybeans. Traffic along the Southern Branch of the Elizabeth River and the U.S. Navy mothball fleet can be seen at the top of this c. 1959 picture.

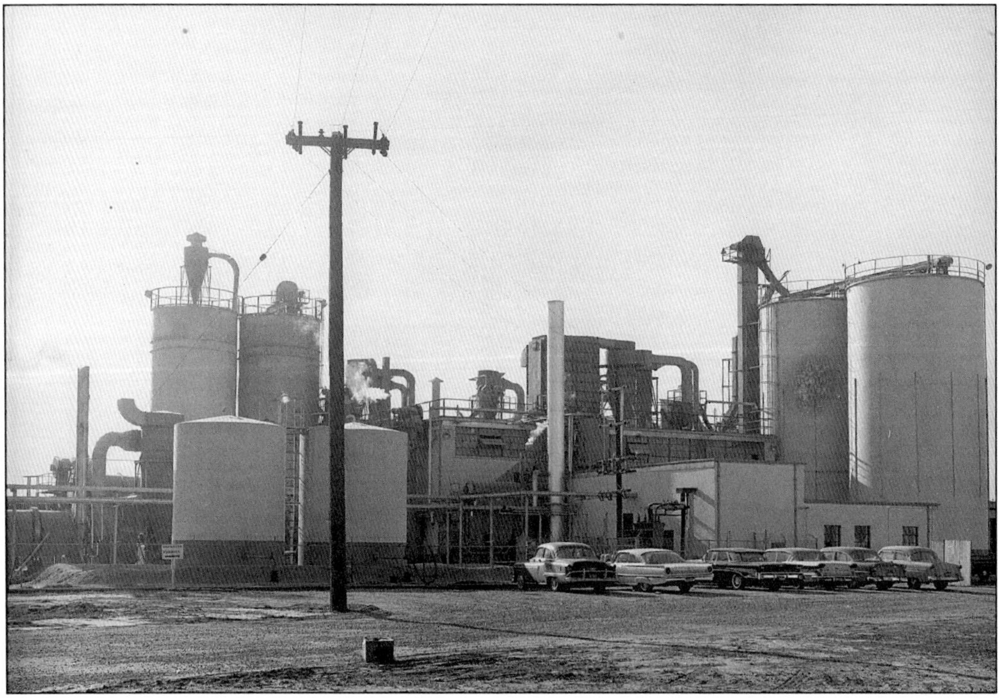

Seen here, *c.* 1959, is the vegetable oil plant, another part of Cargill's operation on Barnes Road in South Norfolk.

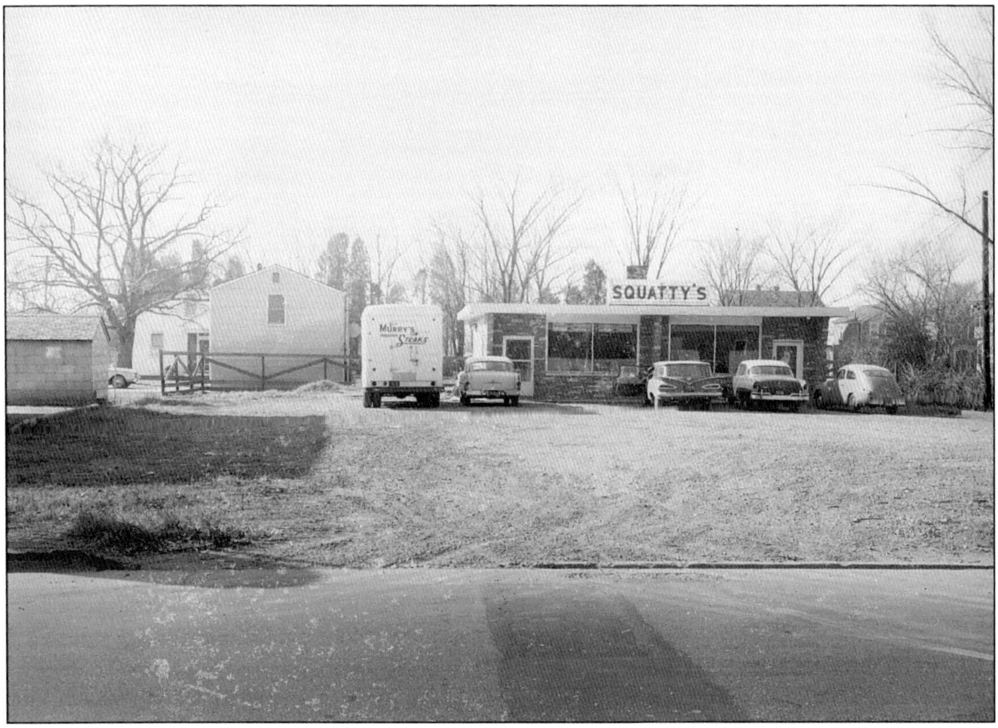

Squatty Ferrell's Restaurant was at 2014 Bainbridge Boulevard in the area that was, at one time, known as Jones' Switch. The building is now the location of Grace's Beauty Salon.

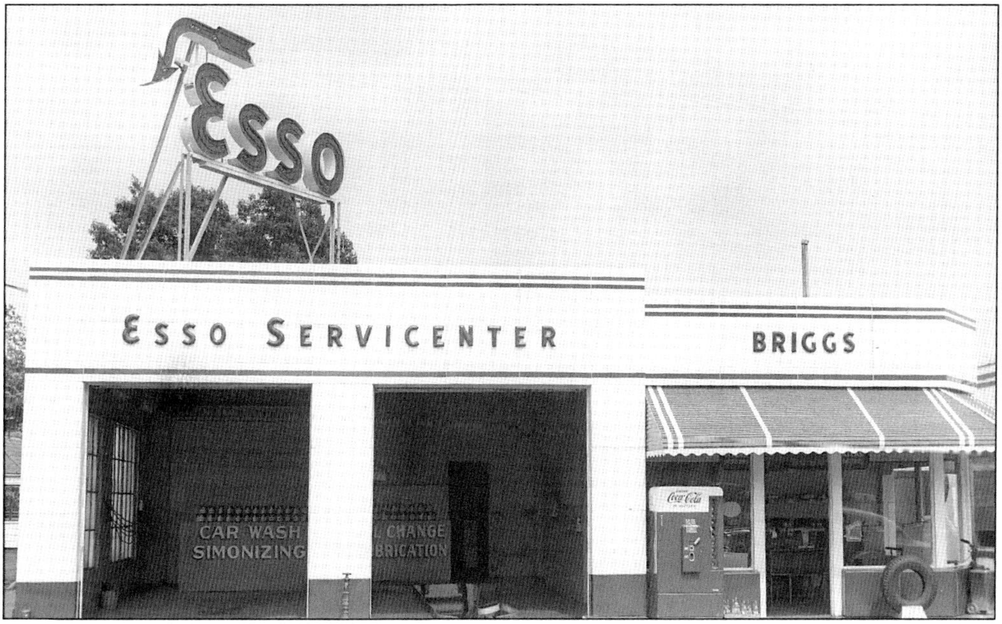

Linwood Brigg's Esso Servicenter, pictured here in 1957, was located at the corner of Bainbridge Boulevard and Chesapeake Drive. (Orby G. Kelley Jr., photographer.)

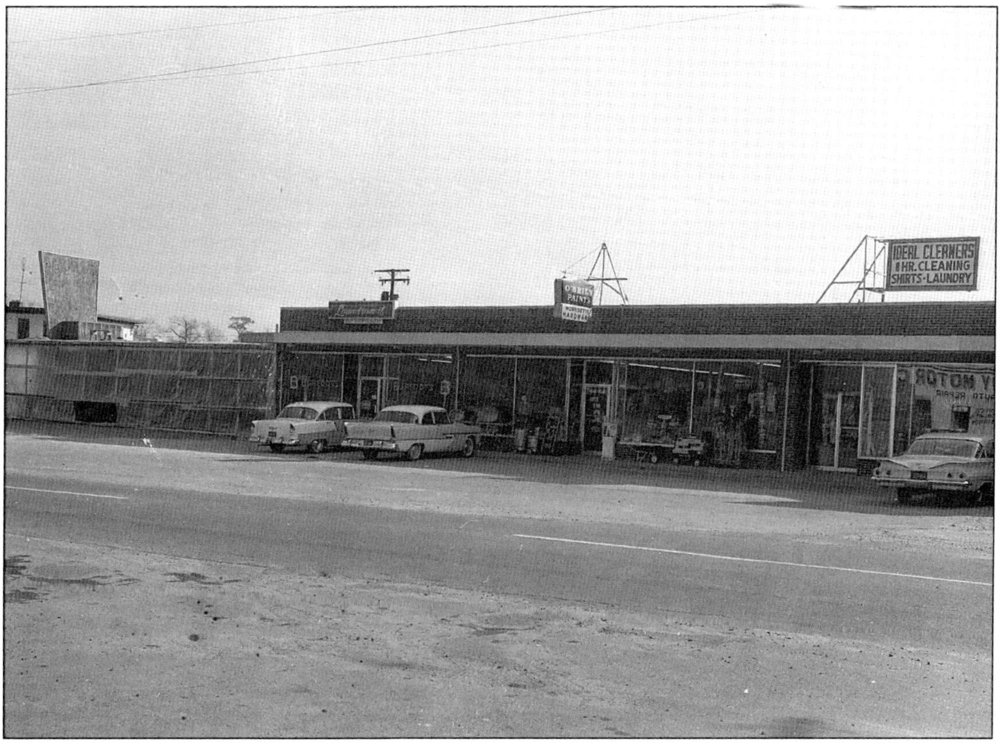

John Burfoot built this row of stores on Chesapeake Drive in 1957. The three tenants shown here are Mr. Burfoot's laundromat, John Morrisette's hardware, and Marie West's Ideal Cleaners. The reflection of Midway Motor Co., located across the street, can be seen in the front window of the Ideal Cleaners.

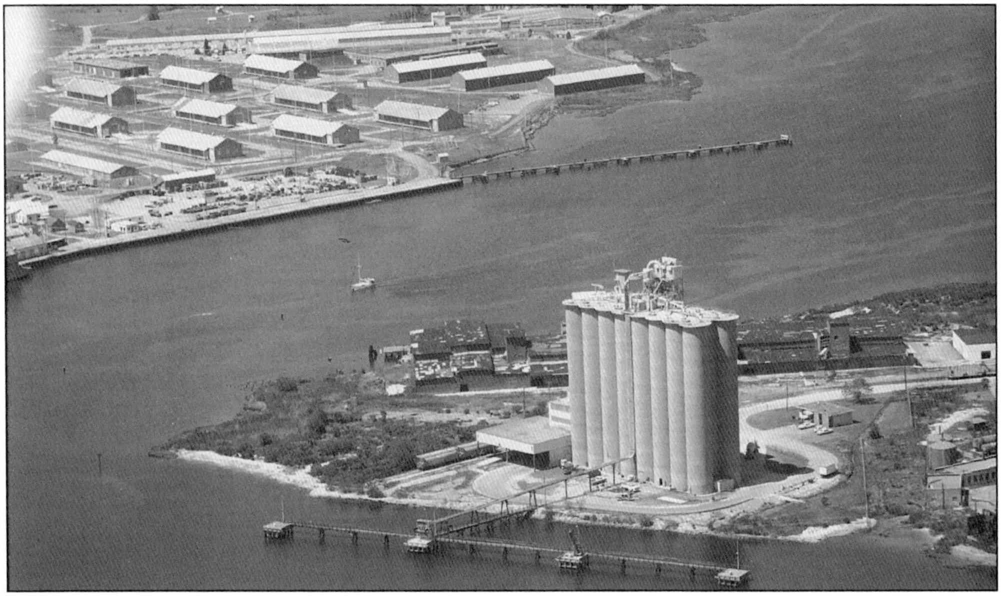

Construction of the Atlantic Cement Company in Money Point was begun in 1962. By February of 1963, production was well underway. This aerial view shows portions of the plant, the Southern Branch of the Elizabeth River, and buildings of the St. Julian Creek Ammunition Depot. The cement company's name has since been changed to the Blue Circle Cement Company.

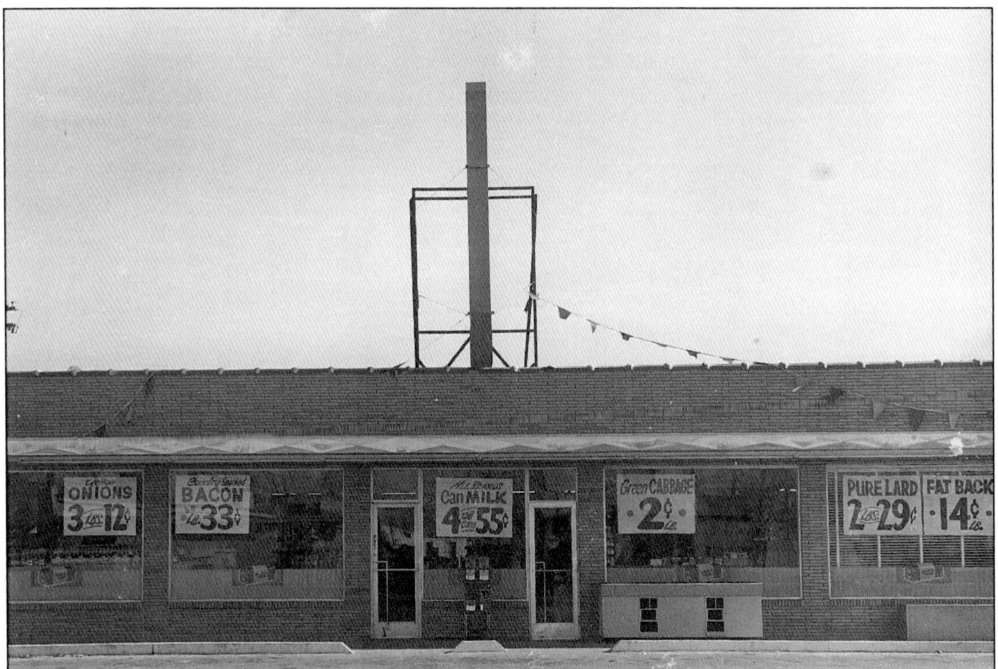

Harrell's Market was located on Campostella Road in South Norfolk. Grocery prices were considerably lower in 1957 than they are in 1999; you could buy a pound of bacon for 33¢ in 1957. In addition to the advertised specials in the windows, the market was also advertising Nolde's Bread. Nolde's Bakery was on Hampton Boulevard in Norfolk.

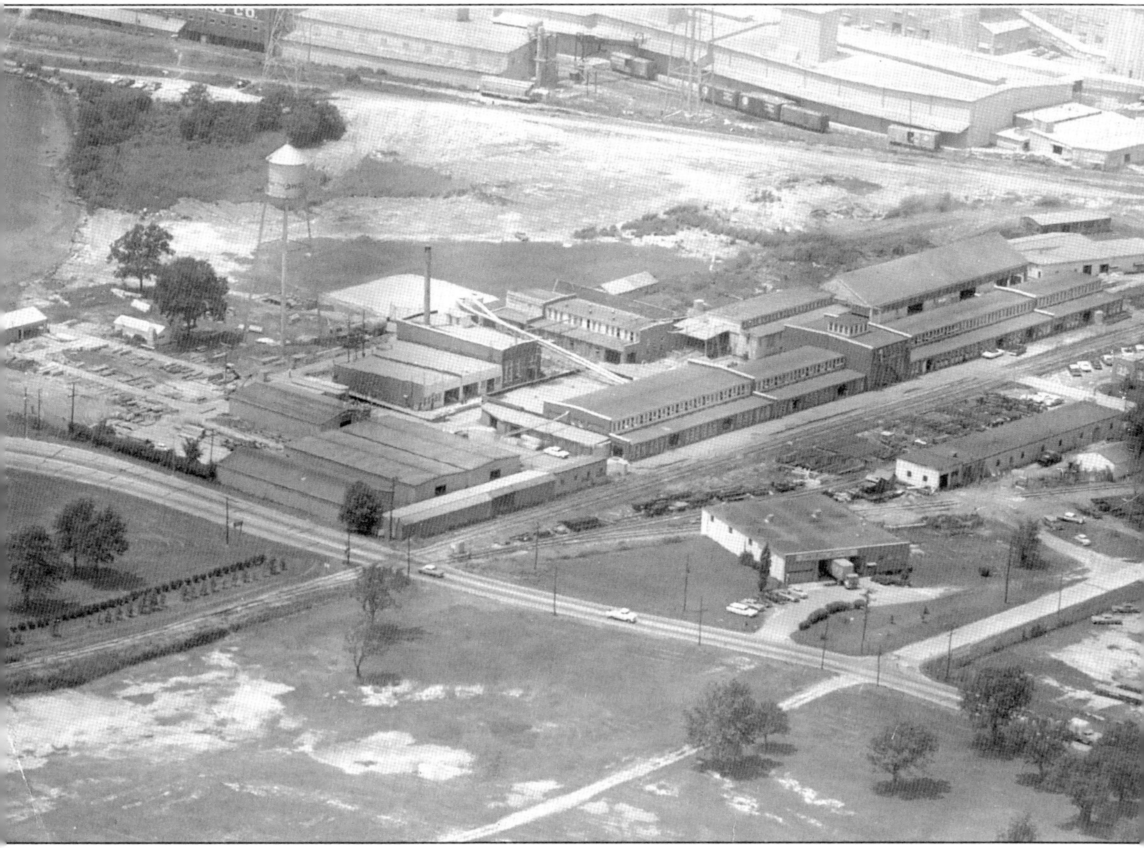

This aerial view shows a small part of the industrial area of South Norfolk. In the upper left is the Royster Guano Co., and the large group of buildings in the center is the J.G. Wilson Co. The square building near the bottom right (with the truck backed into the entrance) is the Sunshine Biscuit Co. This photograph once hung in the office of the now defunct J.G. Wilson Company.

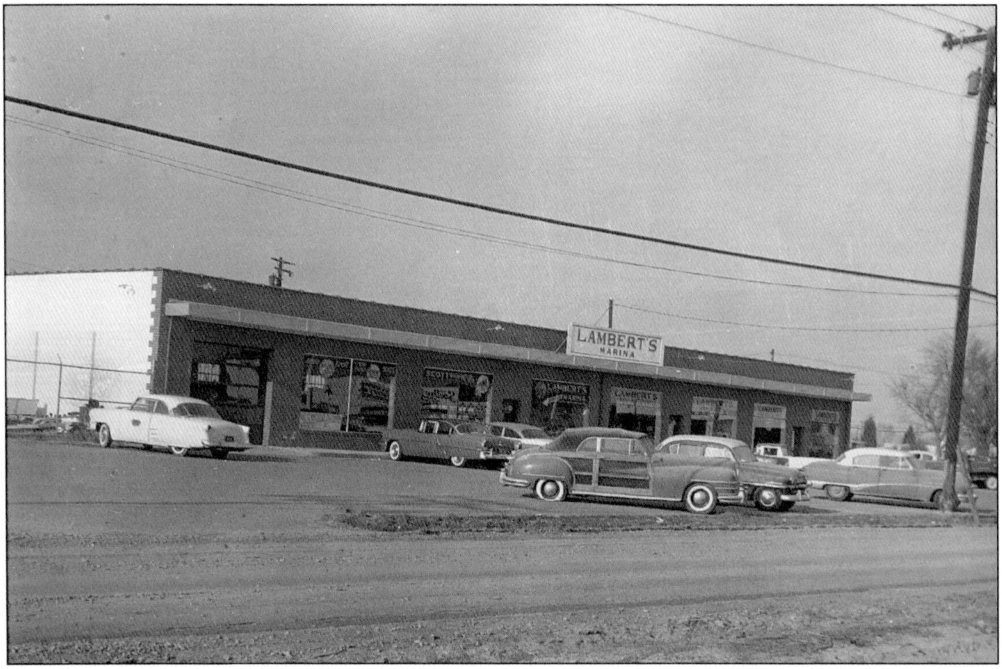

Lambert's Marina and Auto Parts was built at Edmond's Corner in South Norfolk in 1957. The marina part of the name was unusual in that the nearest water and boat basin were several miles away.

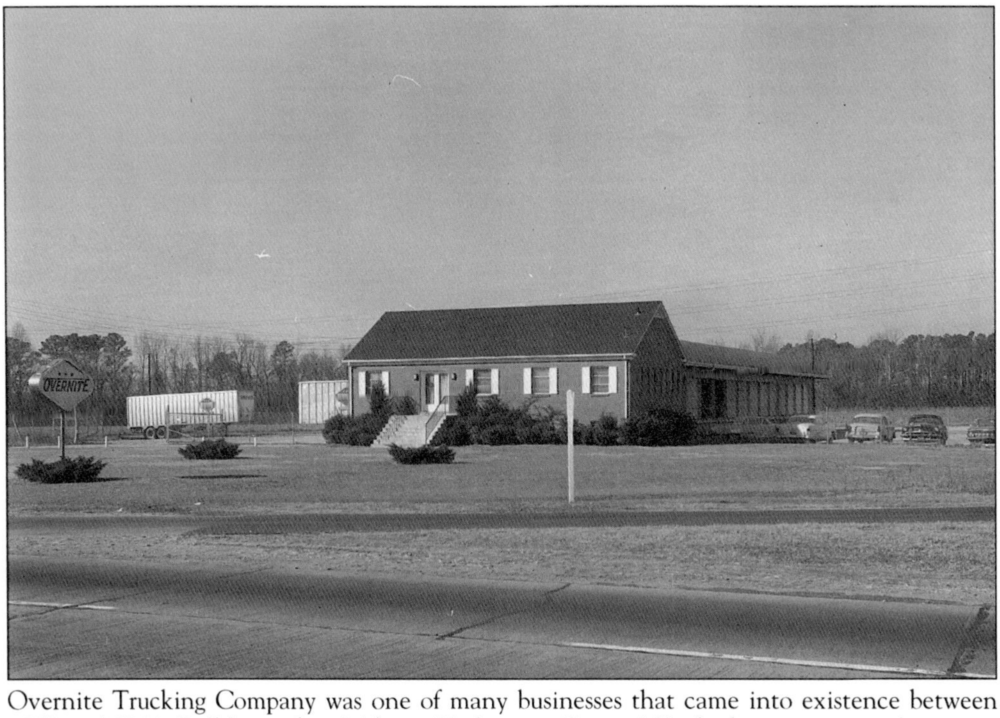

Overnite Trucking Company was one of many businesses that came into existence between 1957 and 1961. Still located on Military Highway at Route 168, the business is now known as Overnite Transportation Company.

Three

Government And Public Safety

Before becoming a town, the village of South Norfolk was part of the Washington Magisterial District of Norfolk County. A supervisor represented South Norfolk on the Norfolk County Board of Supervisors, which held monthly meetings at the county courthouse in Portsmouth. On September 11, 1919, South Norfolk became a town. The town government consisted of a mayor and nine councilmen. At its first meeting, the council elected Mr. Q C. Davis Jr. as mayor. On January 1, 1921, South Norfolk became a city of the second class, and 30 years later it would become a city of the first class.

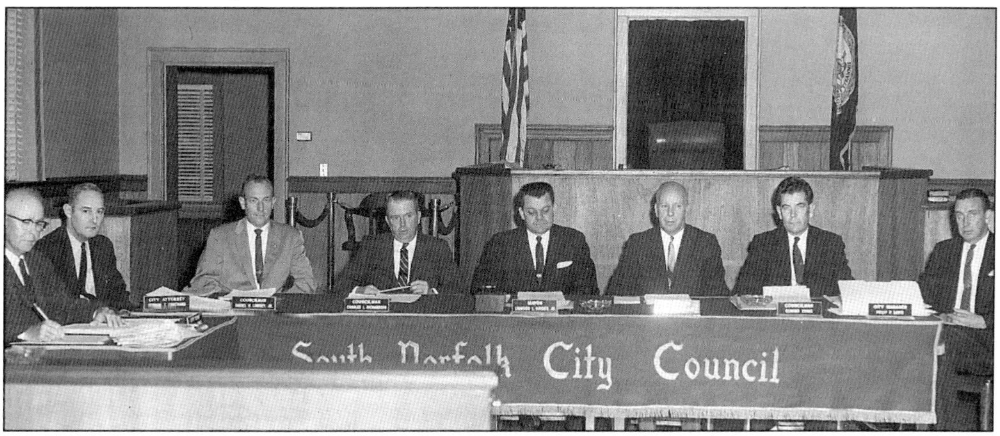

Here we have a meeting of the South Norfolk City Council in the courthouse on Liberty Street. Those present are, from left to right, Raymond Spence, city clerk; Vernon T. Forehand, city attorney; Daniel W. Lindsey Jr., councilman; Charles L. Richardson, councilman; Mayor Linwood L. Briggs; Vice Mayor Jesse McCloud; Osman Evans, councilman; and Philip P. Davis, city manager. Mr. Briggs served as mayor from 1957 to 1961.

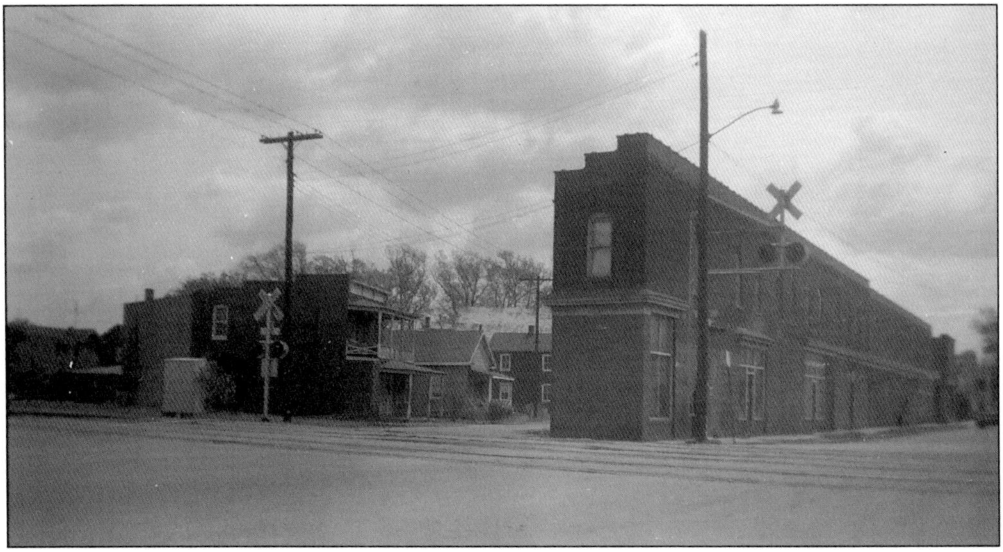

This building was located between Liberty and St. James Streets near the Belt Line Railroad and was known as the Flat Iron building or Berlin Block. In early South Norfolk, all local government offices and courts were housed there. There was also a movie theatre during the days of silent films in one part of the building, but no one remembers the theatre's name. Information has it that there was a saloon on the first floor that was frequented by the local justice of the peace during court session. This photograph was taken in May 1959 just prior to the building's demolition.

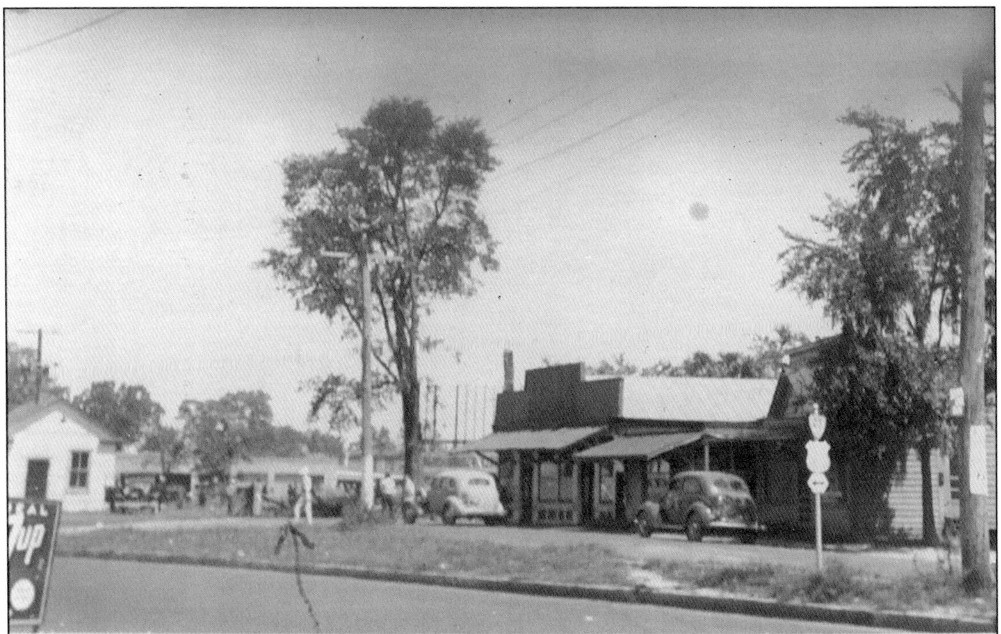

This was St. James Street before the South Norfolk overpass was constructed in 1937. The city garage and a few remaining stores can be seen, as well as a sign on the left advertising 7 Up soda.

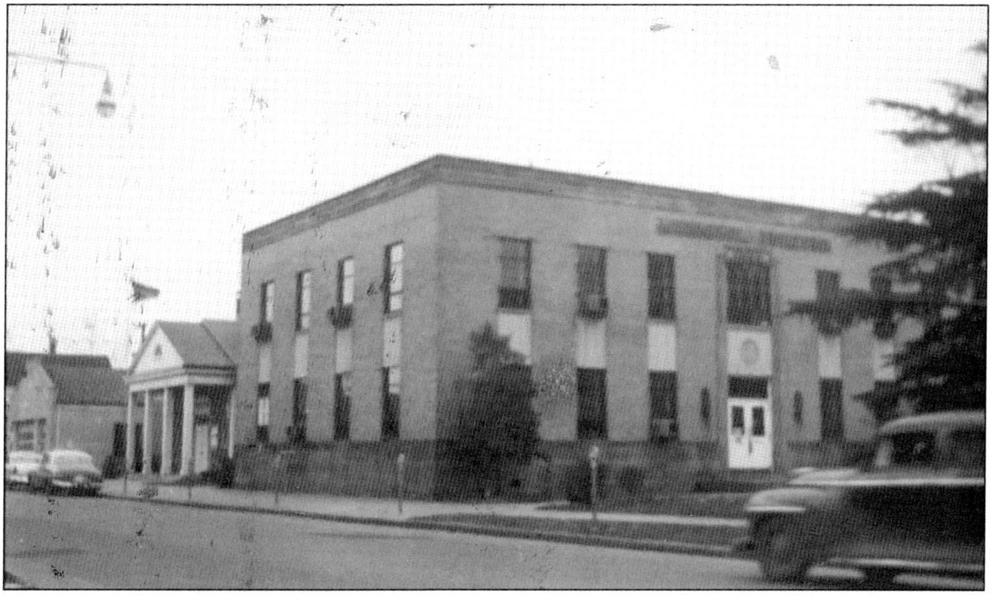

The three buildings seen here are, from left to right, the fire station, the new courthouse, and the municipal building on Liberty Street as they appeared in March 1957. A close look reveals the controversial parking meters, citizens banded together and forced their removal. Also, it is obvious from the many window units that the municipal building did not have central air conditioning.

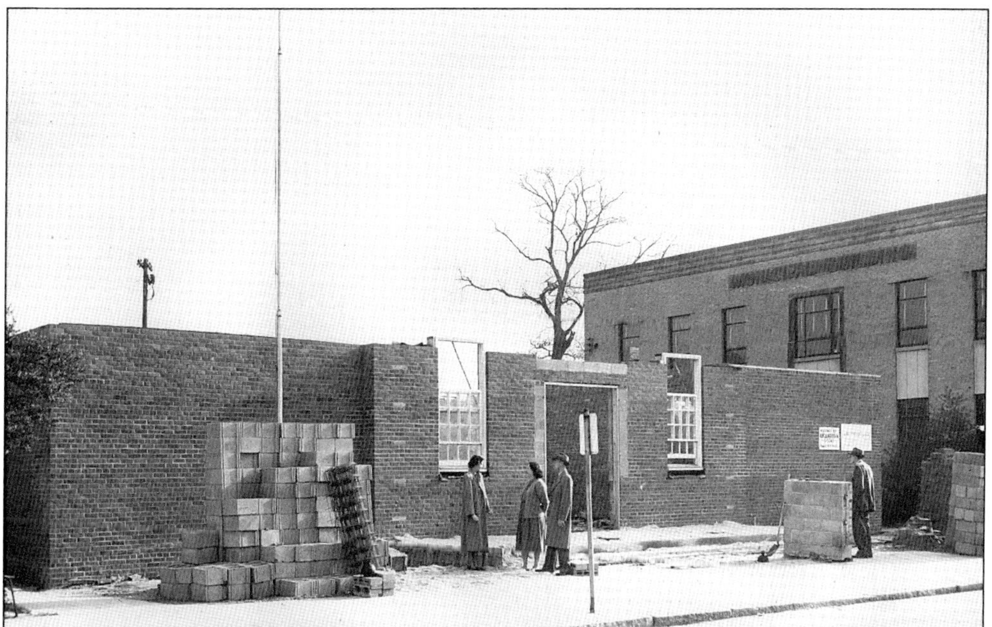

Marion White Nichols, Lil Hart, and Julian Raper check construction of the South Norfolk Corporation Court building on November 30, 1953. An unidentified gentleman stands on the right. Ms. Hart is now clerk of the circuit court for the City of Chesapeake.

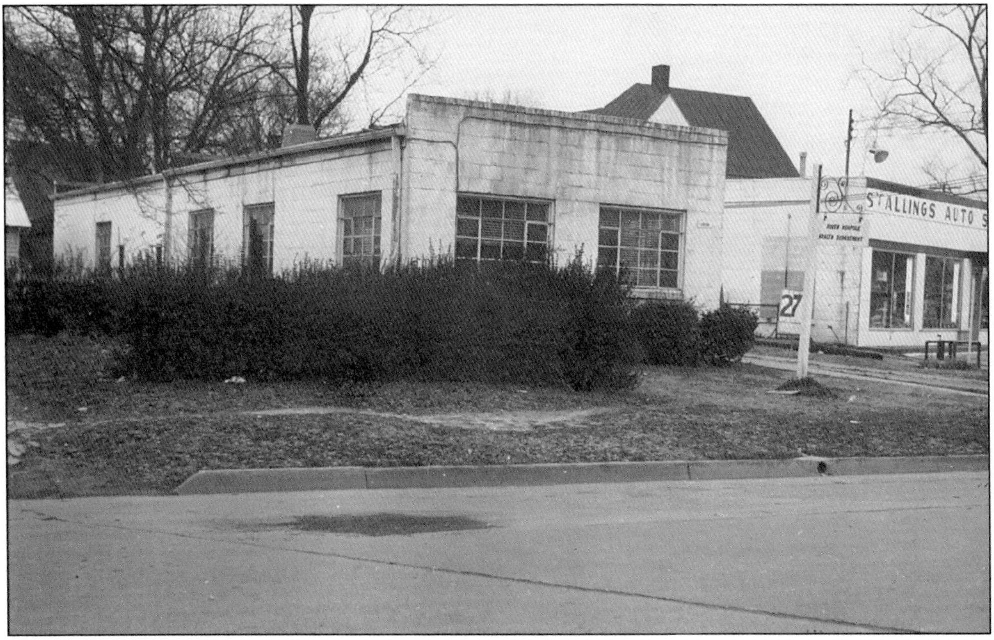

The South Norfolk Health Department was located at 1010 Poindexter Street when this picture was taken. Stallings Auto Supply is on the right at the corner of Poindexter and Stewart Streets. As can be seen, gasoline was only 27¢ per gallon.

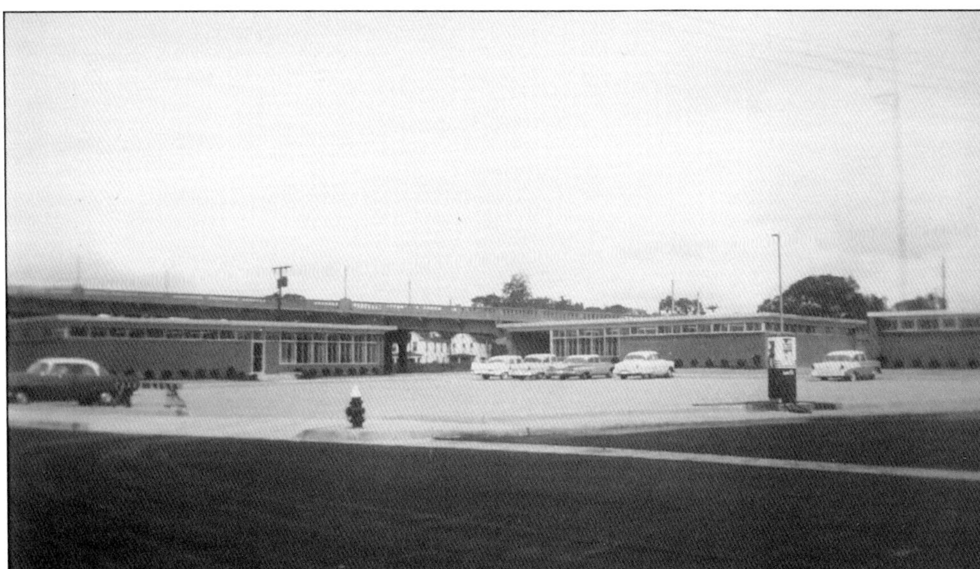

When the Health and Welfare buildings and the police station were completed in June 1961, all three were free of debt.

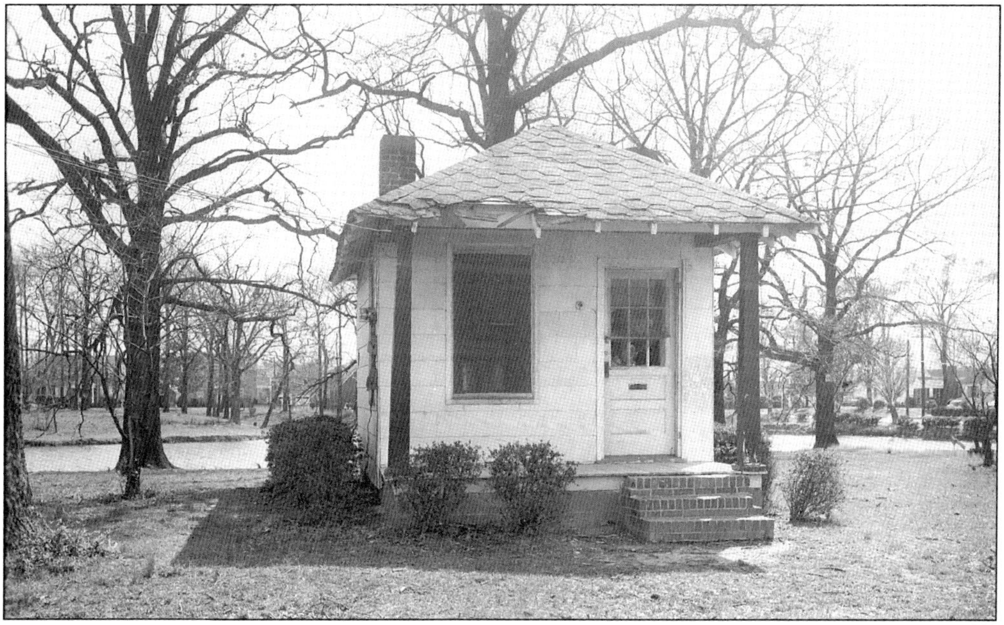

The first South Norfolk Public Library was in this small, two-room building in Lakeside Park that had previously served as a health center beside the Portlock Fire Station. At that time, the city council could appropriate only $1,500 to get the project started. The library started August 20, 1952.

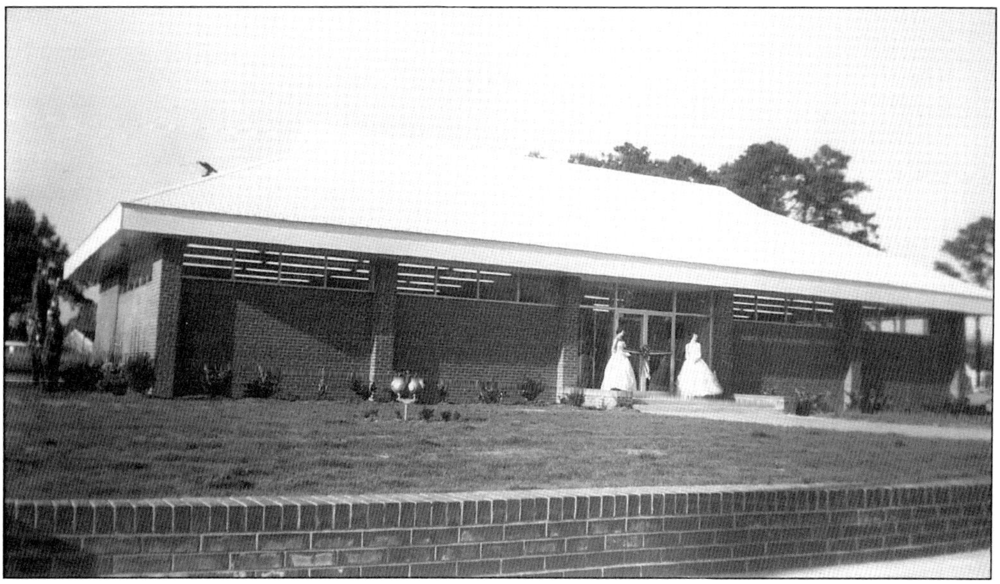

The South Norfolk Memorial Library is pictured here on the day of its dedication. Two young ladies were stationed at the entrance to welcome those in attendance.

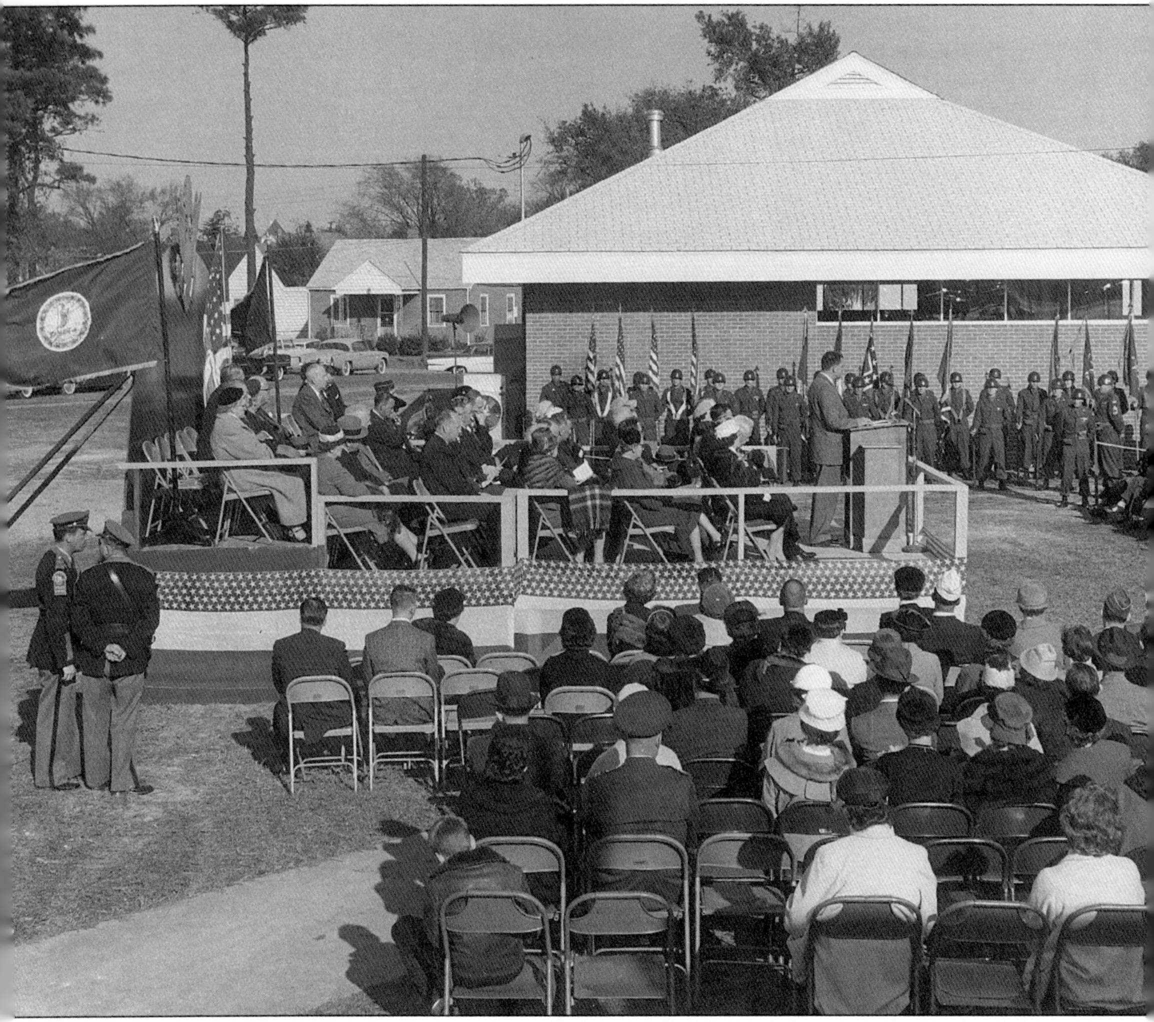

Mayor Linwood L. Briggs Jr. stood on the platform and addressed those present at the dedication of the South Norfolk Memorial Library on Poindexter Street. Governor J. Lindsey Almond and Mrs. Josephine Almond are seated directly behind the mayor. Mrs. Almond was the keynote speaker on that day, November 8, 1958.

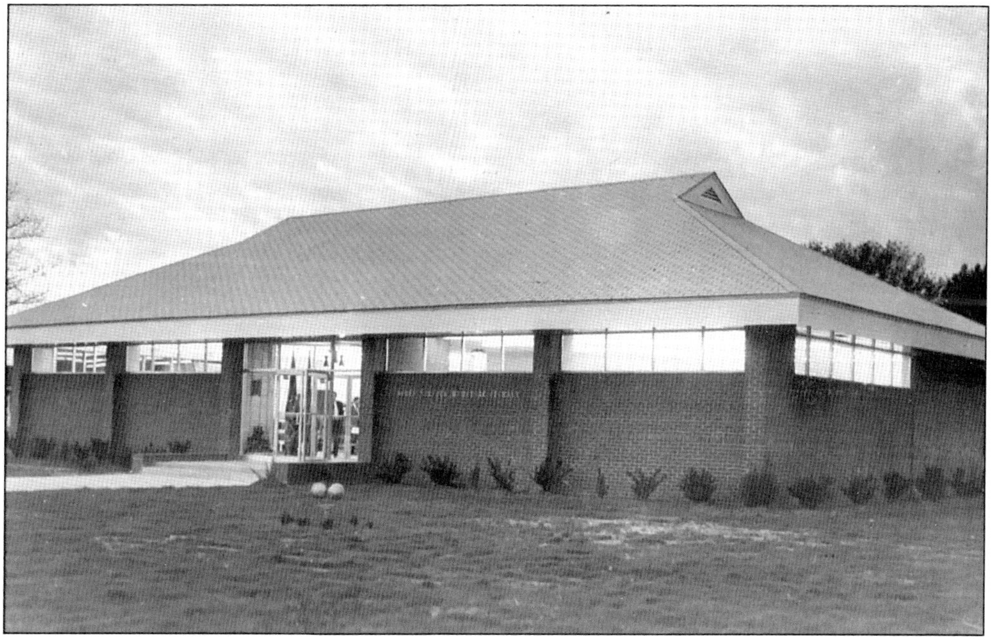

The sun sets on the busy dedication day of the new library. There have been many changes and modifications to the library since that day in November 1958.

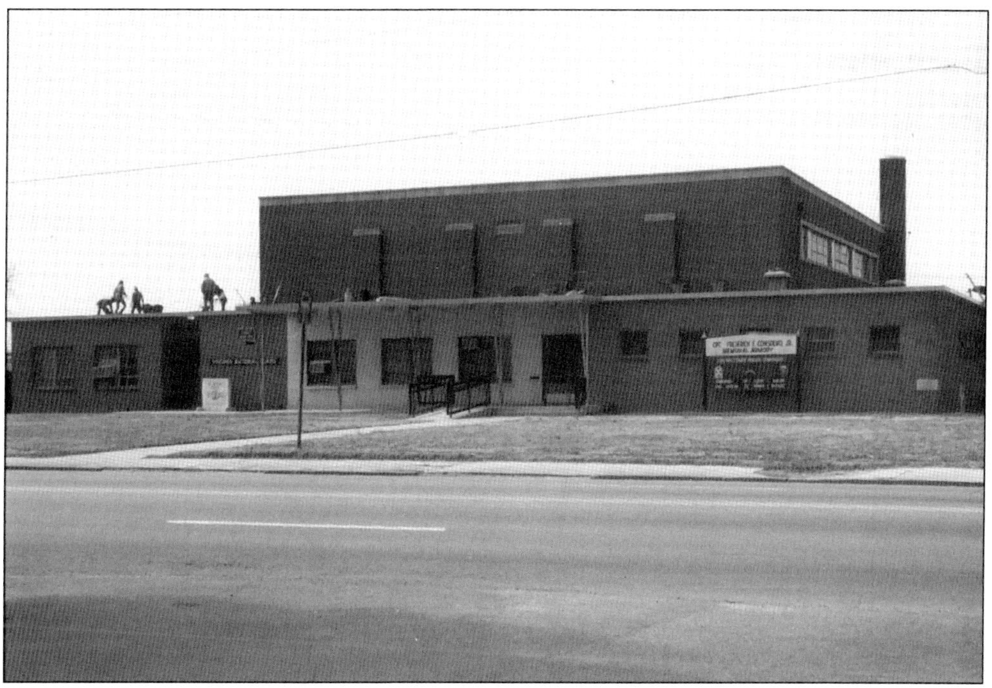

Pictured here is the Captain Frederic E. Consolvo, Jr. Memorial Armory, which was built at 1800 Bainbridge Boulevard. The 5-acre site was acquired from the American Oil Company in exchange for 5 1/2 acres on the water front plus $20,000. The armory was dedicated on May 12, 1956.

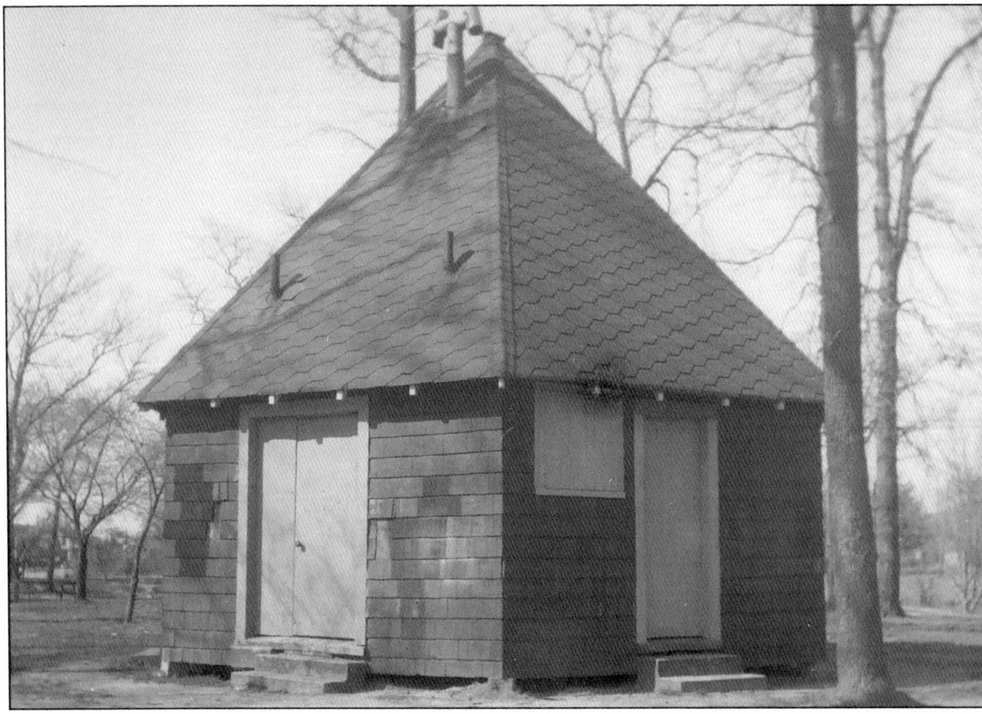

This small building in Lakeside Park on Holly Street was used as a voting precinct. This picture was taken June 1958.

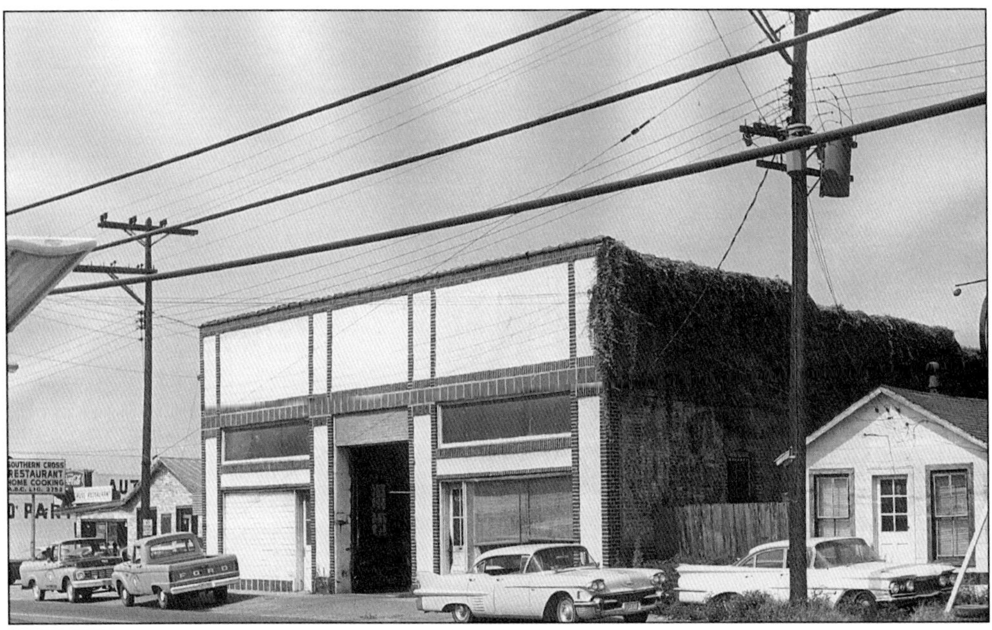

This large, ivy-covered structure was on Bainbridge Boulevard near the corner of Freeman Avenue in Portlock and served many purposes during its existence. The building housed both a stable and the city garage. The small building to the right was used, in earlier years, as a police station for the Norfolk County Police Department. This entire area is now the location of a Hardees restaurant. (Gordon Mitchell, photographer.)

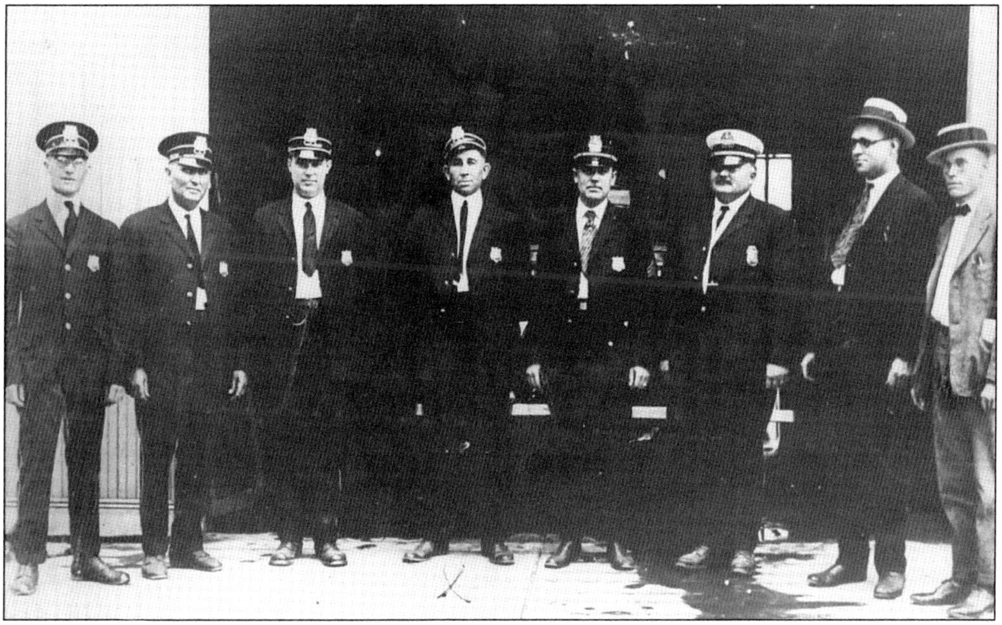

These men enforced the law in early South Norfolk. Pictured c. 1921, the officers and city officials are, from left to right, Clayton C. Ansell; Will Harris; Vernon Sprull; Bill Horton, motorcycle officer; Sergeant Sam Duvall; Chief of Police Paul (Polly) Warden; Mayor Floyd Rowland; and Bill Madrin, clerk of the court.

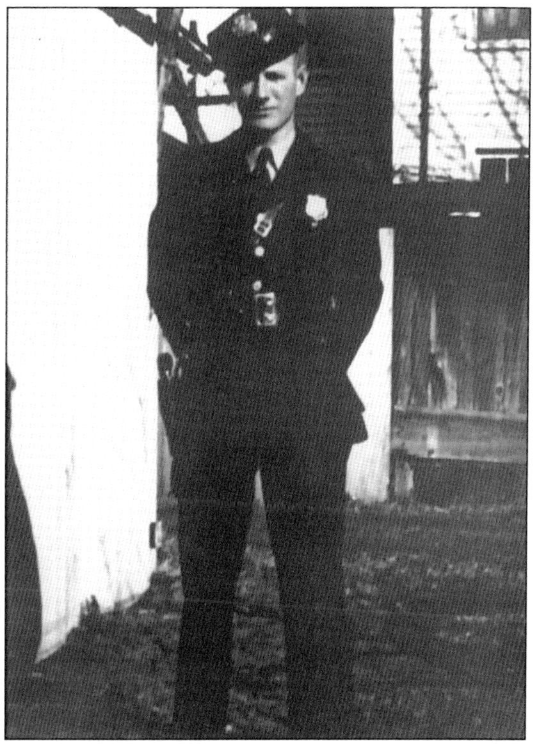

Henry I. Scheuerman was a member of the South Norfolk Police Department and served as its chief from 1944 to 1948. Mr. Scheuerman was later employed by the Virginia Department of Motor Vehicles; he was also a photographer and took several of the pictures used in this book.

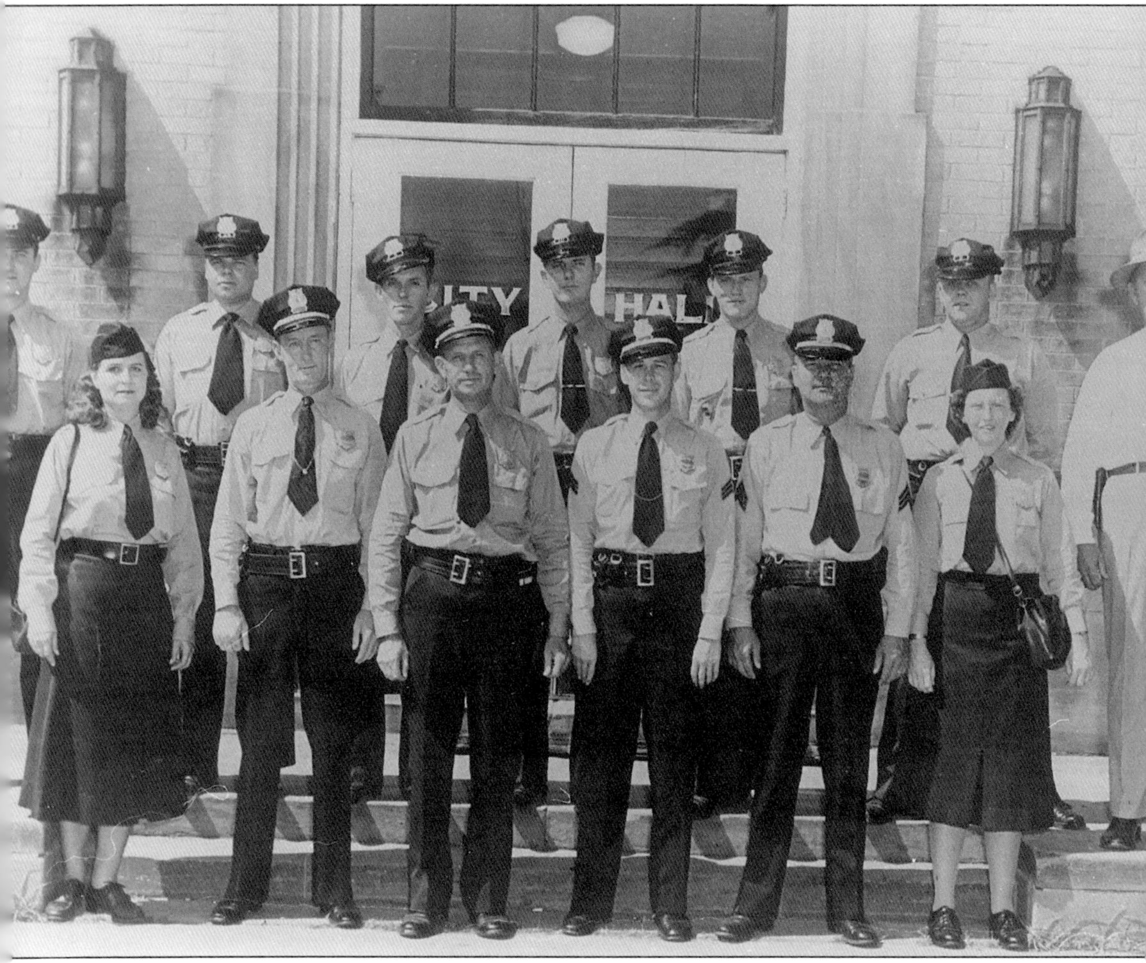

The members of the South Norfolk Police Department in 1952 are, from left to right, (front row) Beatrice Fisher, Chief William E. Beedie, Captain A.R. (Gudgeon) Bryant, Sergeant ? Disbrow, Sergeant R.C. (Chet) Hardy, and Irene Ellsworth; (back row) ? Simpson, Mike Dozier, David McPherson, William Vaught, Bernard (Bunky) Womack, ? Dorsett, and Detective ? Stryker.

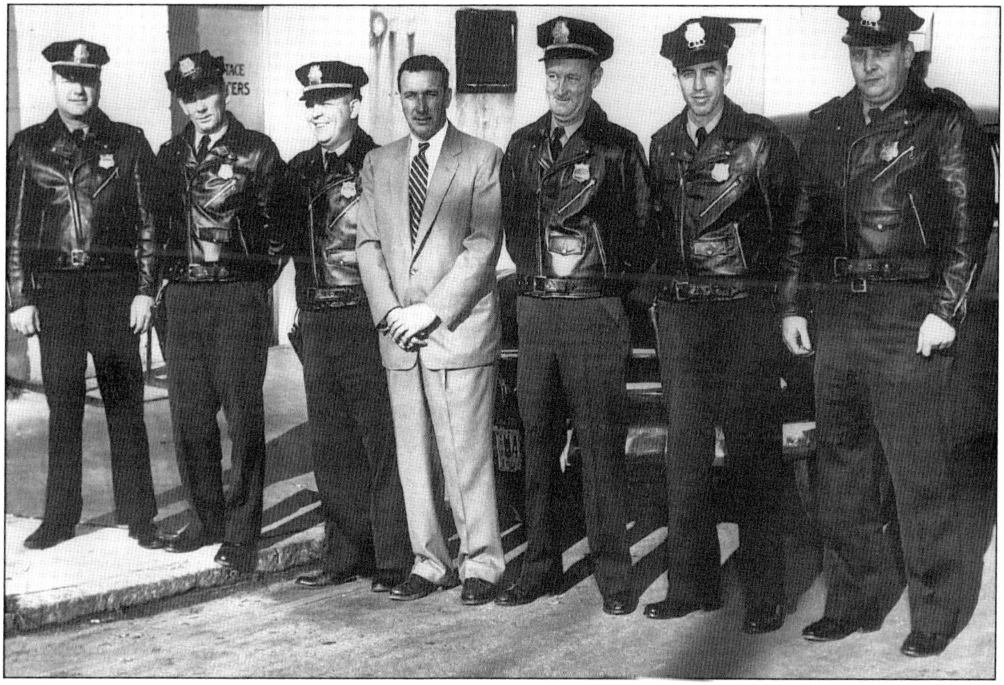

This photograph of a group of South Norfolk police officers was taken in the 1950s. Pictured are, from left to right, R.C. (Chet) Hardy, Vernon Eure, Waverly Phelps, city manager Phil Davis, Bill Beedie, Bud Guess, and John Schafer.

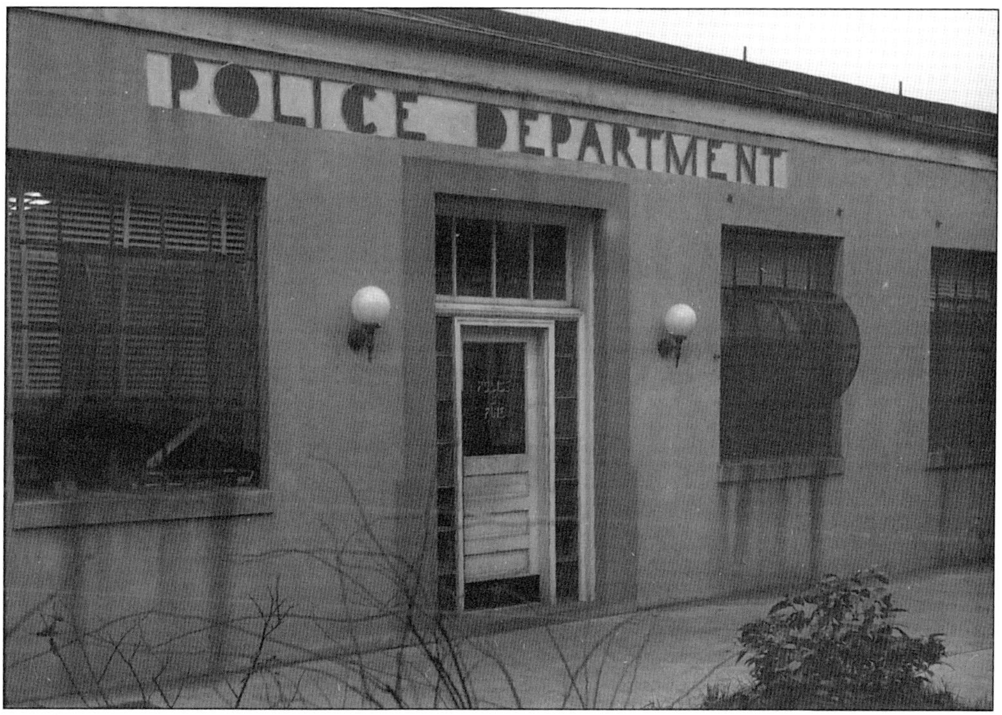

South Norfolk's Police Department shared the building on Liberty Street with the fire department. This picture was taken in 1960; a new police station was completed in 1961.

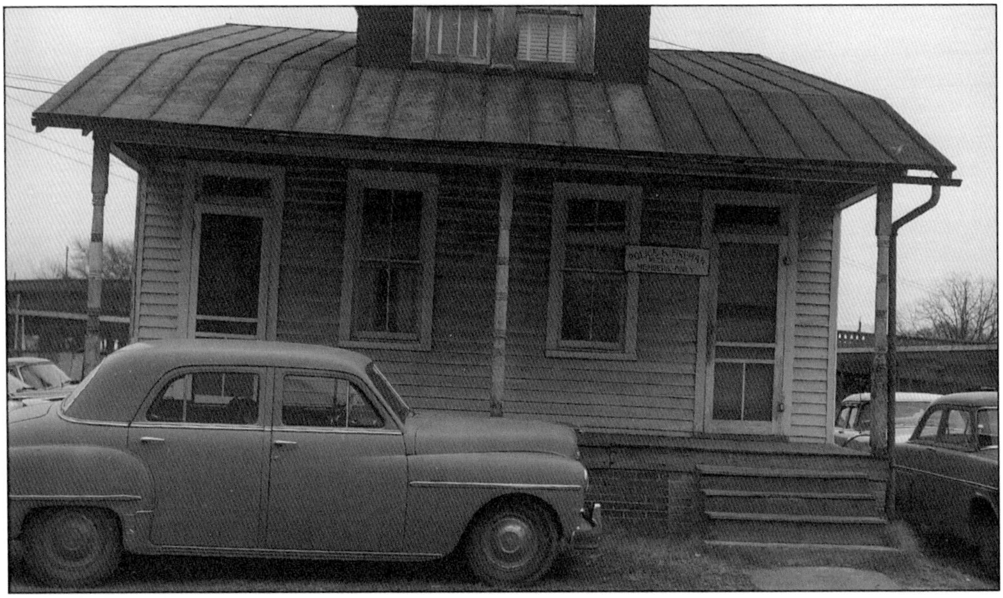

This old house at 701 St. James Street provided a meeting place for Troop 54 of the Boy Scouts of America. In May 1942, the Office of Price Administration (O.P.A.) opened its office on the first floor. The structure was later used as recreation quarters for members of the police and fire departments and eventually became the barracks for the first full-time firemen. The car on the front lawn belonged to Beatrice Fisher of the police department. Ms. Fisher was the first female officer in the South Norfolk Police Department.

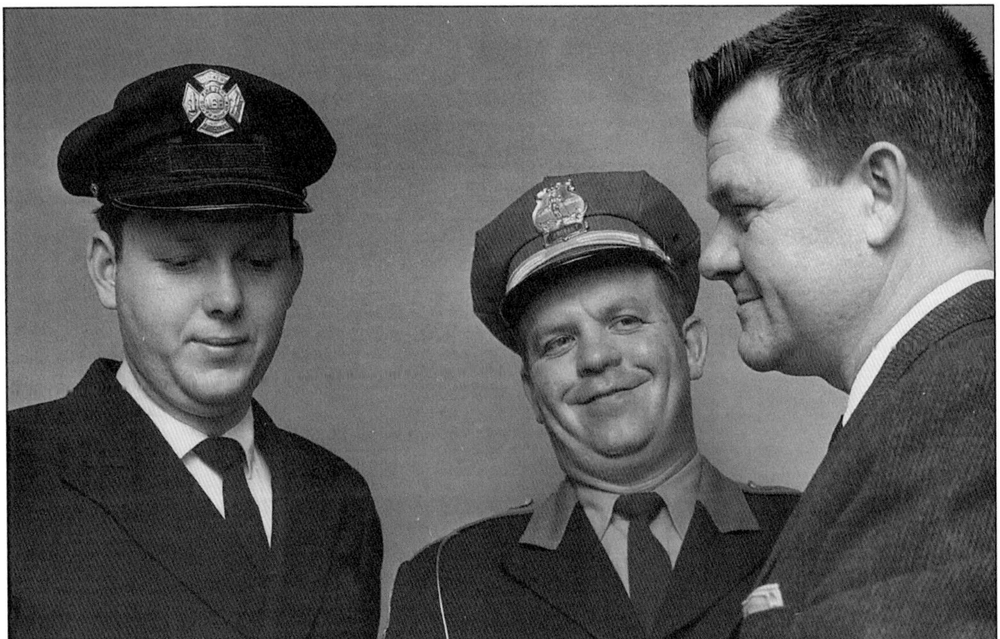

Shown here c. 1959, David Smith of the South Norfolk Volunteer Fire Department and Waverly Phelps of the South Norfolk Police Department receive medals from Mayor Linwood L. Briggs. (Orby G. Kelley, photographer.)

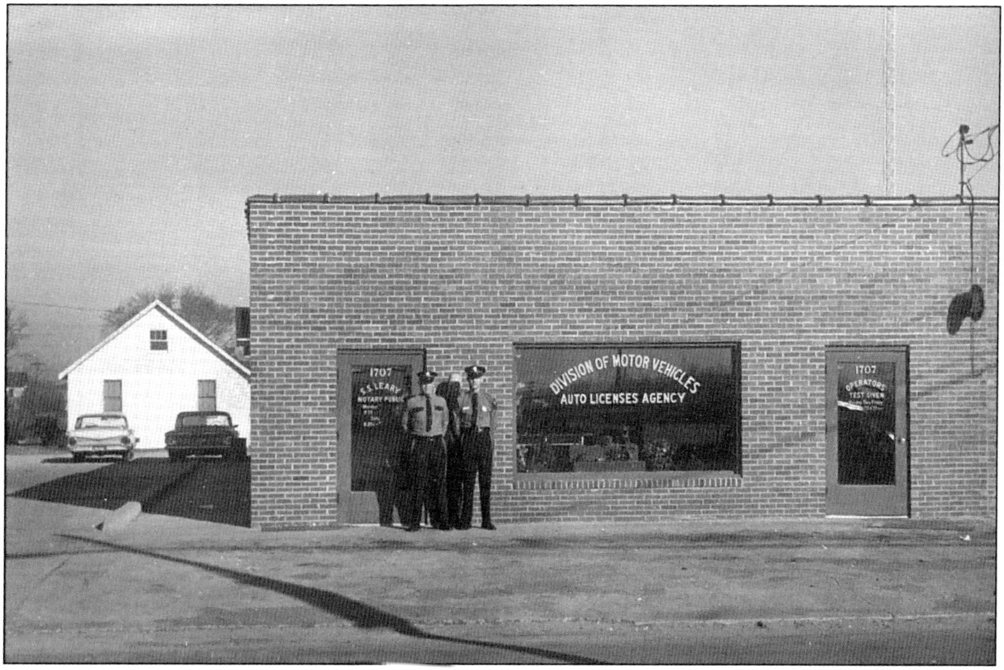

The Division of Motor Vehicles was at 1707 Park Avenue near the corner of Hawthorne (now Hoover) Avenue, and Mr. S.S. Leary operated the agency in the 1950s and '60s. Two unidentified state troopers are waiting patiently to administer driving tests to applicants desiring a driver's permit c. 1950s.

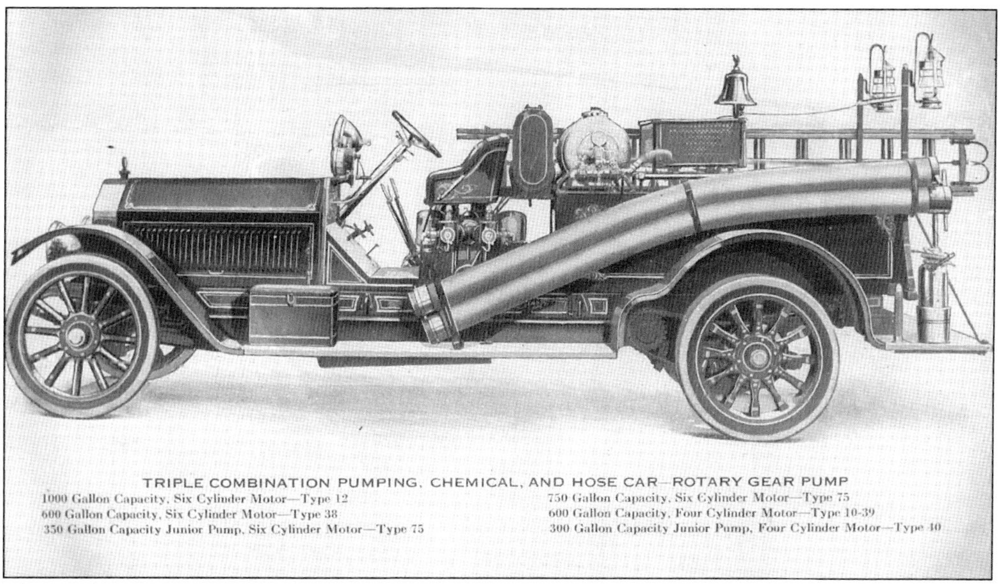

This early American pumping engine was manufactured at the Waterous Engine Works in St. Paul, Minnesota. The gearshift and hand brake were installed on the right side of the vehicle.

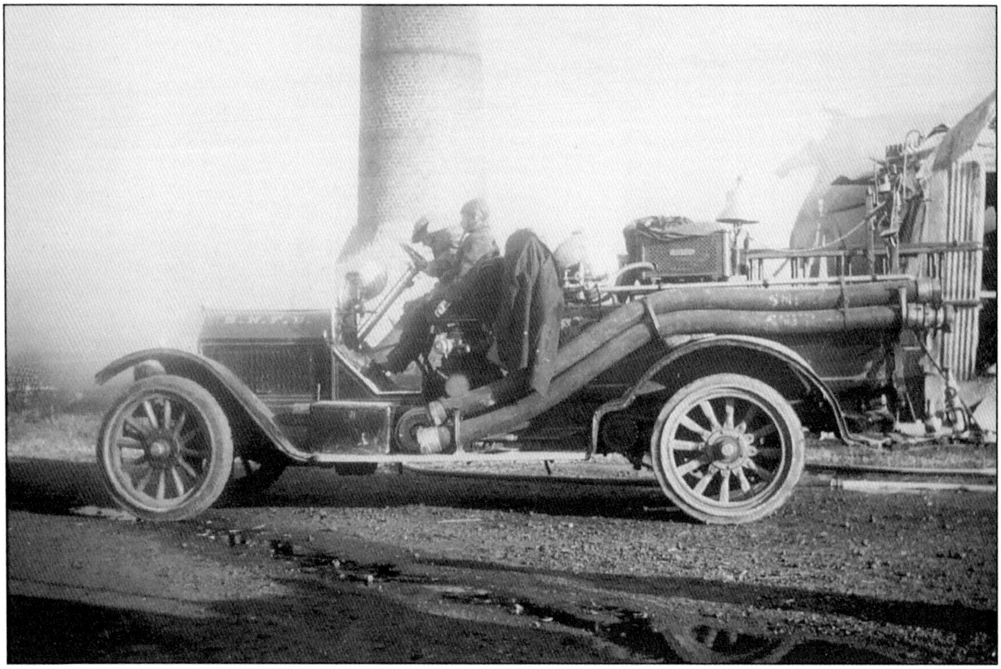

This is South Norfolk's first motorized fire engine after extinguishing a major conflagration c. 1917.

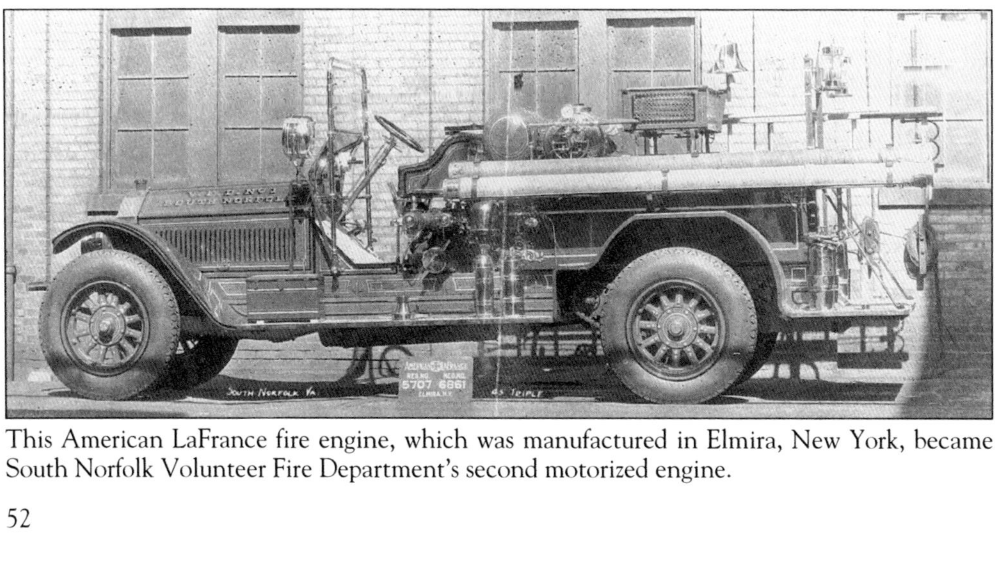

This American LaFrance fire engine, which was manufactured in Elmira, New York, became South Norfolk Volunteer Fire Department's second motorized engine.

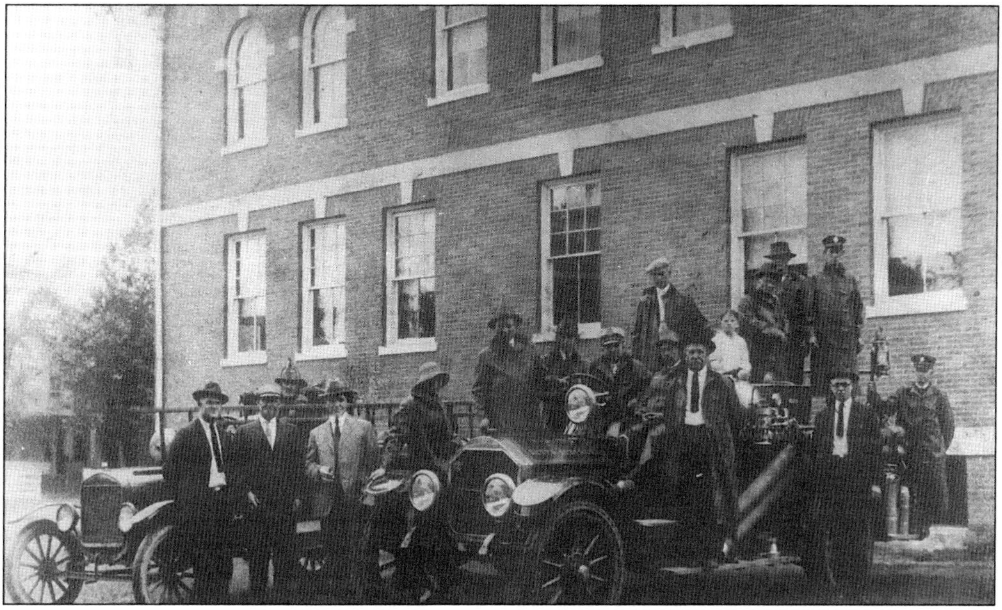

This photograph of the South Norfolk Volunteer Fire Department was taken in 1916 on the grounds of the South Norfolk Grammar School on "B" Street. The members are, from left to right, Harvey Bunch, P.G. Etheridge, T.R. Keller (sitting in the fire engine), L.H. Newberry, A.M. Spivey, H.A. Stewart, Ralph Stewart, S.H. Dennis (chief), D.E. Gregory (seated beside the chief), Jack Brown, R.G. Reber, Richard (Billy) Morgan (mascot), M. Parron, Russel Garrett, C.L. Sykes, F.L. Rowland, and W.F. Morgan. The engines are, from left to right, a 1914 Model T Ford and an American LaFrance 500-gallon-per-minute (GPM) pumper.

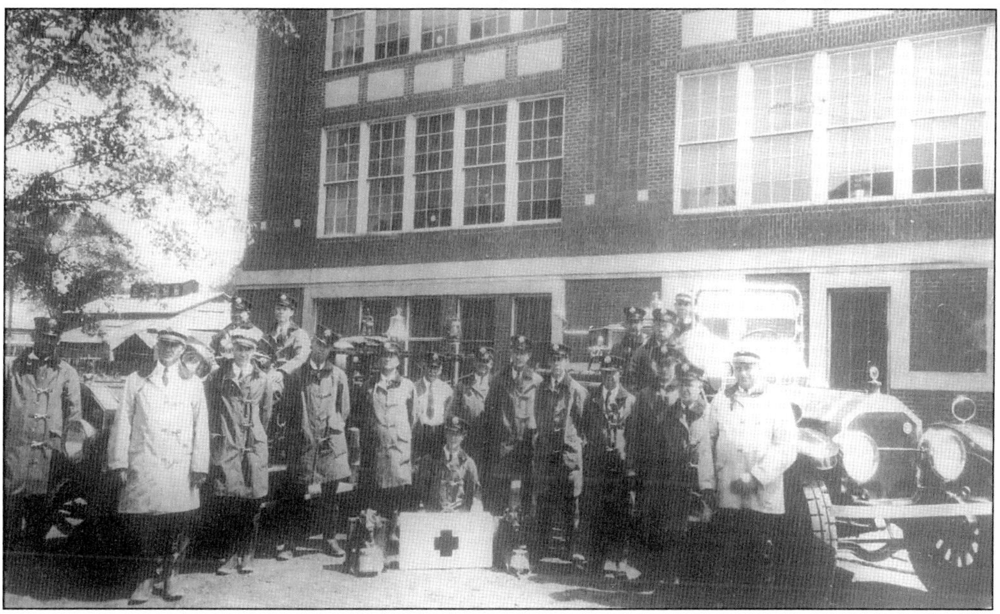

The members of the South Norfolk Volunteer Fire Department are pictured here in their new turnout clothing in 1936. The department reached its peak in numbers and performance in 1936, and remained so until 1945. Due to the efficiency of the fire department, the city received an excellent rating from the National Board of Fire Underwriters.

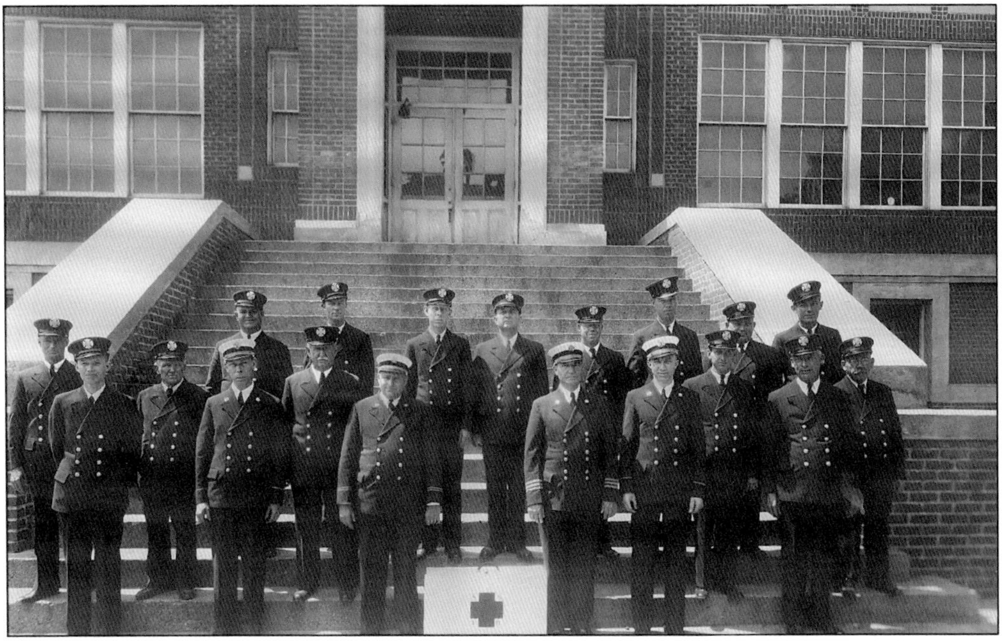

The members of the volunteer fire department dressed in their new uniforms to have this picture taken in 1936. The stone steps of the grammar school provided the background for many pictures. The members were, from left to right, (first row) Howard Jones, Cecil Gregory, Forest Williams, L.H. Newberry, Winston Dunning, and Jack Brown; (second row) John Humphries, Billie Morgan, R.G. Reber, Aubrey Harrell, and D.E. Gregory; (back row) Harvey Bunch, Herman Powers, Herbert VanVleek, John Jernigan, A.M. Kriss, William Nicholas, Harry Stewart, and Churchill Brown. (Photo taken by Atlantic Photo Studio, Norfolk.)

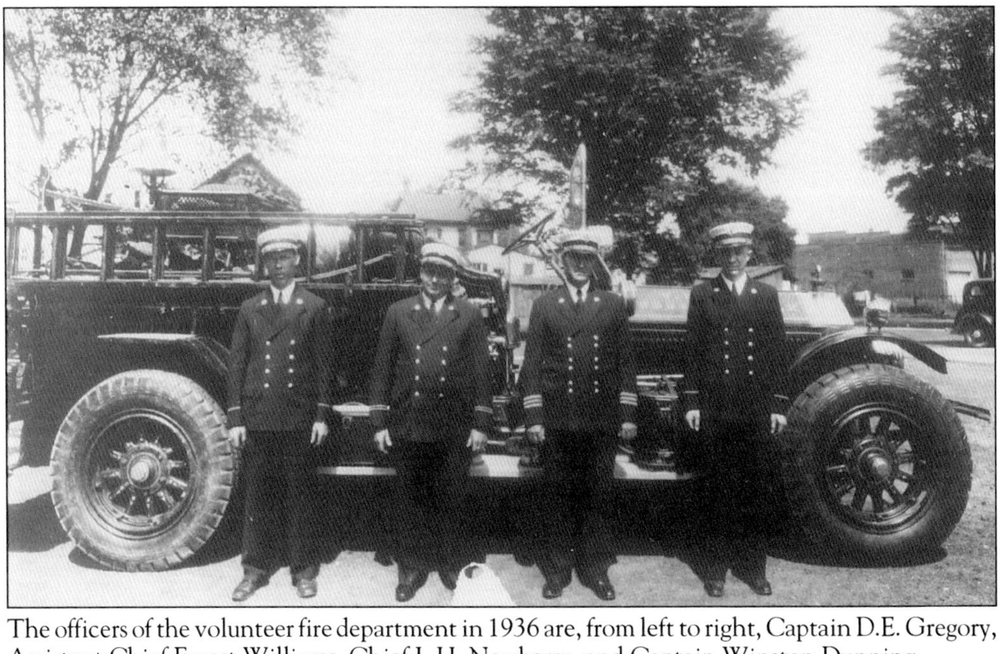

The officers of the volunteer fire department in 1936 are, from left to right, Captain D.E. Gregory, Assistant Chief Forest Williams, Chief L.H. Newberry, and Captain Winston Dunning.

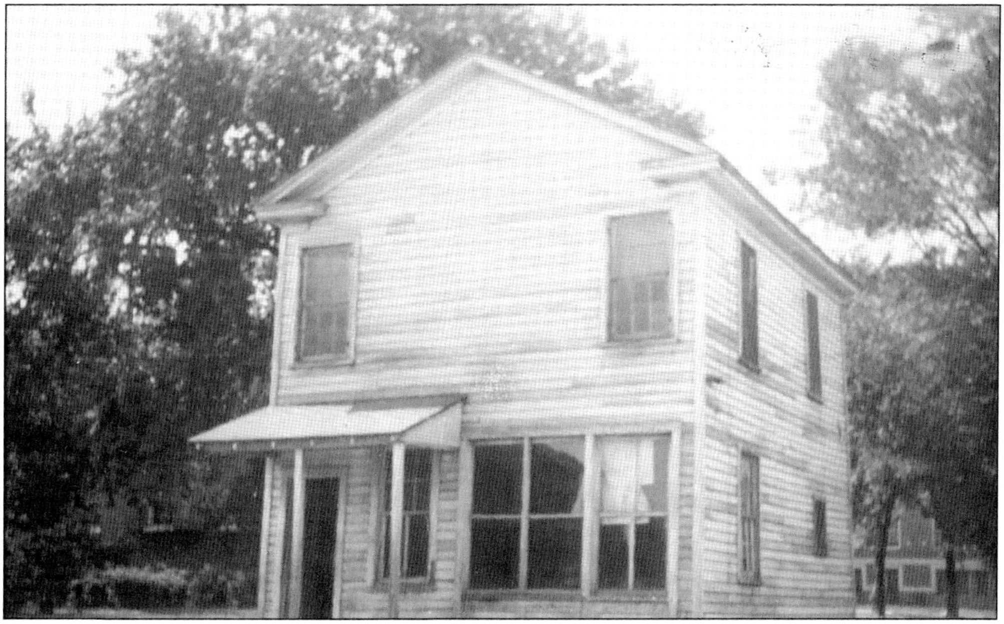

This old house in the corner of the schoolyard at Twenty-second and "A" Streets was originally the home of Bill White's parents. In 1892, it became the first fire department headquarters. The building was later used by the school as domestic science classrooms, and the building also served as the welfare department during the Depression era. The boy scouts met there at one time, and the boy's club used it for a wood working shop. This photograph was taken August 13, 1937.

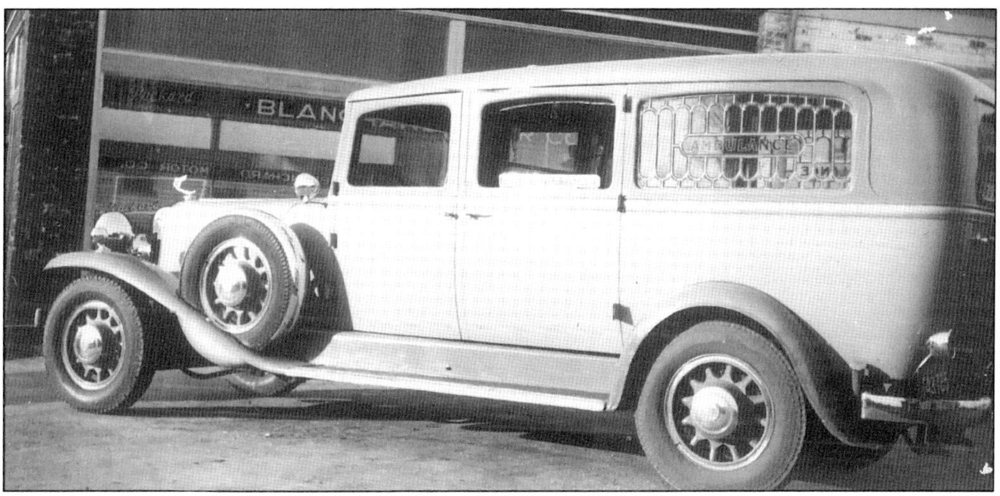

South Norfolk's first ambulance was parked at Blanchard Motor Company, a Packard dealer on Liberty Street. This ambulance was probably purchased, as were several others, with contributions from the citizens of South Norfolk.

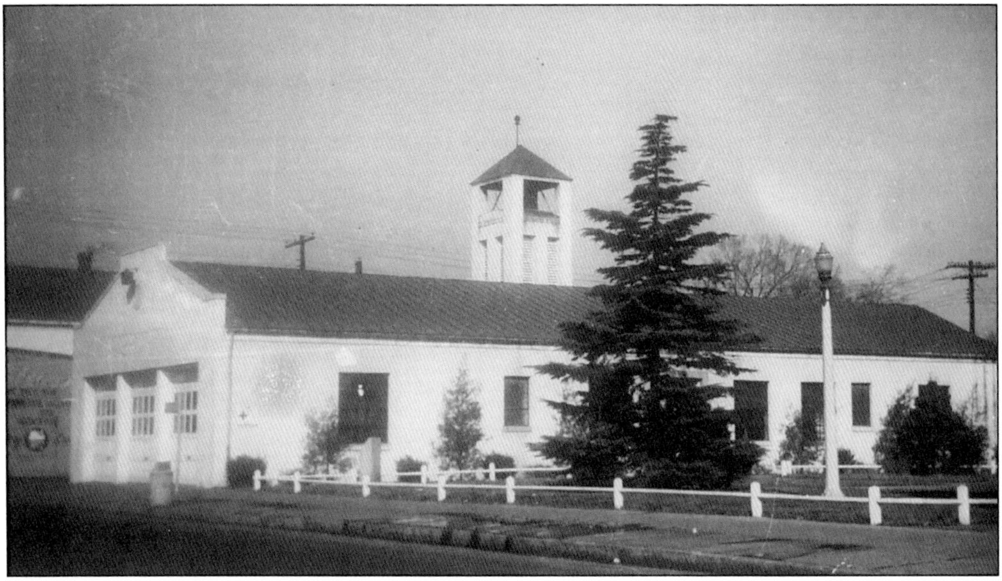

The fourth fire station was built on the corner of Liberty and Twentieth Streets around 1938. Prior to the construction of this station, the corner was occupied by Blanchard Motor Company.

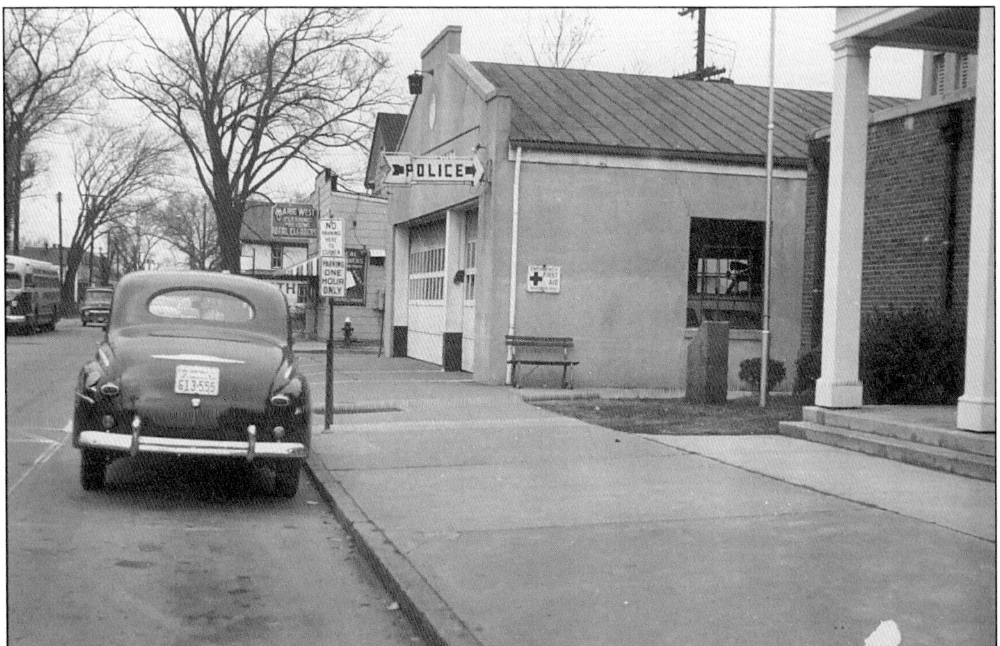

This photograph was taken around 1959. In 1953, the court building was constructed beside the fire station. By that time, a sign had been installed that identified the location of the police station. The automobile parked in front of the courthouse belonged to Mr. Paul Sykes, a member of the fire department.

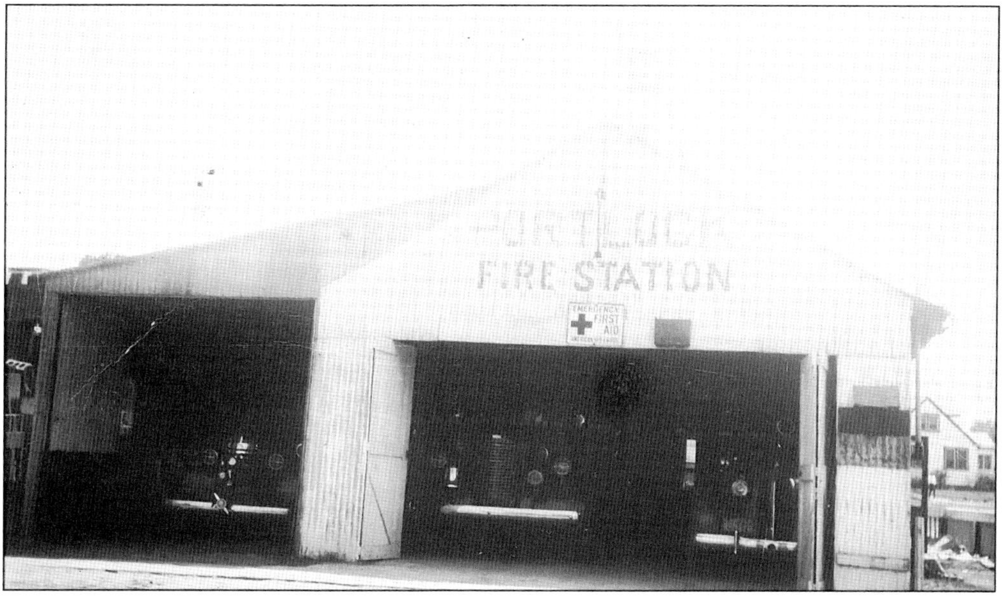

This old tin garage served as the fire station for the small village of Portlock, which was part of Norfolk County when this picture was taken in April 1944. Portlock became part of the City of South Norfolk in 1951.

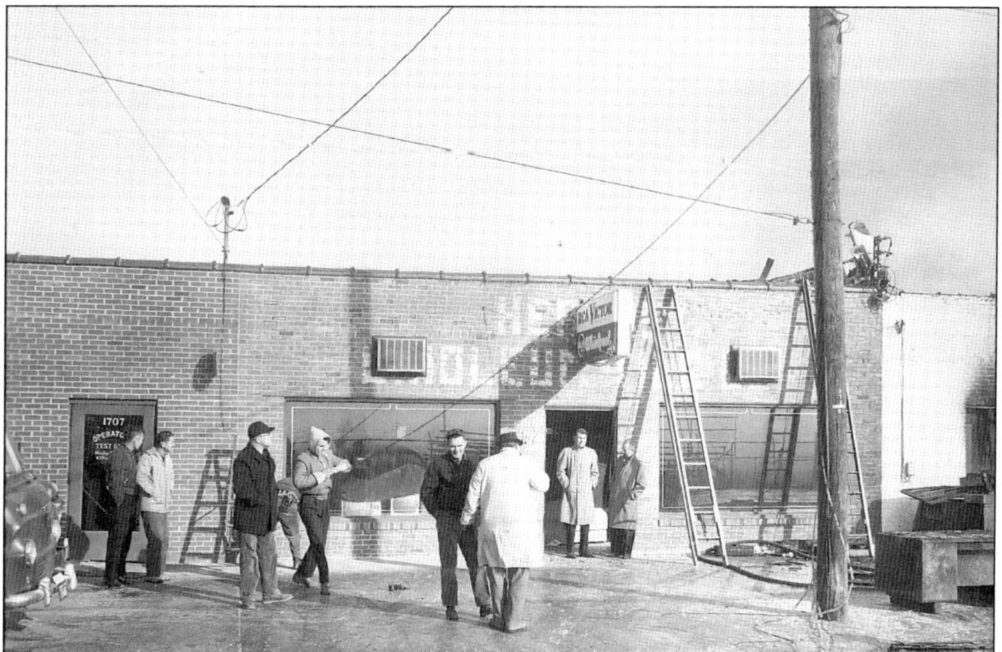

Greenough & Company was a wholesale building material business in the 1700 block of Park Avenue, next to the Division of Motor Vehicles. Fire broke out on one of the coldest nights of the year, c. 1960, and destroyed most of the building and its contents. Water from the fire hoses froze as soon as it hit the building and the surrounding streets. This photograph, which was taken the next day, shows ice on the street and sidewalk.

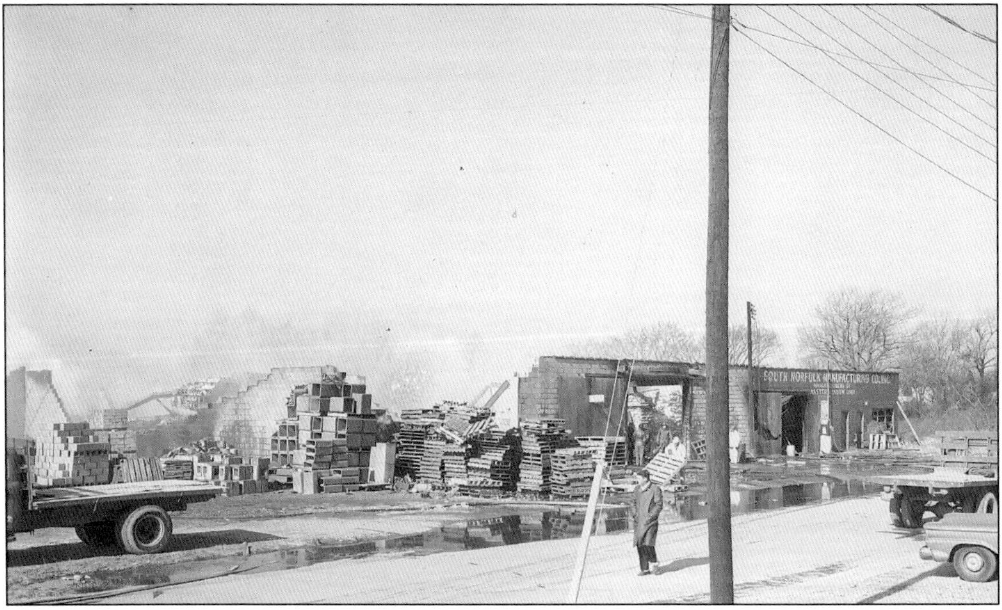

This picture of the Greenough fire was taken from Transylvania Avenue and shows additional destruction of the building.

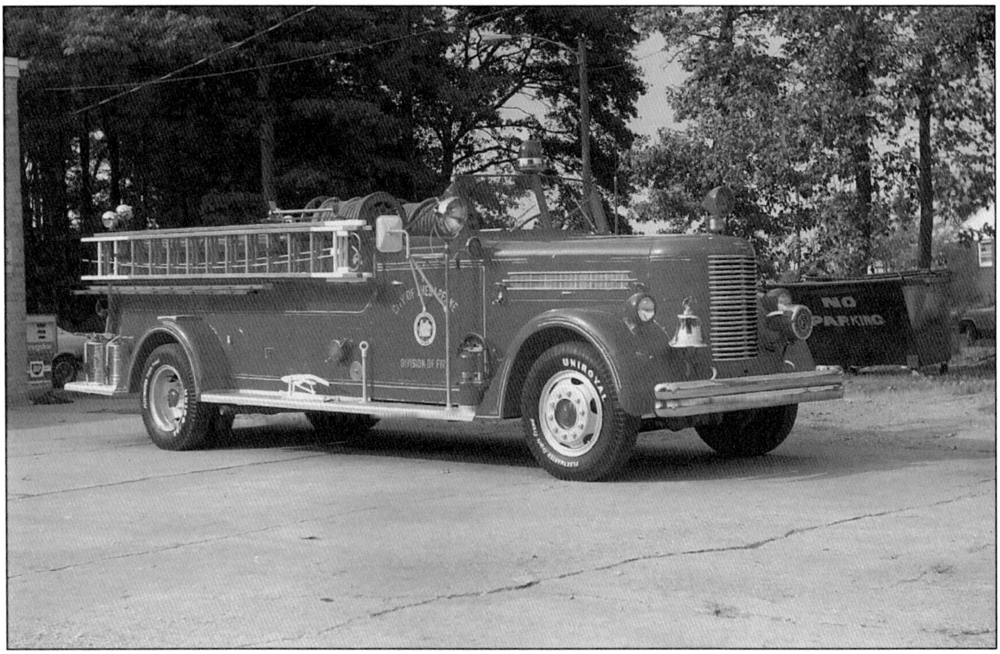

This 1941 model Peter Pirsch fire truck was top of the line, and two were ordered for South Norfolk in October 1941. When the United States entered WW II, production of the trucks for civilian use was soon terminated; however, one was delivered to the Portlock volunteers in May 1942. It is possible that this one was delivered to South Norfolk after the war and went on to serve the City of Chesapeake.

Four

CHURCHES AND CONGREGATIONS

Many community activities revolved around the early churches of South Norfolk and Portlock. The local churches served not only as places of worship, but also hosted such events as school graduations, picnics, and many other happenings of the day. During the latter part of the 19th and the early 20th century, about a dozen churches were established in the area. Among them were the Liberty Street Methodist, South Norfolk Baptist, South Norfolk Congregational Christian, South Norfolk Church of Christ, First Presbyterian, Southside Baptist, Providence Christian, Rosemont Christian, Raleigh Heights Baptist, Portlock Methodist, Bethel Assembly of God, and South Norfolk Pentecostal Holiness Church.

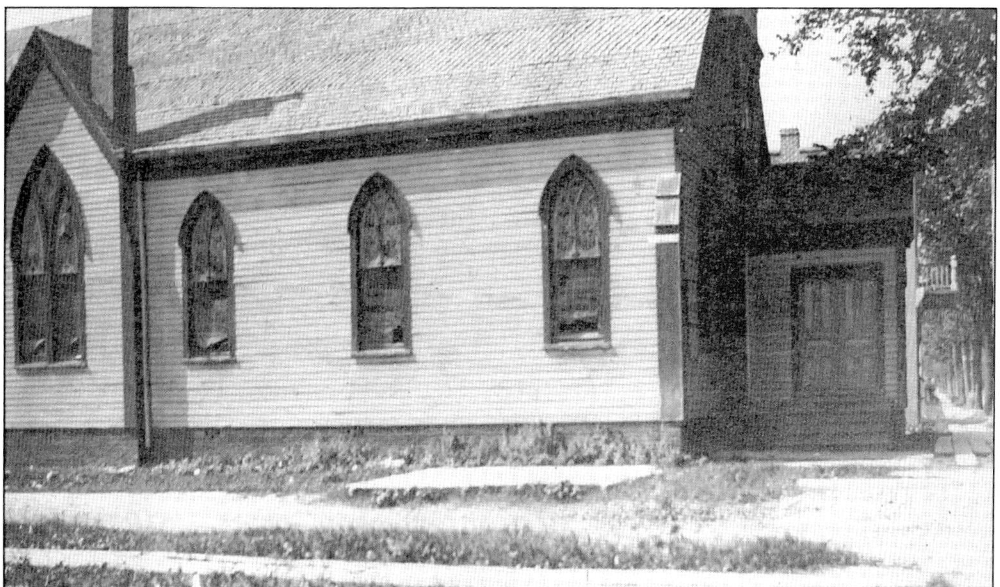

The Liberty Street Methodist Episcopal Church, South, was the first church in South Norfolk, established at the corner of Liberty and Twenty-second Streets in 1892. At that time, Liberty Street was a dirt road with wooden boardwalks and young tall trees. The streetcar ran down its middle, taking people to and from Berkley and Norfolk. Many members of the congregation rode the trolley to church services on Sunday and at other times.

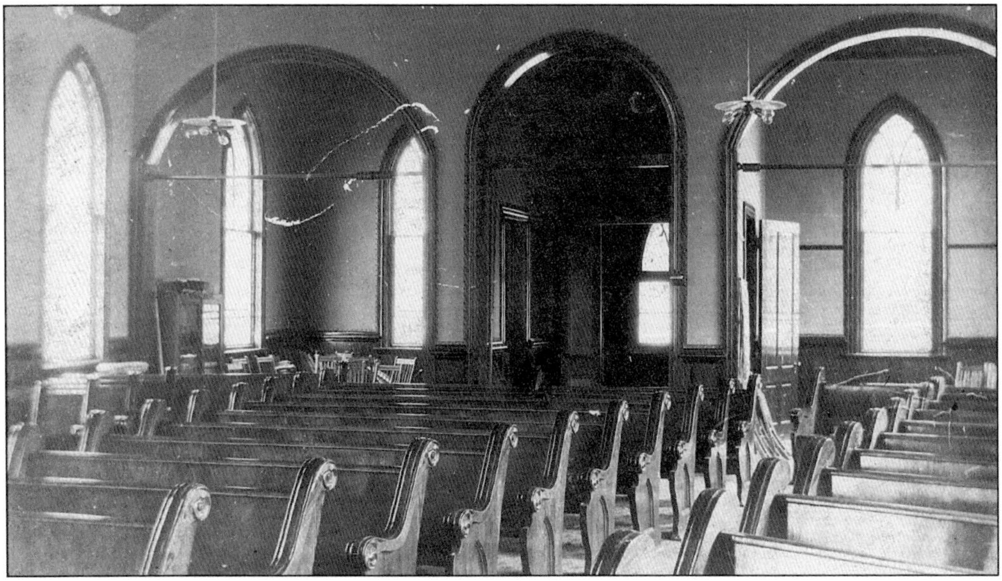

The interior of the Liberty Street Church consisted of one large room with wooden pews and light bulbs mounted on fixtures hanging from the ceiling. On Sunday morning, the congregation met together, then divided into classes, and each class had a designated corner where they went for Sunday school. After Sunday school, everyone came back together for a church service.

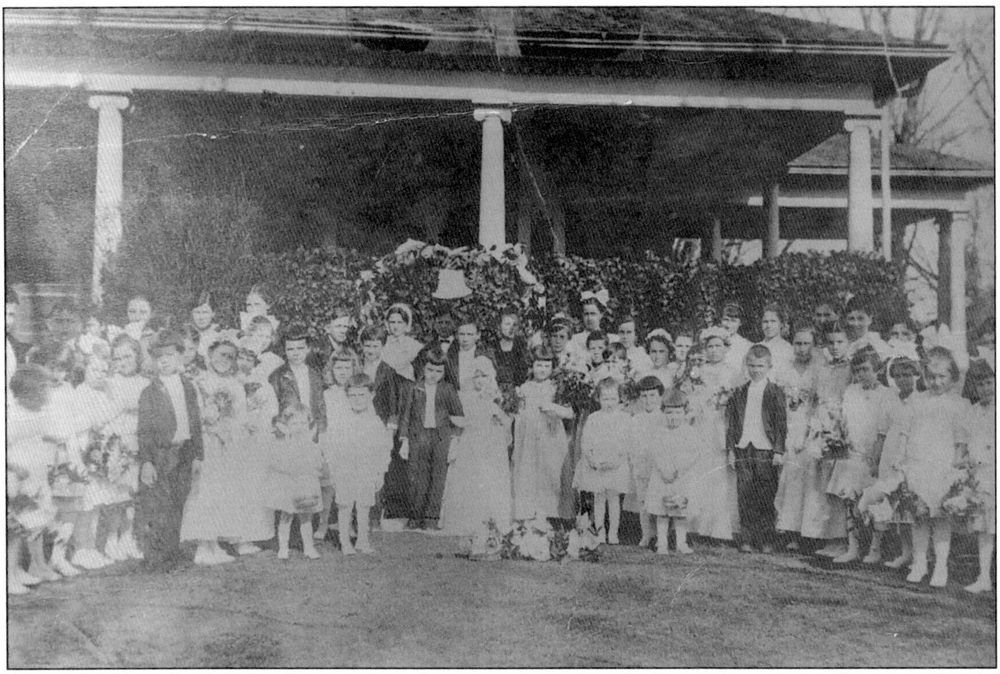

Around 1916, the Liberty Street Church was having financial problems. Mrs. Winnie Heath, the pastor's wife suggested a Lilliputian wedding as a means of raising funds. The mock wedding, which consisted of some 56 children, was held on the side lawn of the Forehand home at the corner of Chesapeake Avenue and Ohio Street. The bride was Mildred Simpkins, and the groom was Melvin Young.

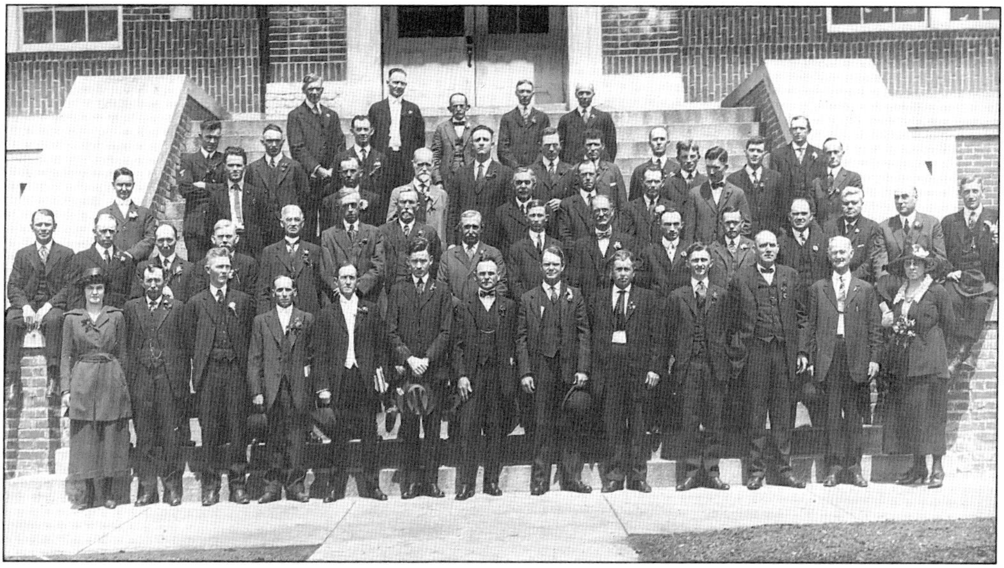

The Beacon Bible Class of the Liberty Street Methodist Church used the stone steps of the old grammar school to have this picture taken in May 1920. Unfortunately, no one can identify all the members of this class.

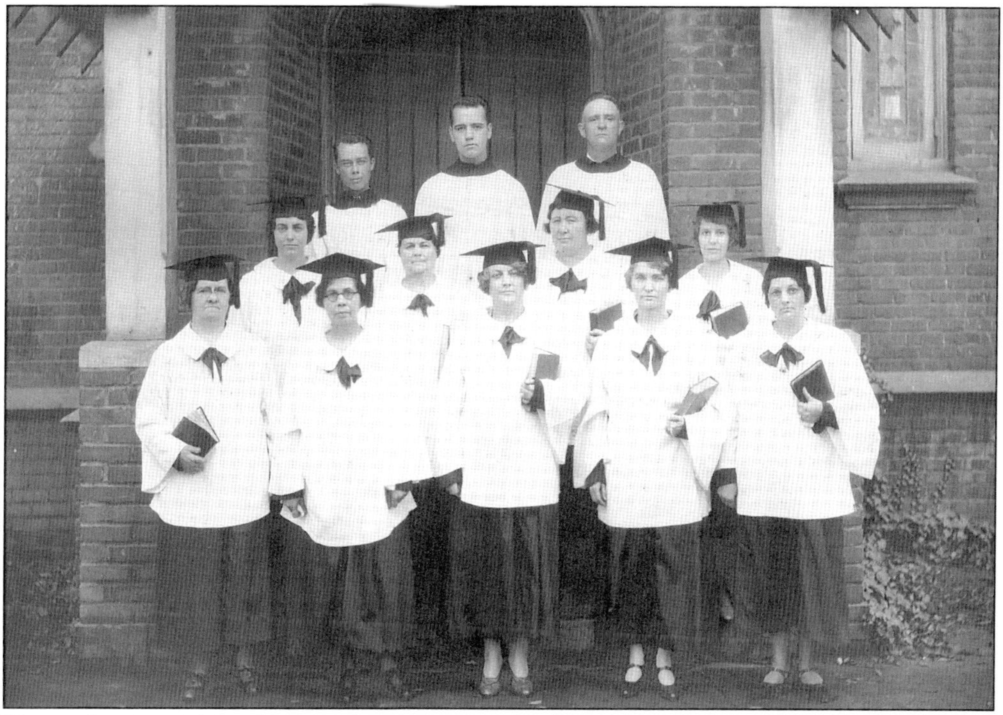

This is the choir of the Chesapeake Avenue Methodist Episcopal Church, South, c. 1922. The new church building was completed in 1921, and the Liberty Street Methodist Church became the Chesapeake Avenue Church. Again it is not possible to name all the members seen here. However, in the first row is Mrs. Ethel Townsend Warden (fourth from the left), in the second row is Mrs. A.Guy Hall Sr. (third from the left), and in the third row are, from left to right, Poppy Beale, A. Guy Hall Jr., and A. Guy Hall Sr.

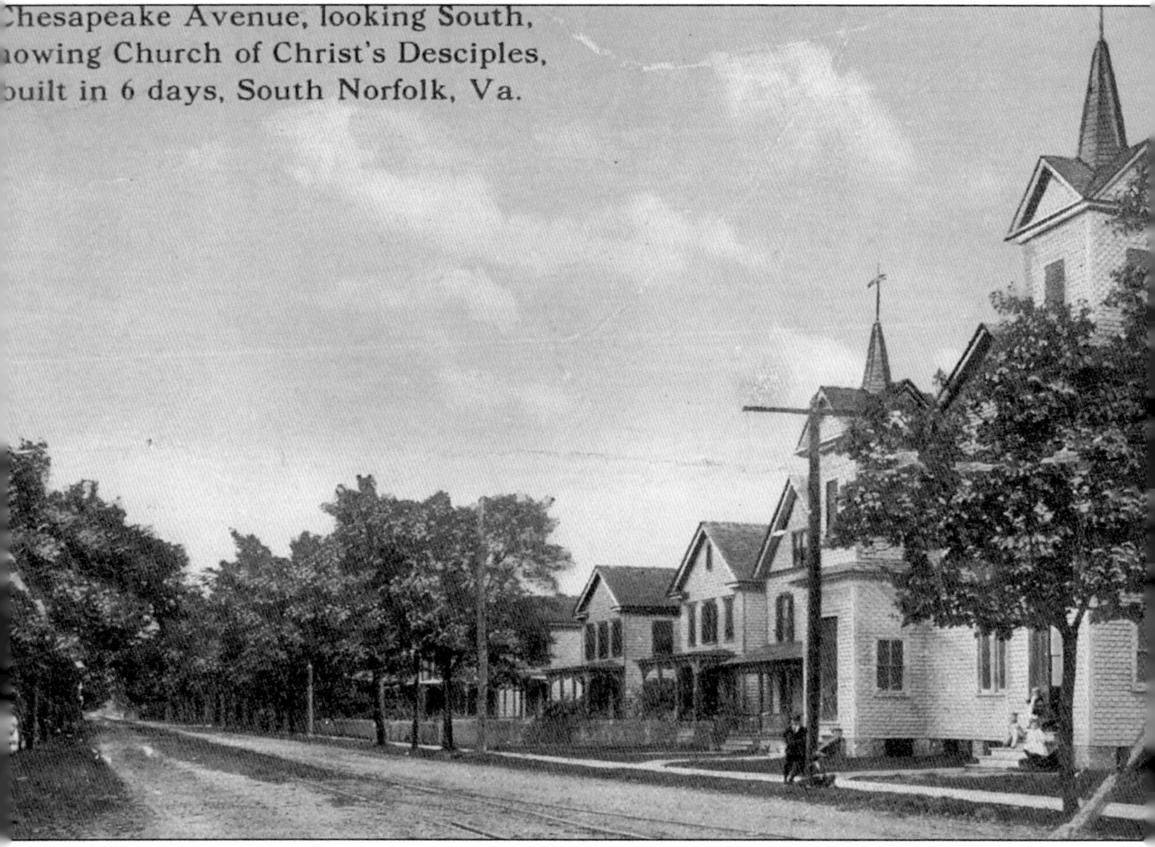

This image was made from a postcard. The message in the upper left corner almost says it all, but, as can be seen, the word 'disciple' has been misspelled. The Church of Christ's Disciples was built at the corner of Chesapeake Avenue and Poindexter Street when the streets were still dirt with the streetcar tracks down the middle. The postcard is dated *c.* 1910.

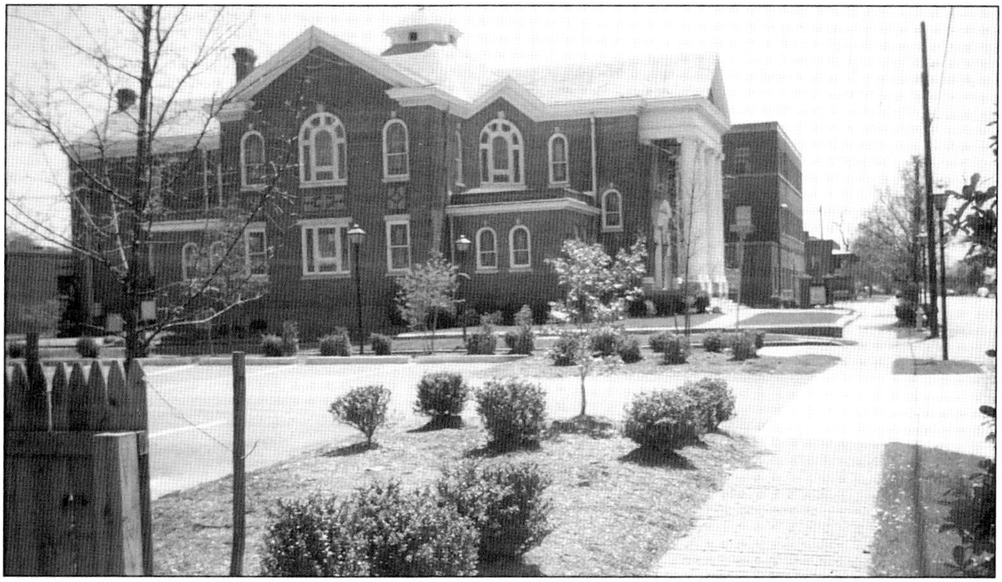

On September 9, 1891, the Berkley Avenue Baptist Church appointed a committee to investigate the possibility of acquiring lots in South Norfolk for the erection of a church. On April 1, 1892, it was reported that Mr. Thomas Synon had offered to donate the lots, and by July 1, 1892, a contract was awarded to build a 20-by-60-foot chapel at a cost of $1,660. The building opened for worship on January 5, 1893, and the formal dedication was held on June 11, 1893. This is a recent photograph of the South Norfolk Baptist Church.

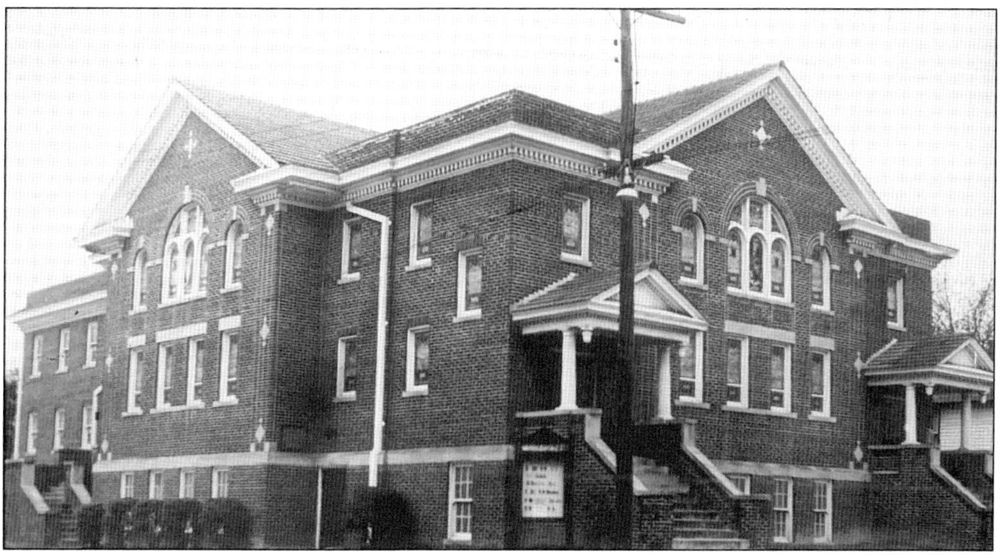

In the fall of 1903, a Sunday school was organized in the South Norfolk school in the 1100 block of Jackson Street. The Sunday school continued to grow, and on May 29, 1904, the South Norfolk Christian Church was organized with 16 charter members. In 1906, lots were purchased at the corner of Jackson and Guerriere Streets; a house of worship was erected and formally opened in November of the same year. This picture of the South Norfolk Congregational Christian Church was taken June 6, 1926.

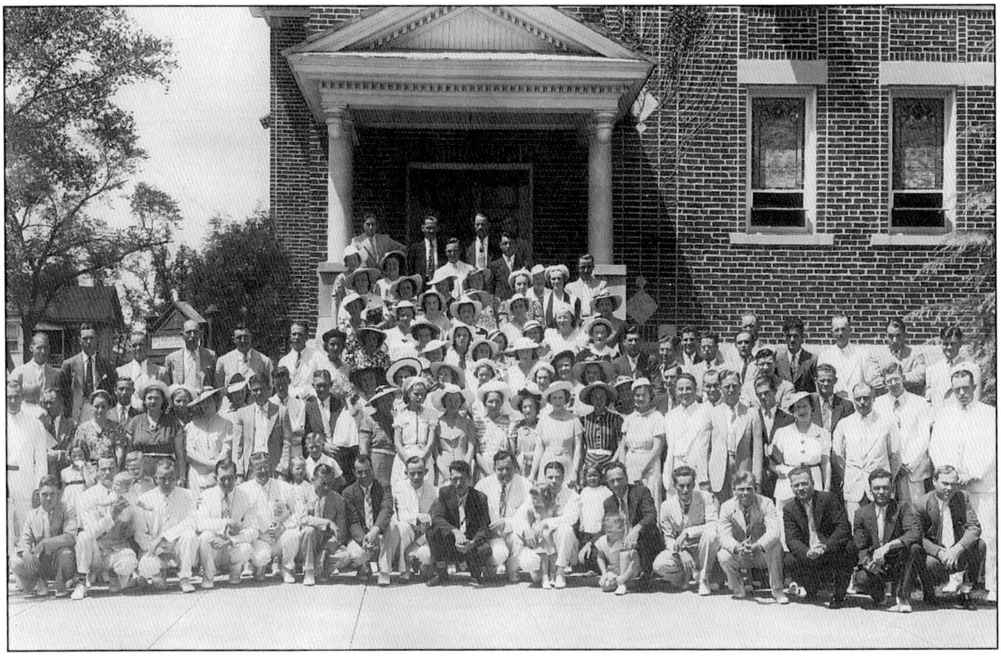

Members of the Sunday school gather in front of the South Norfolk Congregational Christian Church to have this c. 1940 photograph taken. The Reverend O.D. Poythress, in his white suit, is the fifth man from the left in the first row.

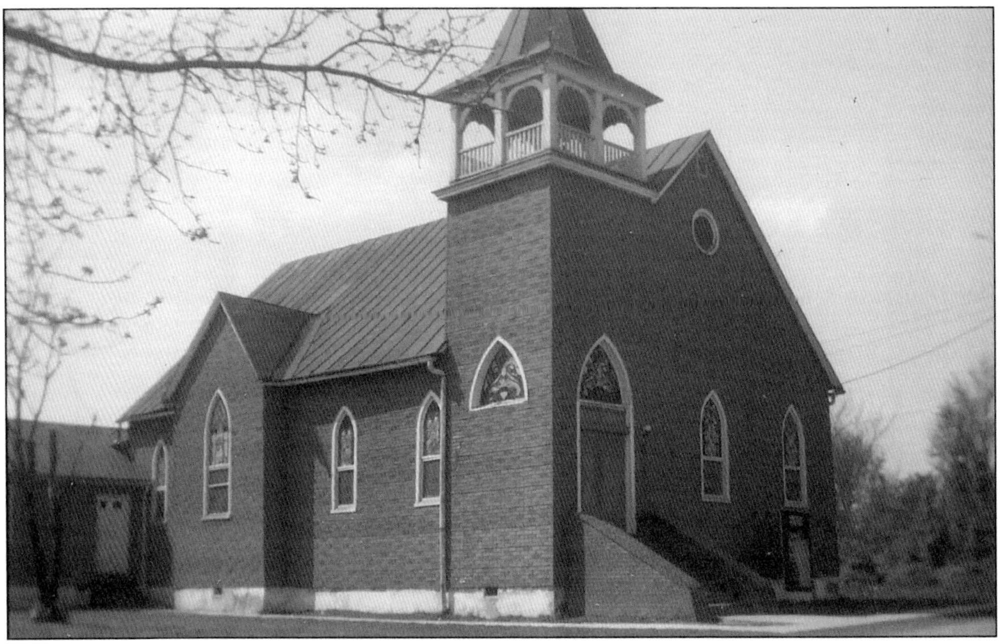

This church, located on St. James Street at the corner of Hodges Road, is pictured here in May 1961.

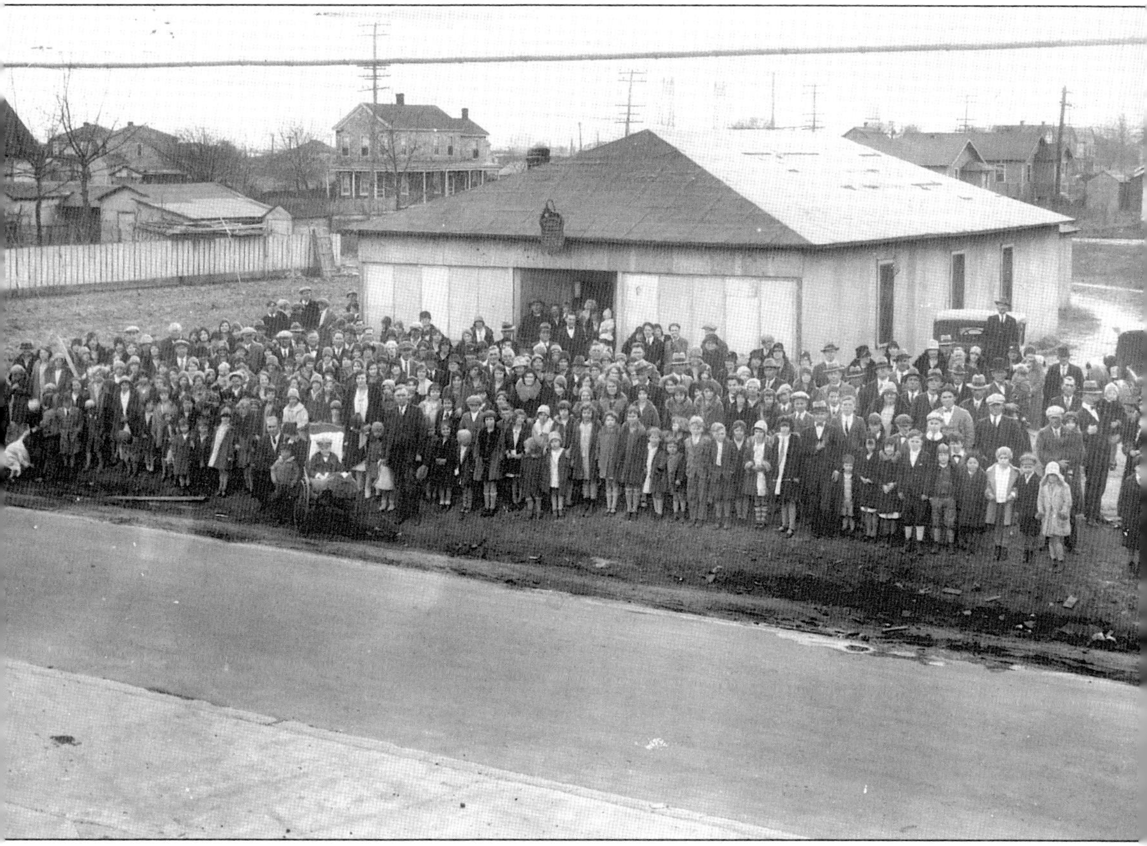

Members of the South Norfolk Assembly of God met in this converted garage at the intersection of Bainbridge Boulevard and Poindexter Street in 1930 with their pastor, J.M. Oliver. The church later became the Bethel Assembly of God and is now located at the corner of Decatur and Grady Streets.

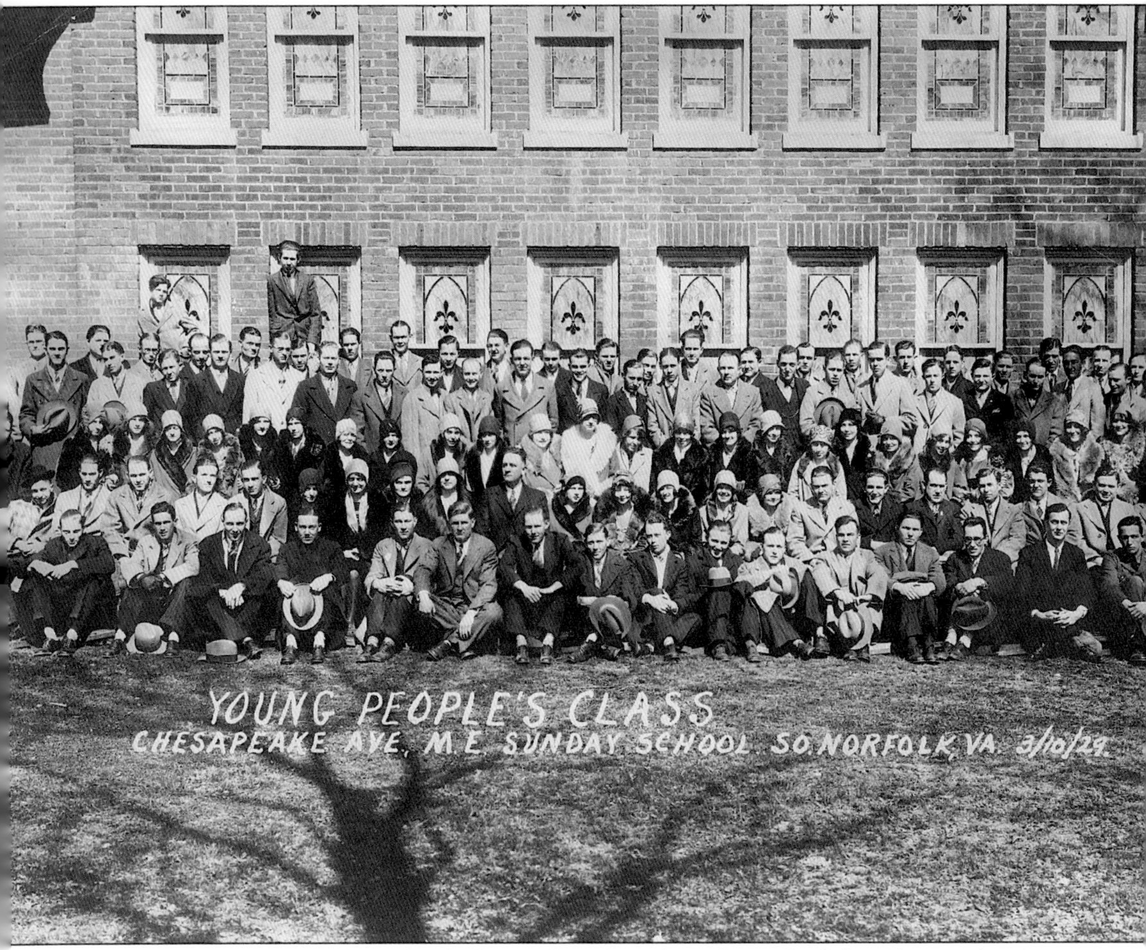

This rather large Sunday school class gathered in the side yard of the Chesapeake Avenue Methodist Episcopal Church on Sunday, March 10, 1929, to pose for this picture. The teacher is Mr. A. Guy Hall Sr., and the young man standing in the second window from the left is Wilbur Curling.

Five

Residences and the Historic District

The South Norfolk Historic District has the largest number of historic structures in the City of Chesapeake. The district has more than 600 contributing structures and more than an additional 100 have been identified outside the district. Many of the homes featured here no longer exist, but will be of interest to current and former citizens of South Norfolk.

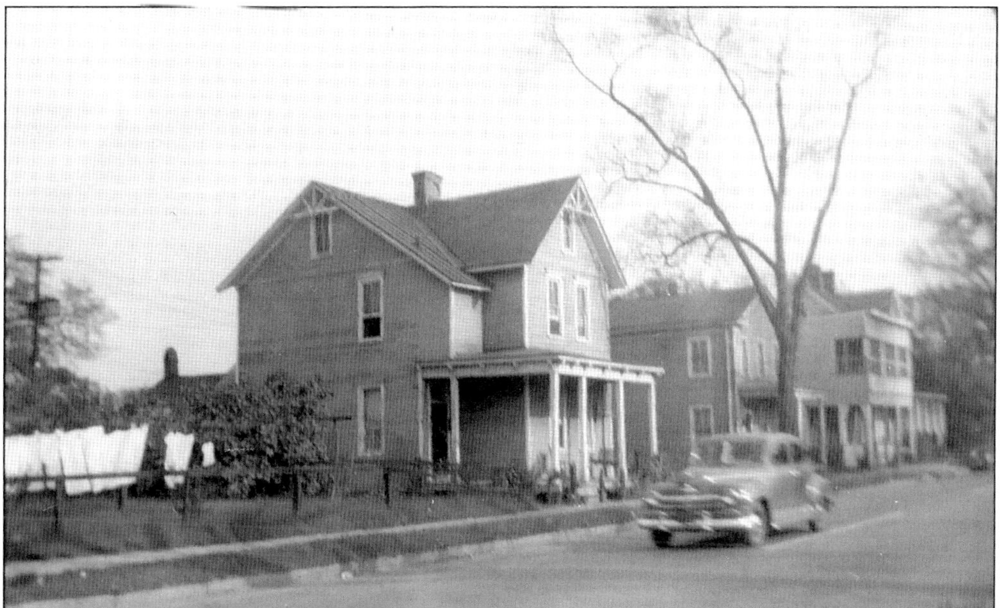

The homes shown here are in the 100 block of Liberty Street between the Belt Line Railroad and Eighteenth Street. They were demolished around 1961.

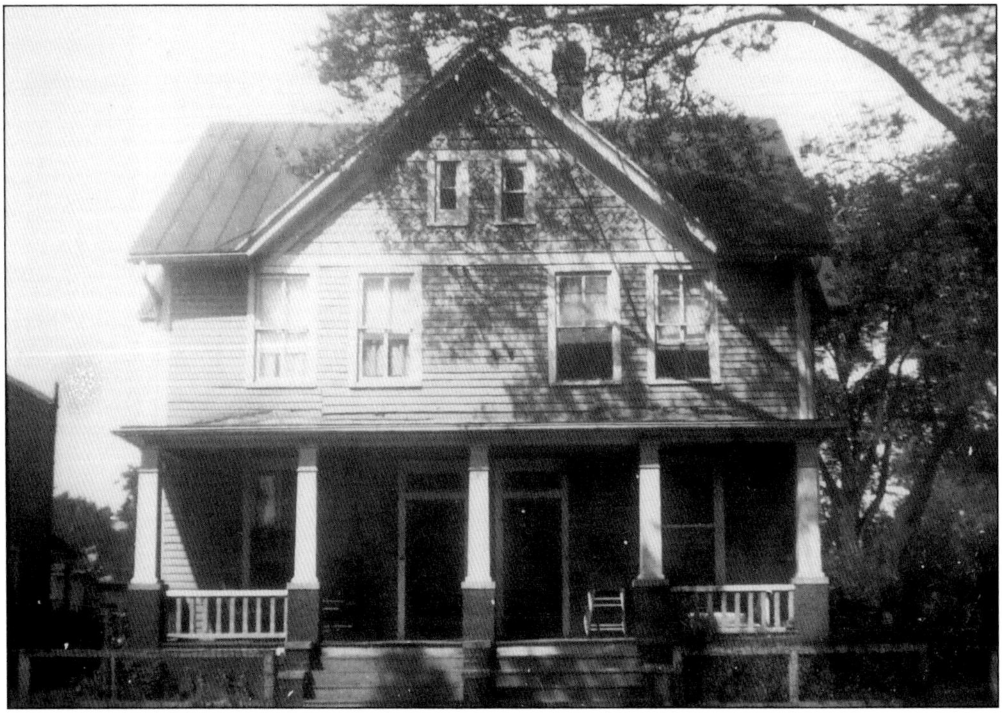

This was the home of Sam Zedd and his family at 319 E. Liberty Street.

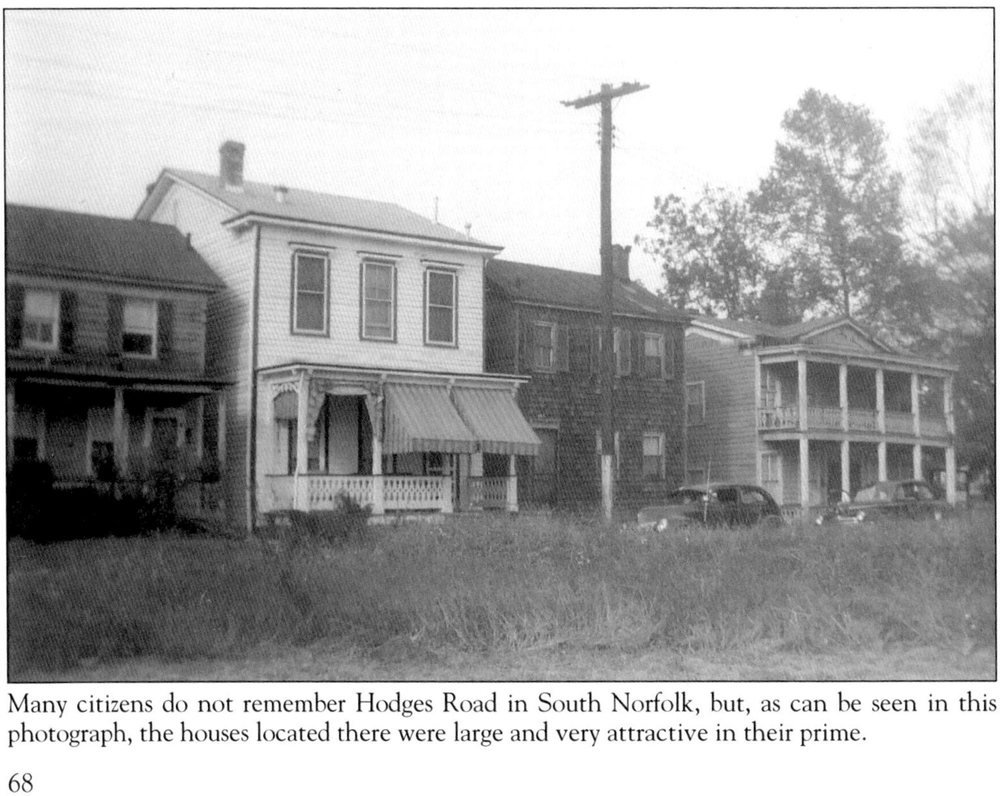

Many citizens do not remember Hodges Road in South Norfolk, but, as can be seen in this photograph, the houses located there were large and very attractive in their prime.

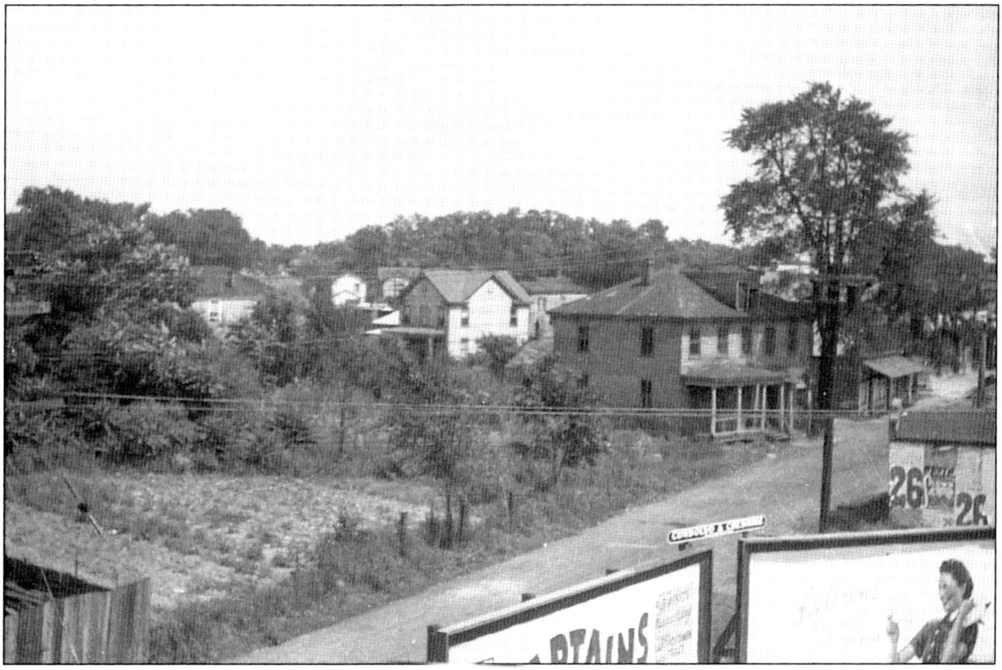

These pictures of St. James Street were taken on July 5, 1937, shortly before the construction of the South Norfolk overpass was begun. Originally, the area was filled with large fashionable homes, but slowly, businesses and their billboards crept in and made slums of the area. A large part of St. James Street was lost when the overpass was built.

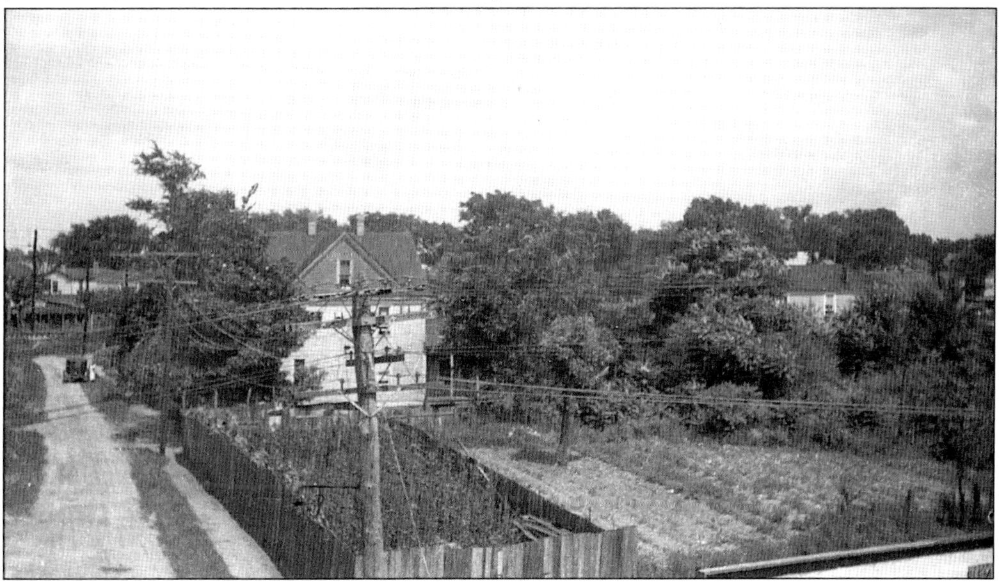

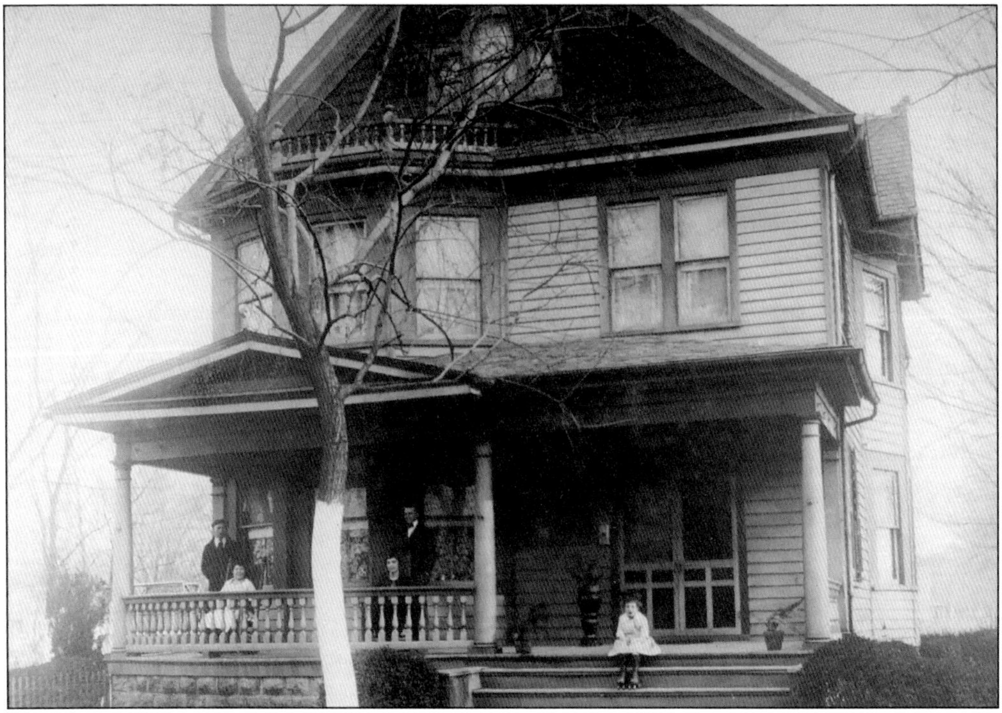

This large home was built for Sam Wilson at 64 "D" Street in 1907. Wilson encountered many obstacles when trying to hire tradesmen for this project because most of them were involved in the construction of buildings for the Jamestown Exposition. The small girl with roller skates, sitting at the top of the steps, is Eloise Wilson.

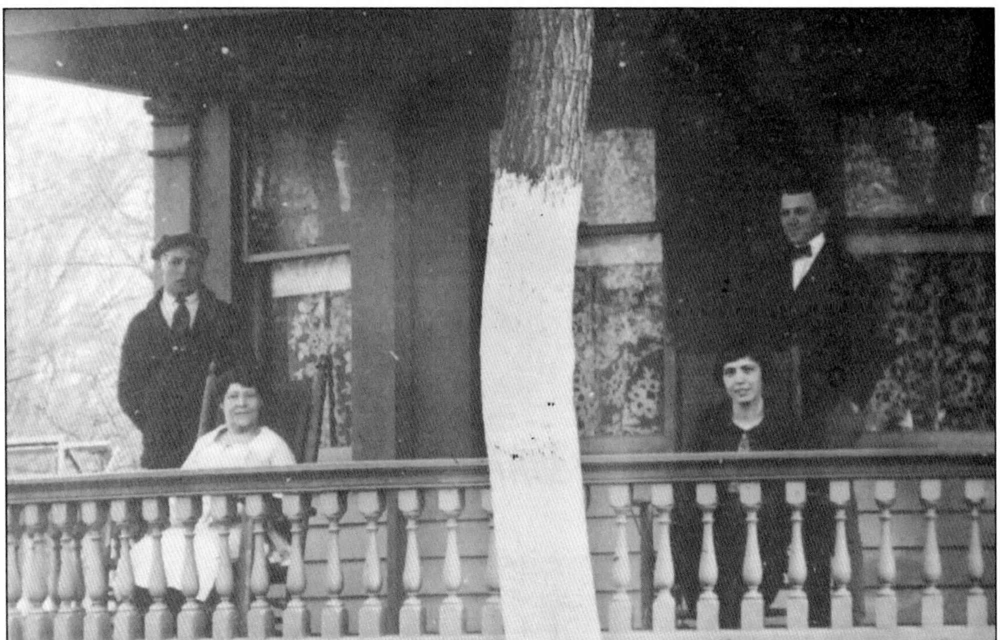

Those relaxing on the porch of the Wilson home are, from left to right, Luton (standing behind his mother), Jennie Wilson, and Bill Darden (standing behind Christine Wilson).

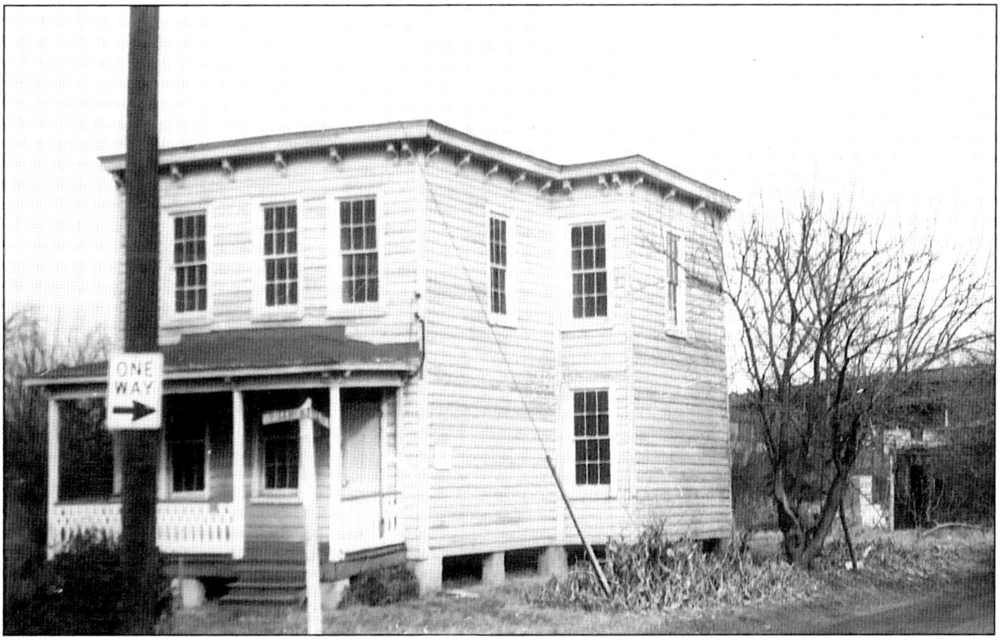

This old home, pictured in January 1960, was located at the corner of St. James and Twentieth Streets. It stood behind Marie West's Ideal Cleaners and was catty cornered from the fire and police stations. The building gave way to the slum clearance that began in 1961.

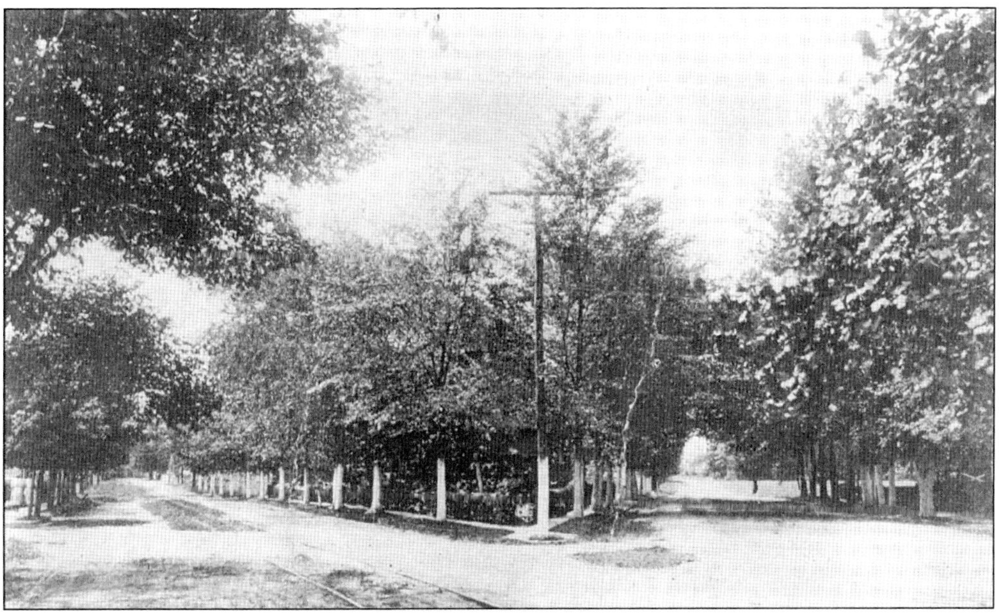

This image was made from a postcard, but the original picture was taken at the intersection of "D" and Decatur Streets and shows how the area looked shortly after 1907. Trees hid the home of Mr. Sam Wilson. The streetcar traveled "D" Street on its way to and from Norfolk. Two ladies can be seen on the sidewalk to the left of the streetcar tracks. The whitewash used on the trees added to the neat appearance of both streets.

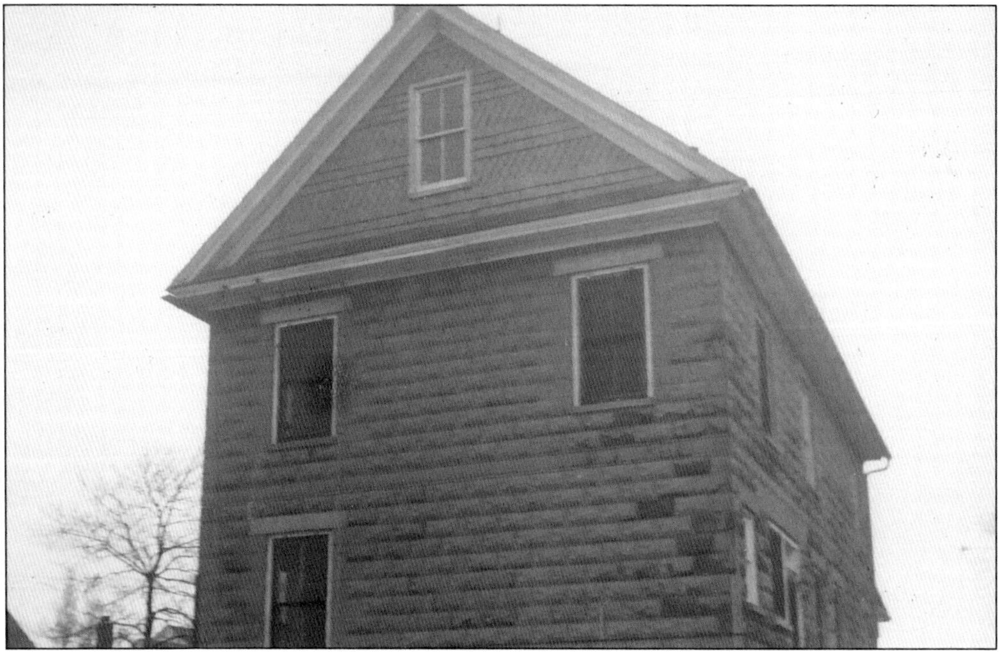

In December 1957, this large, two-story, concrete-block house was moved from the corner of Stewart and Poindexter Streets and placed on a lot at 910 Stewart Street. This was a very unusual sight for those days. This house and the one next to it were eventually replaced by a Gulf service station.

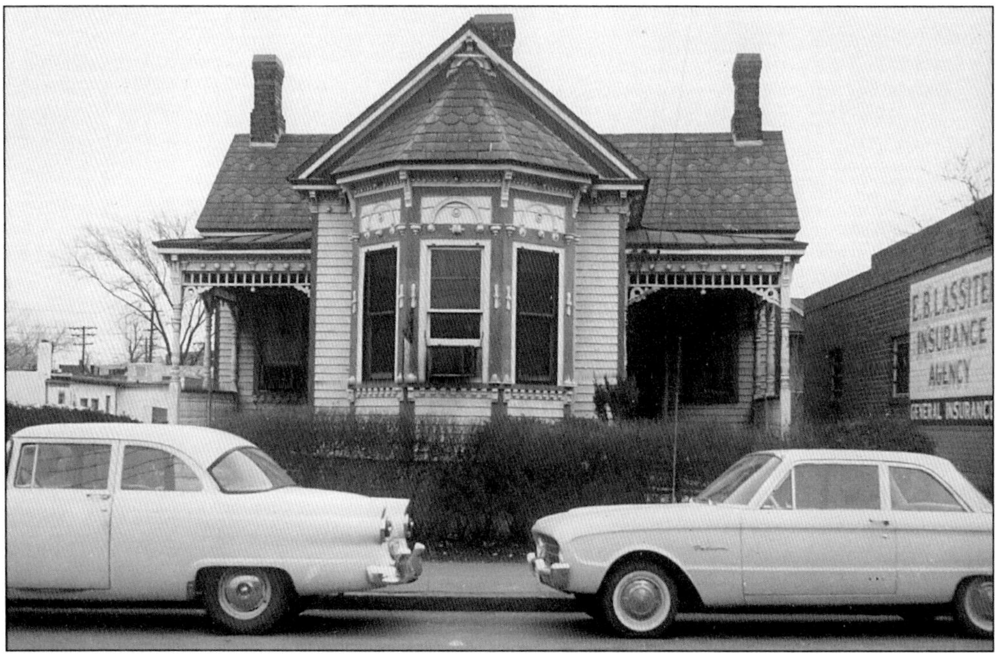

Captain George Funk built this home on Poindexter Street in 1894. The Funk family sold it to "Doc" Monroe. The structure has served as the South Norfolk Welfare Department, Dr. Woodley's office, and is now the office of E.C. Beacham and Associates Accounting and Tax Service.

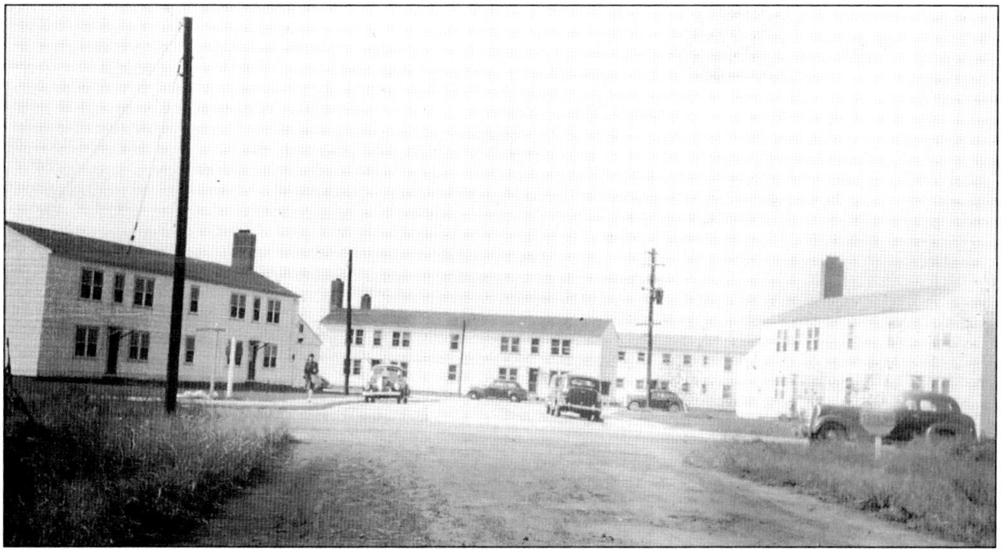

Prior to WW II, Bainbridge Boulevard came to an end at Poindexter Street on the edge of Johnson's woods. During the war, the woods were removed, Bainbridge Boulevard was cut through, and 400 apartments were built. The apartments were constructed on land that, many years before, had been the beginning of Admiral's Road. In light of this fact, a decision was made to name the community the Admiral's Road apartments. This photograph of the main entrance was taken on Sunday, November 12, 1944.

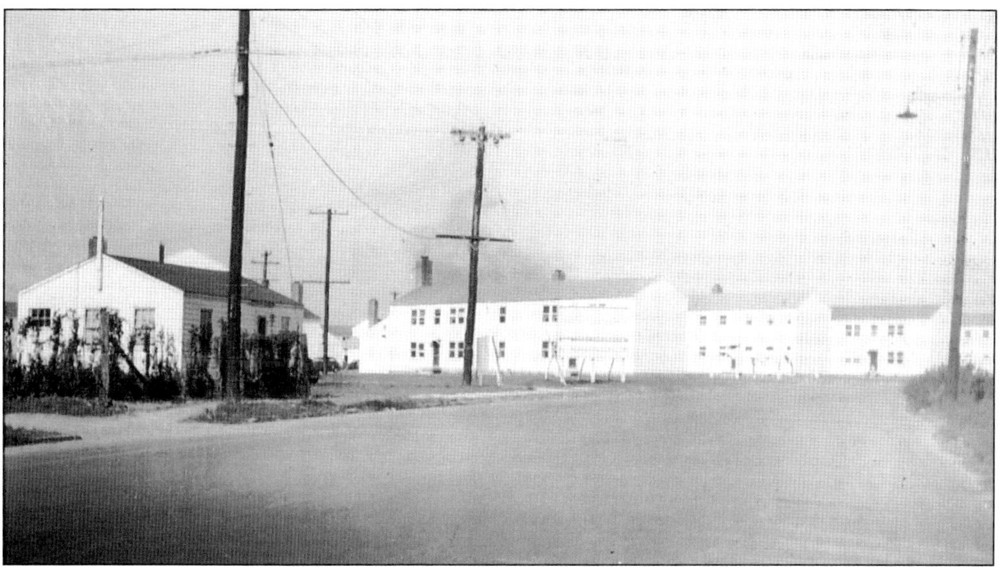

This view of the Admiral's Road apartments was taken from Poindexter Street and Bainbridge Boulevard on Sunday, November 12, 1944.

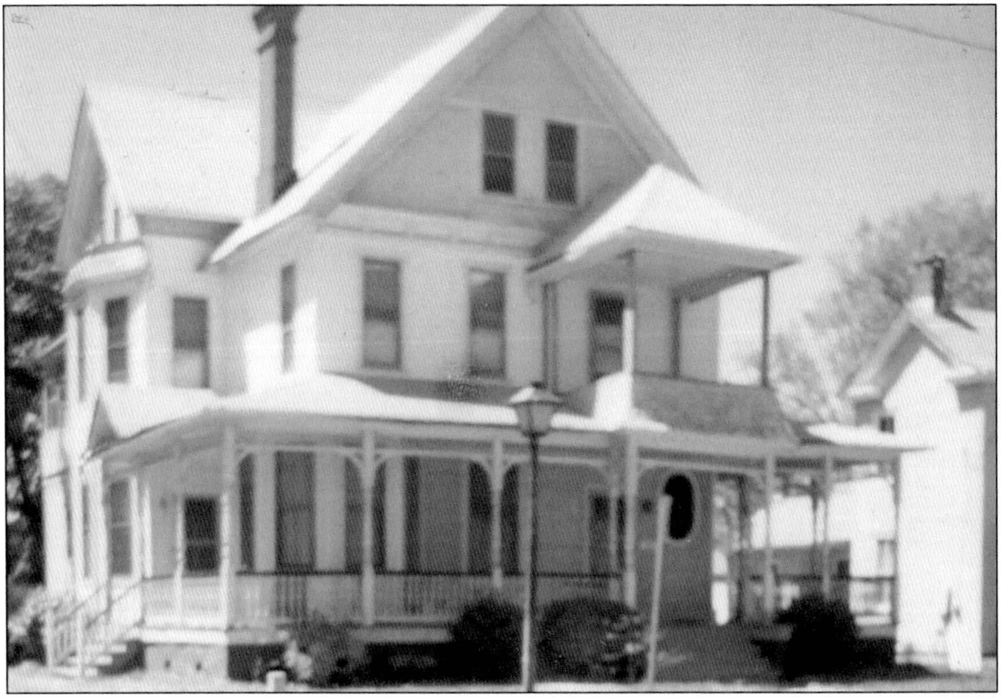

Mr. William Lane built one of the majestic homes in the historic district at 1044 Chesapeake Avenue.

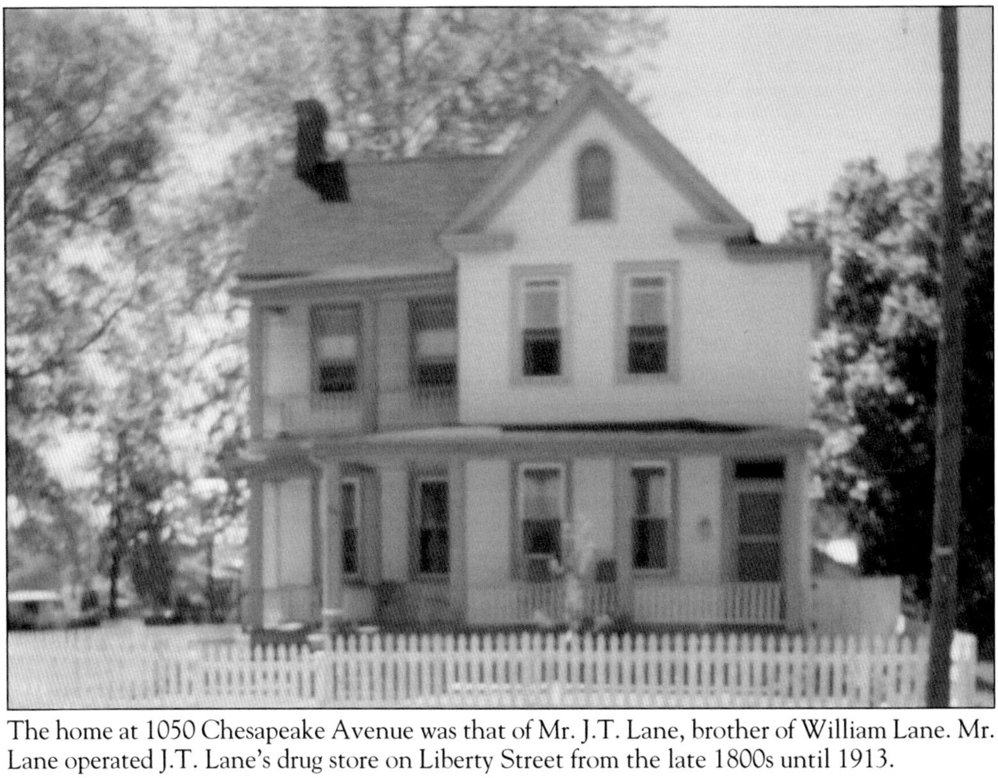

The home at 1050 Chesapeake Avenue was that of Mr. J.T. Lane, brother of William Lane. Mr. Lane operated J.T. Lane's drug store on Liberty Street from the late 1800s until 1913.

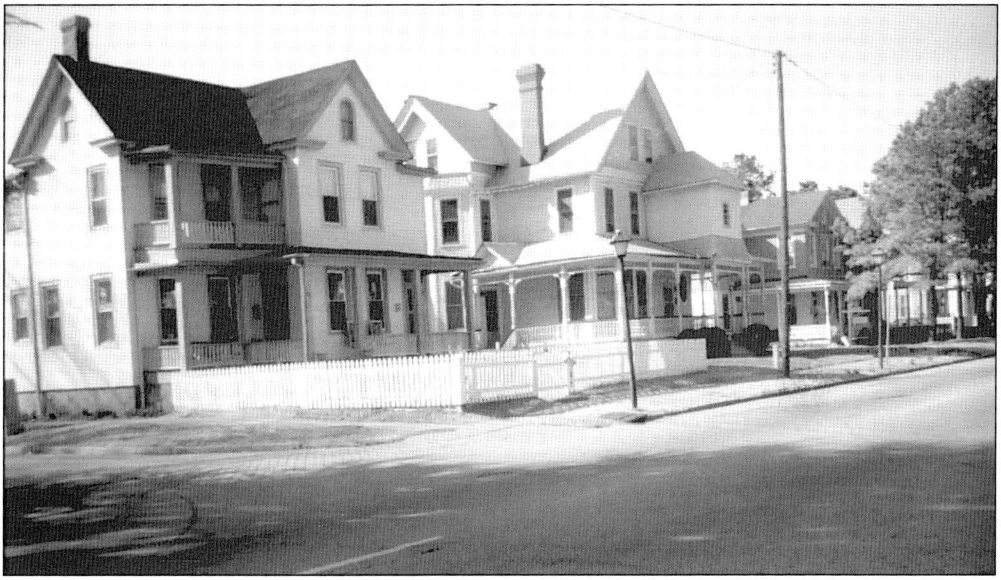

This view shows one side of the 1000 block of Chesapeake Avenue. The corner house was the home of J.T. Lane, and the one next to it was that of his brother William. Many years ago, streetcars rumbled down this street, and beautiful trees lined both sides, meeting in the center to form an arch. A large number of the old homes have given way to the wrecking ball.

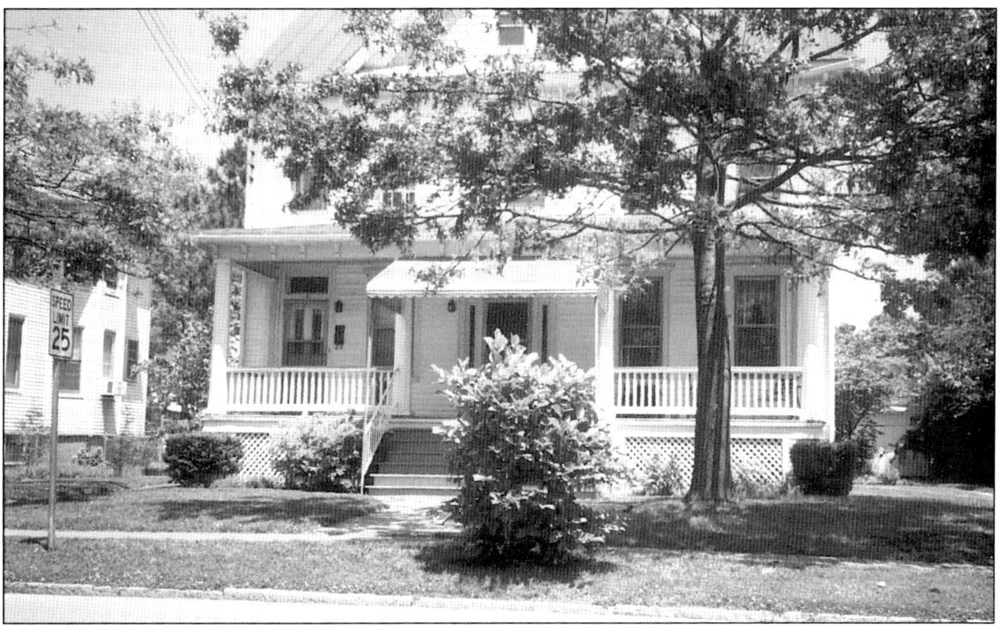

This large house at 1041 Chesapeake Avenue was originally the home of Dr. Jackson, who practiced in South Norfolk in the latter 1800s. Jackson's carriage house faced what became Seaboard Avenue. Later, this building became the home of Dr. T.B. Wood, and, still later, it became the Carva Hall apartments.

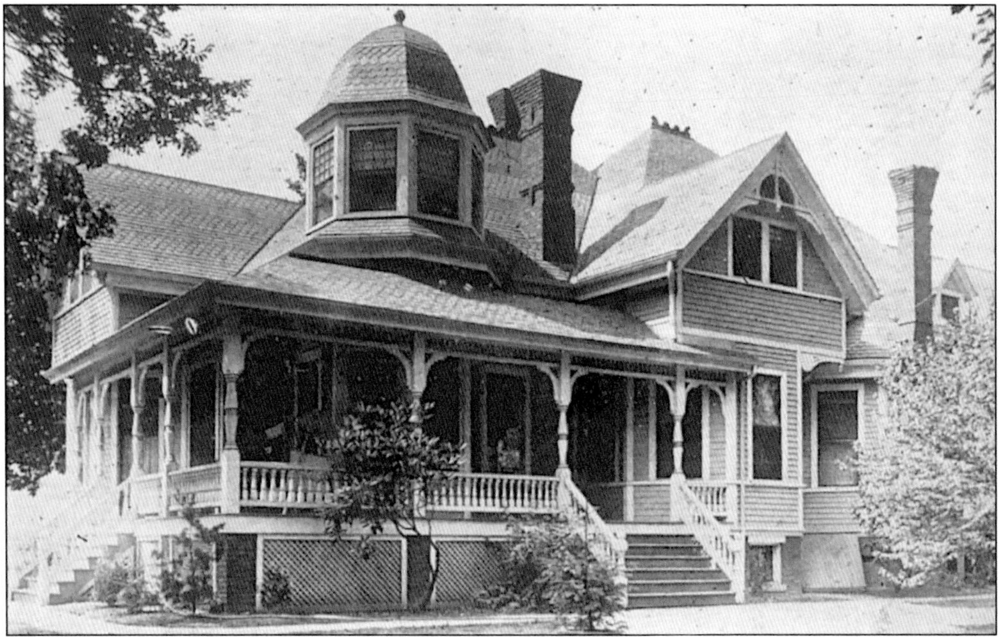

Edward Munro Tilley came to the area shortly after the Civil War and entered into the lumber business along the water front and built this house on Chesapeake Avenue in 1890. This large stately home contained 22 rooms and many fireplaces. The kitchen was off the back of the house and was separated from the main structure by a breezeway. Quarters for the servants were over the kitchen. The carriage house, which faced Guerriere Street, was, in later years, removed to Jackson Street and became a residence. After Mr. Tilley's death on December 21, 1917, Mr. Q.C. Davis Jr. acquired the home.

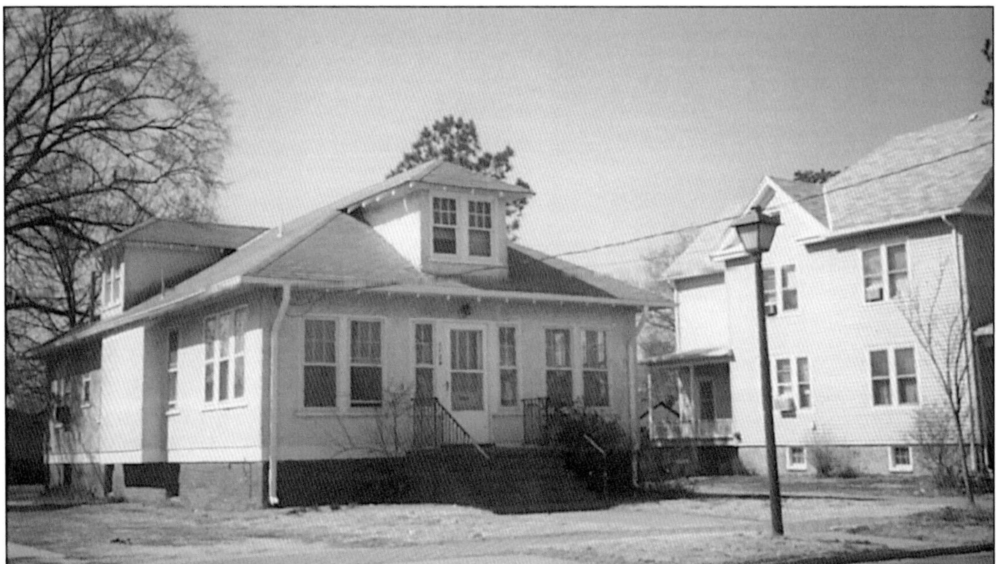

The house at 1126 Chesapeake Avenue was the home of the VanVleek family and then served as the office of Dr. G.W. Simpson for many years. The large house on the right was the home of Waverly Lane.

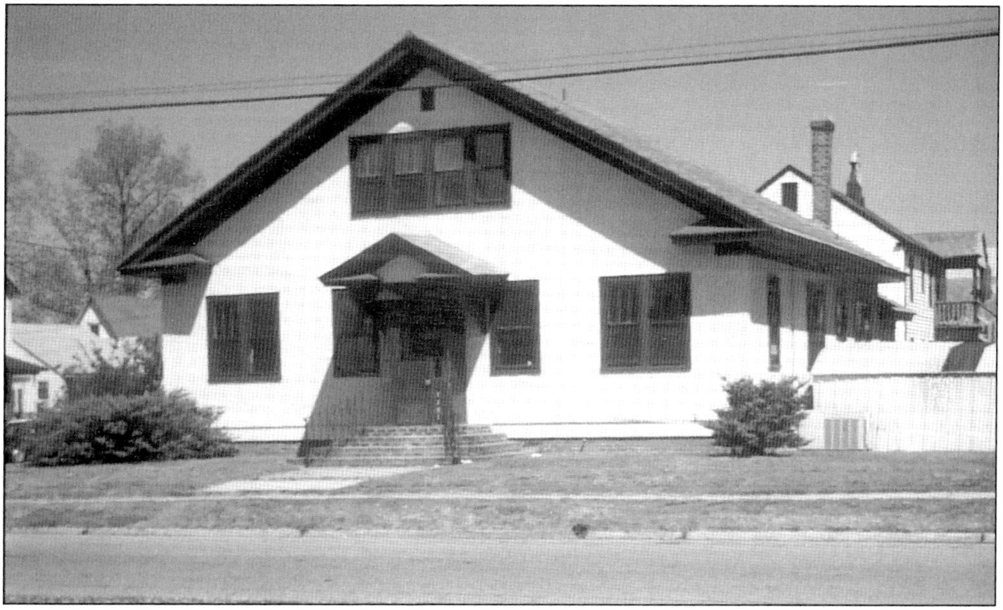

Dr. Horace Ashburn built his clinic at 1301 Ohio Street, and he and Dr. T.B. Wood had offices on the first floor. Dr. Belcher had his dental office on the second floor.

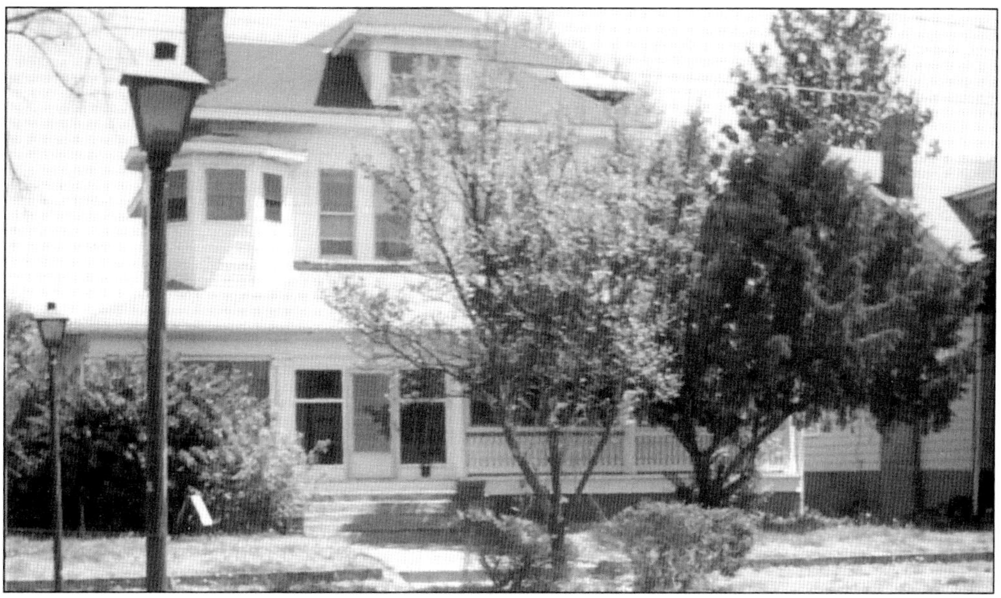

William Sloane, owner of the Chesapeake and Elizabeth Knitting Mills, built this stately home at 1203 Chesapeake Avenue in 1895. In 1907, he built a summer home in Norfolk, which is now the Hermitage Foundation Museum at 7637 North Shore Road. The house in South Norfolk later became the home of Mr. G.W. Forehand.

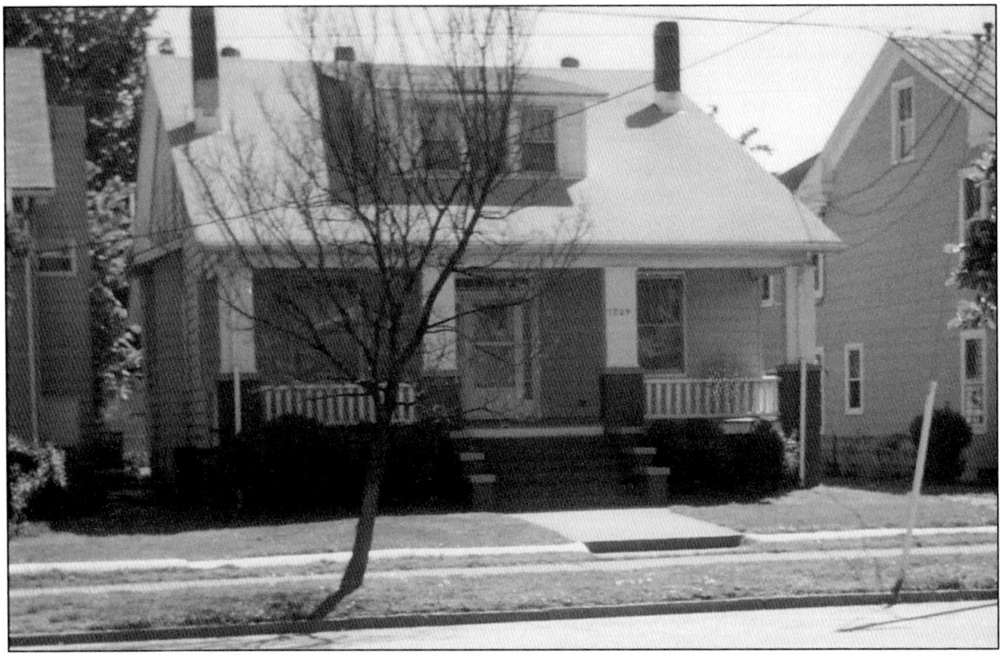

Construction of the house at 1209 Chesapeake Avenue was begun in 1918 and completed in 1919. It was the residence of Mr. E.J. Reass, owner of the Grand Theatre. The house on the left was the home of Bill Darden, proprietor of the Lakeside Dairy.

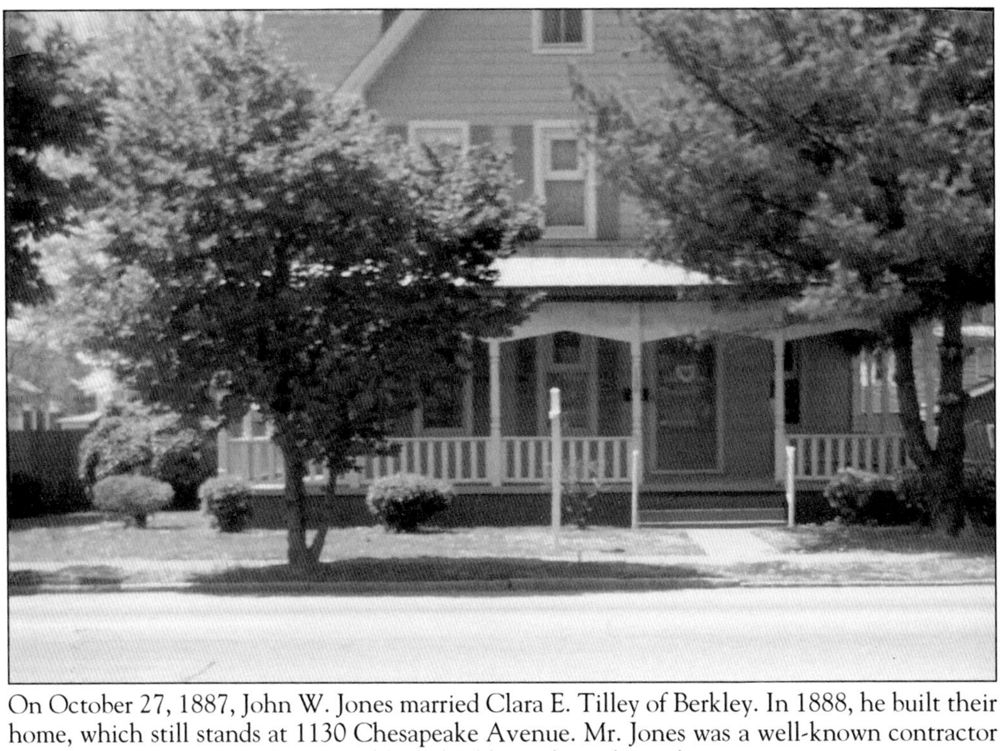

On October 27, 1887, John W. Jones married Clara E. Tilley of Berkley. In 1888, he built their home, which still stands at 1130 Chesapeake Avenue. Mr. Jones was a well-known contractor and built many homes, schools, and large buildings throughout the area.

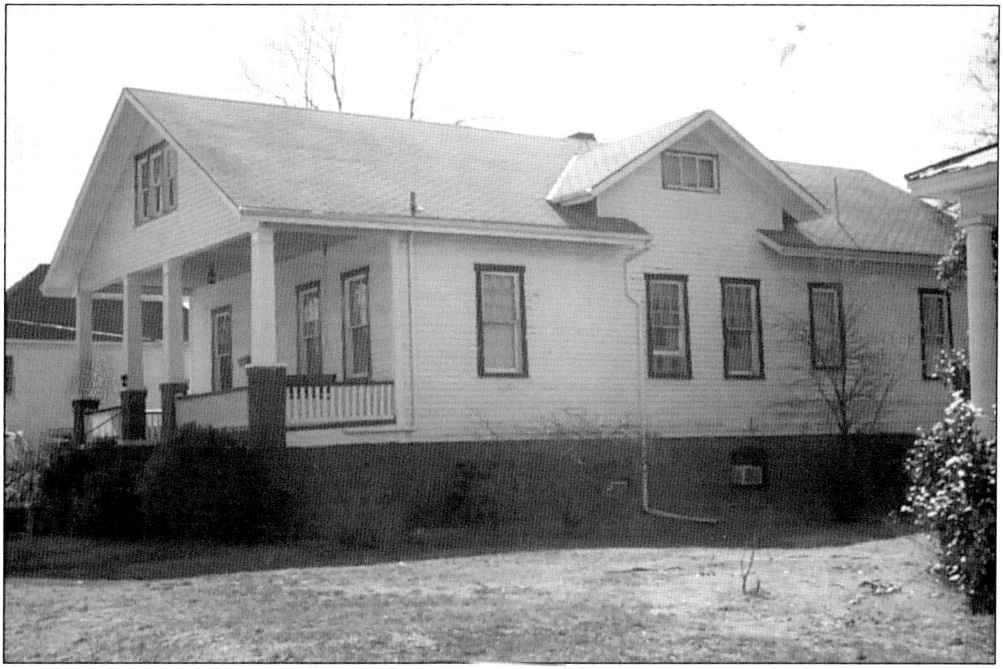

The house at the corner of Chesapeake Avenue and Holly Street was the office of Dr. Chapman. After his death, his medical practice was taken over by Dr. Bocock. Dr. Bocock passed away at an early age, and the practice was passed on to Dr. Jennings, who is there now.

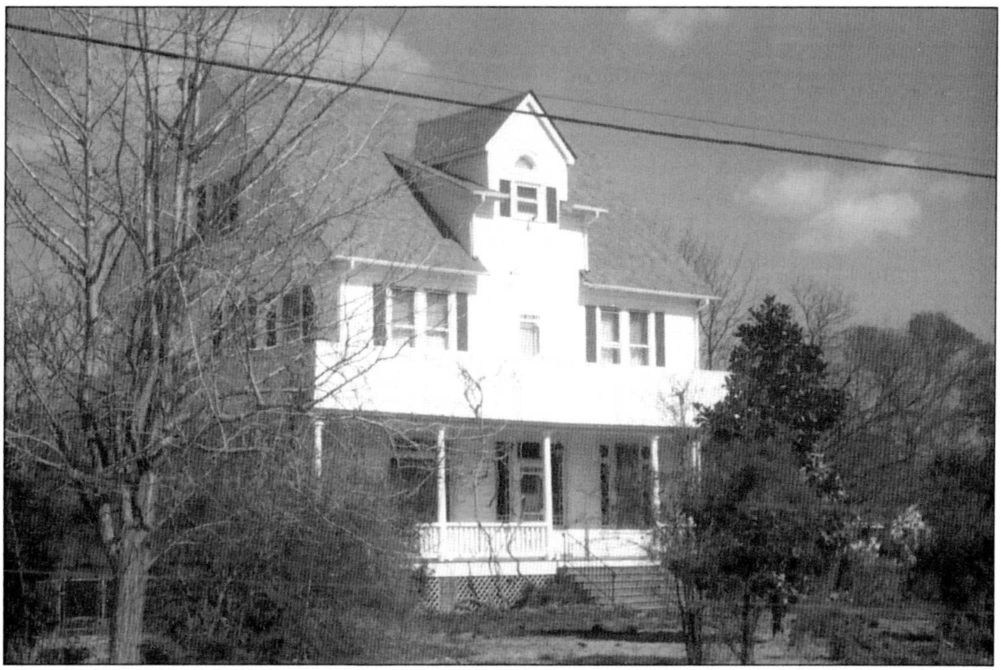

This lovely old building at 1007 Ohio Street was originally the home of William Tilley. Mr. Franklin L. Portlock acquired the house in 1910, and the house remained in the Portlock family until 1972.

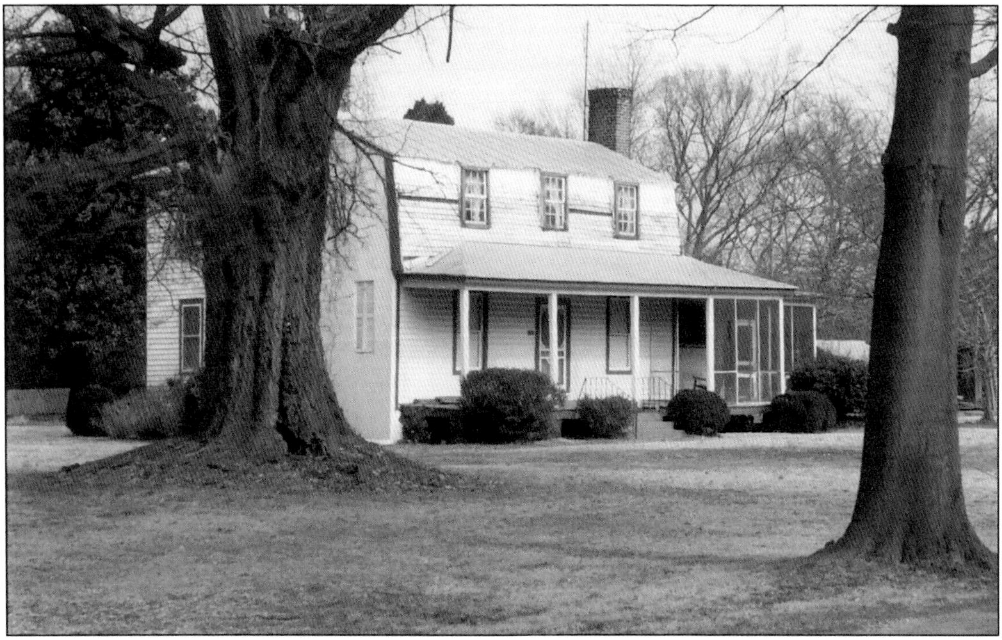

Built around 1798, the Tapley Portlock house on Franklin Street in Portlock was sold to Benjamin F. Gibson in 1884. The porch was added in 1910. A daily chore for the Portlocks was to fetch water from the spring on the property where the Portlock school was built in 1908.

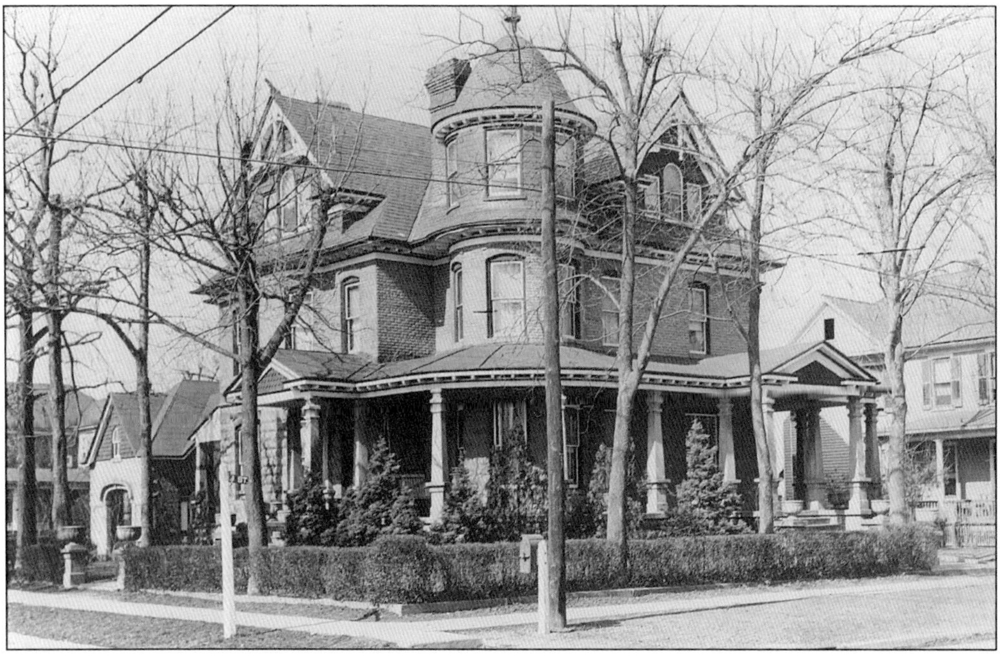

One of the most impressive homes in South Norfolk is this large Queen Anne–style house at 1146 Rodgers Street. Built in 1903 in a combination of cement block, brick, and wood, this was the home of the John Cuthrell family. Francis A. Gay bought the home from Mr. Cuthrell in February 1939 and turned it into a funeral home. In this early photograph, the carriage house can be seen off the back of the main structure.

Six

School Days

For a number of years, the children of McCloudtown, as South Norfolk was then known, and nearby farms attended the schools of Berkley. After the Civil War, during the Reconstruction period, the people who could afford to do so employed tutors for their children. The first school to be established in the village of South Norfolk was a private school. Around 1890, the Elizabeth Knitting Mill was operating on Park Avenue between Perry and Porter Streets, and the children employed at the mill usually worked six days a week. When a depression began in 1893, the mill cut back to three days a week and the children worked only Thursday, Friday, and Saturday of each week. Their parents collectively asked Mrs. Edward Williams if she would teach them. For two years, Williams used the second floor of her home as a classroom, and she received $1 a month for each student.

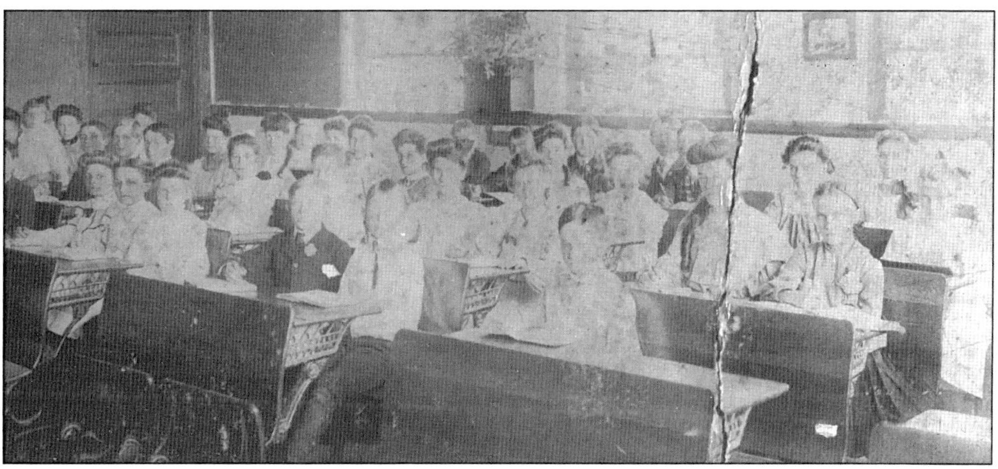

A public school was organized in South Norfolk as early as 1891. Forming an organization called the "South Norfolk School Society," a group of men of the community erected a two-room wooden school building on property acquired from Mr. E.M. Tilley. The school was built on Jackson Street in what is now the 1100 block. The cost, including furniture and out buildings, was approximately $2,200. This picture, which was taken in 1903, was possibly the last day of the school year, as the students were well dressed and a small child can be seen in the first row near the door.

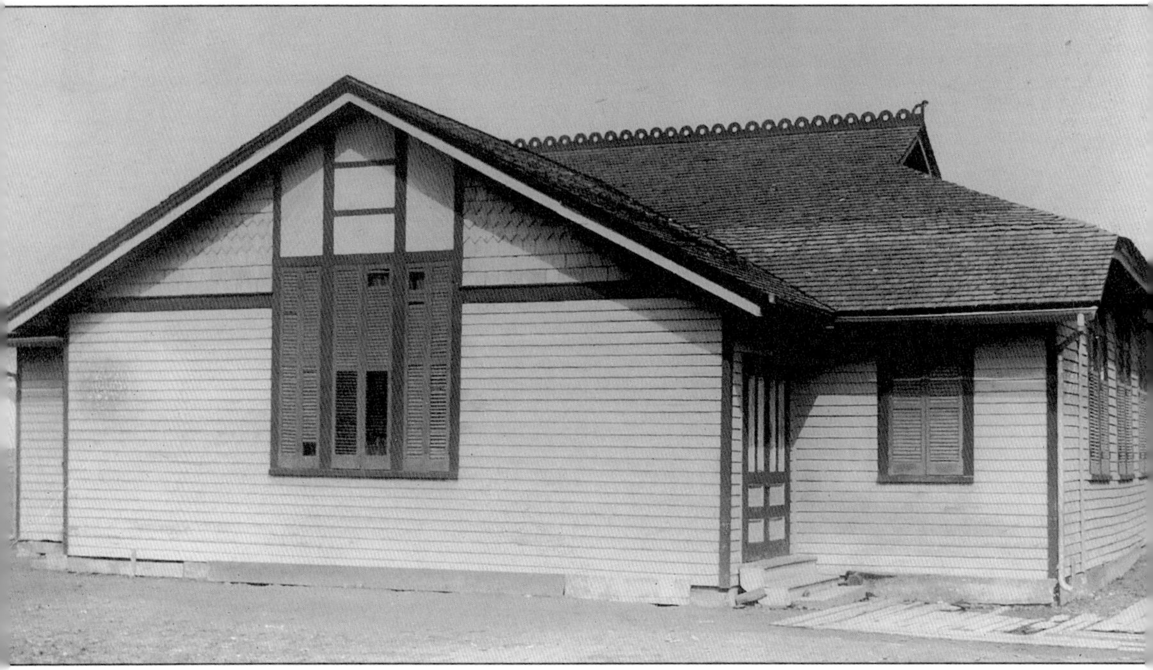

This structure was located on "B" Street next to the first school building. It appears in pictures dated as early as 1909 and was possibly moved there from Jackson Street. The building had no running water, so the larger boys in the school were detailed to carry buckets of water to the classes in the morning and again in the afternoon. One of the outhouses can be seen in the right background.

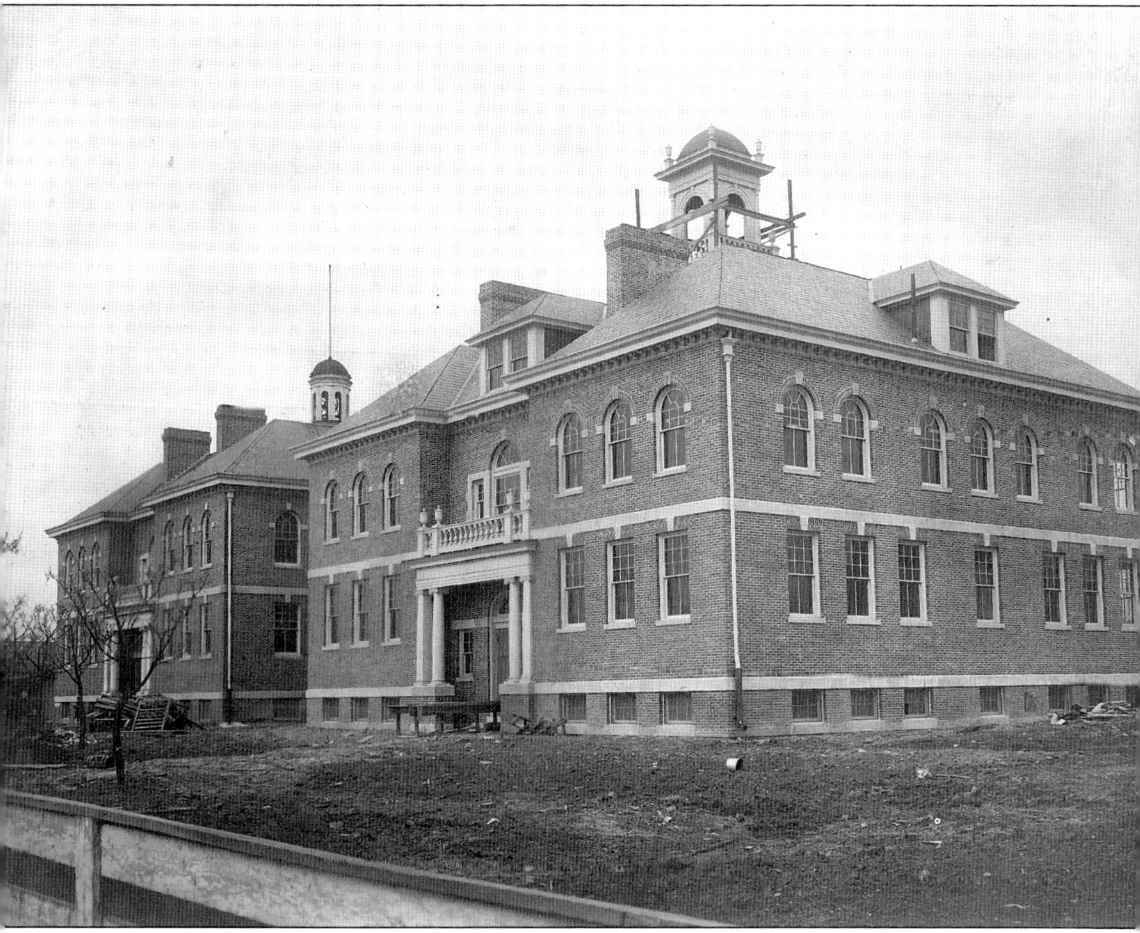

When the wooden building on Jackson Street became inadequate, the members of the school board of Washington District purchased a block of land in Elmsley between "A" and "B" Streets and built the building on the left at a cost of $35,000. This took place around 1902. By 1906, plans were being made for a high school and more room was needed. This photograph shows the second building when it was still under construction, c. 1909, but it was completed in time for the school year, which began in September 1910.

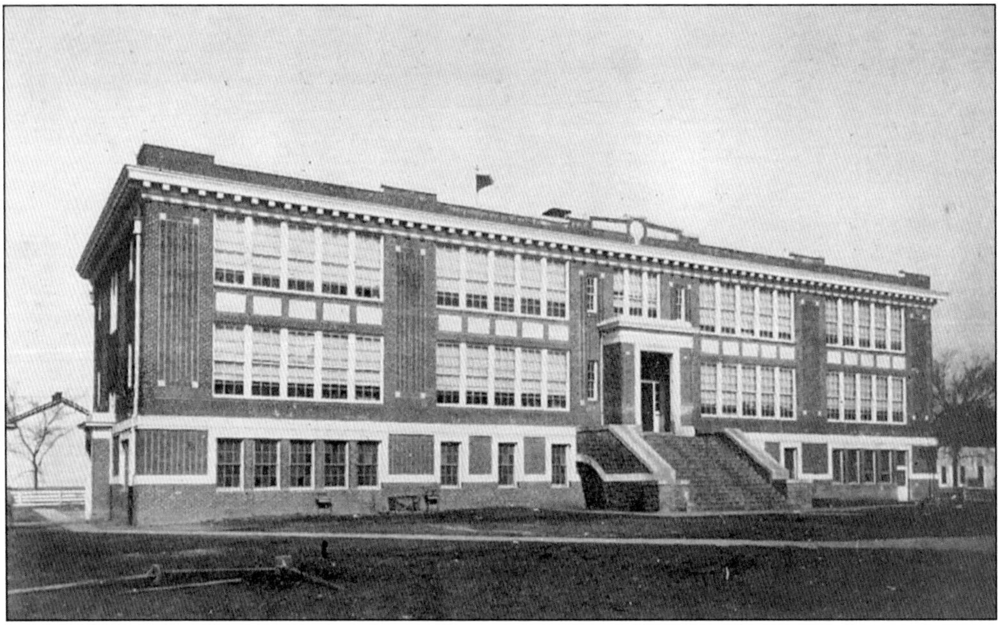

This was the third of the three school buildings that were constructed on "B" Street. This large building was located at the corner of "B" and Twentieth Streets and was put into use in September 1916.

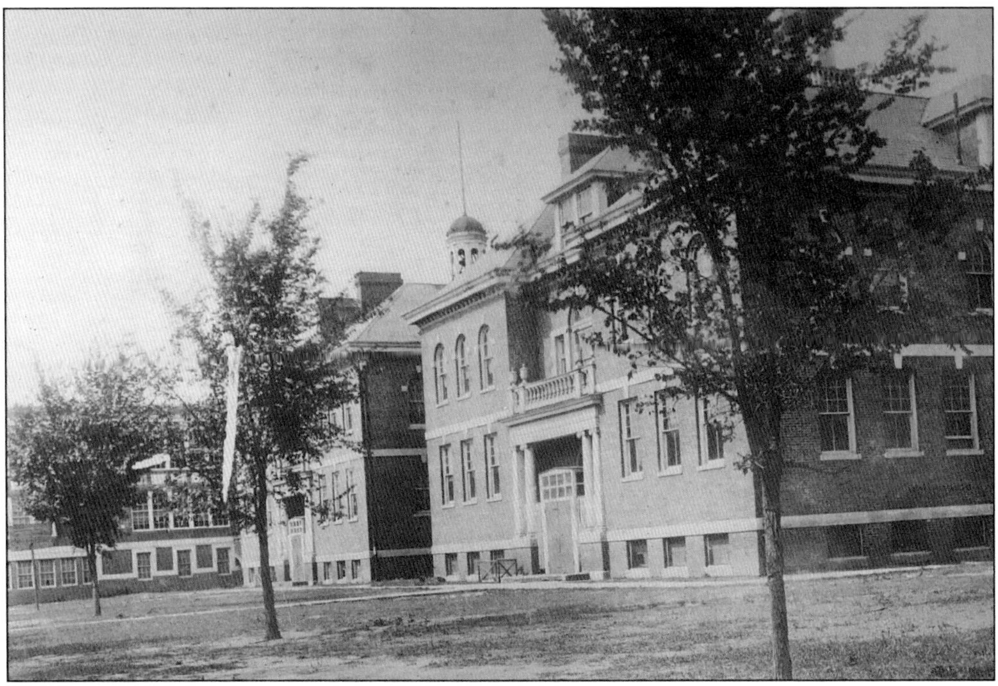

This photograph, taken around 1920, shows all three school buildings on "B" Street in South Norfolk.

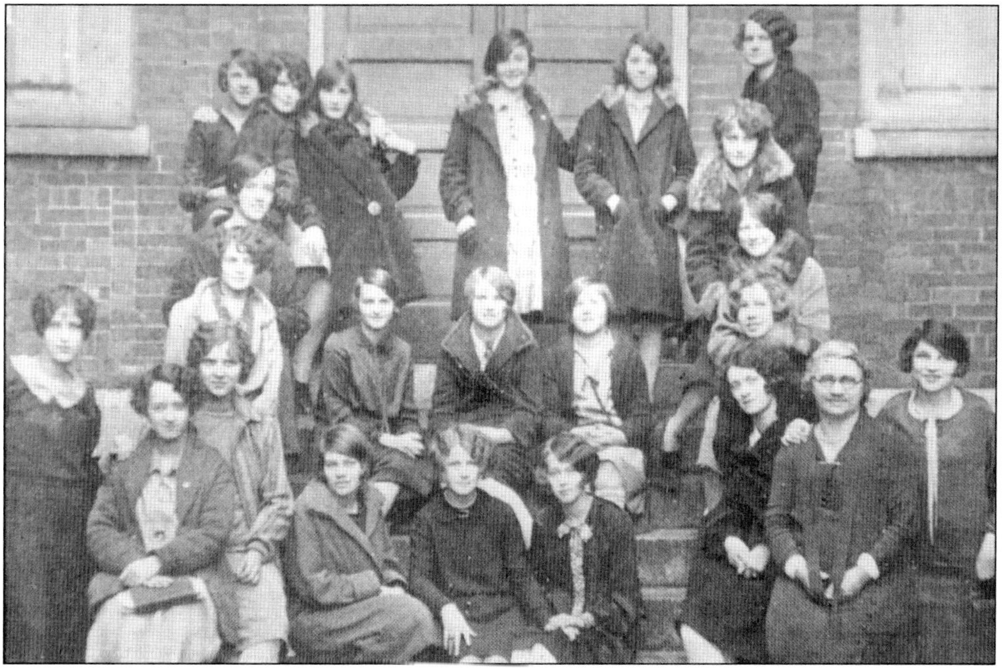

These ladies, pictured c. 1927, are members of the domestic science or home economics class, as it was better known, and Mrs. Julia Parker is their teacher.

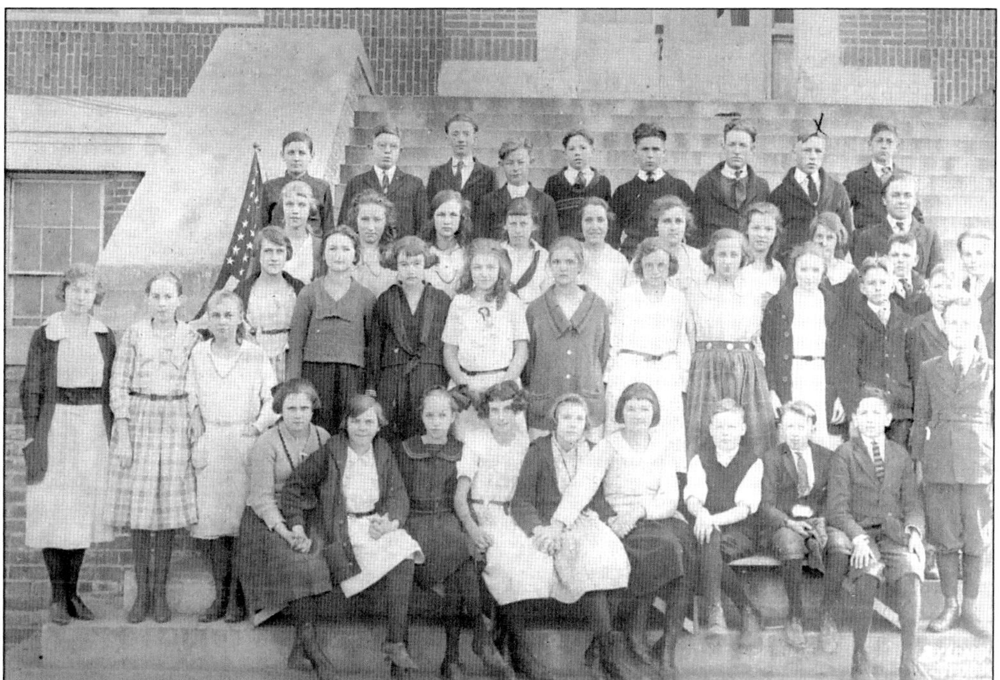

Members of Miss Florence Rountrey's class pose for this picture on the stone steps of the school building on December 7, 1921. The photograph was made by Long Studios of Norfolk, Virginia.

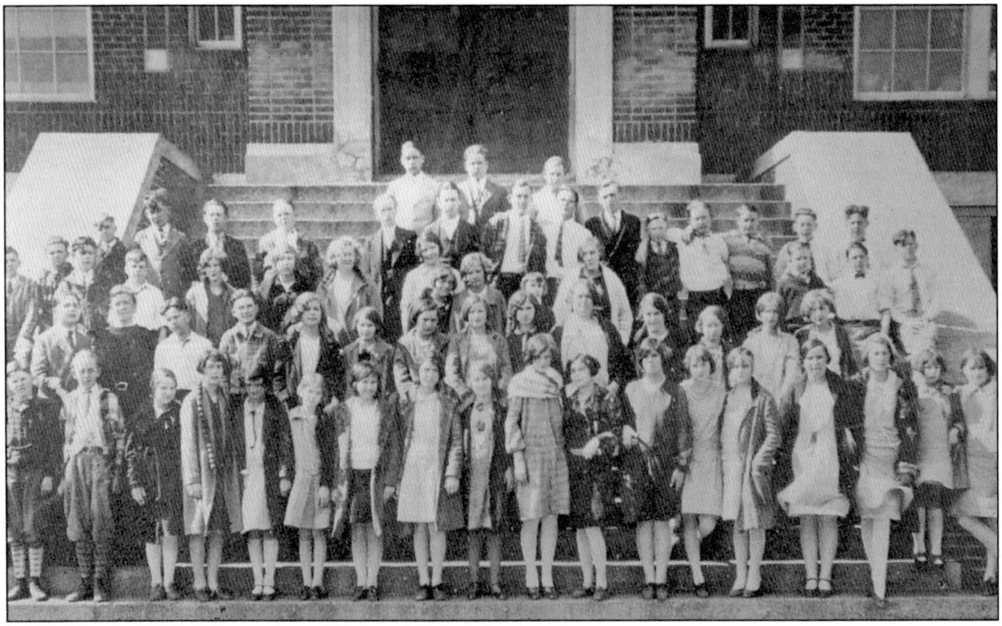

This is the 1928 freshman class of South Norfolk High School.

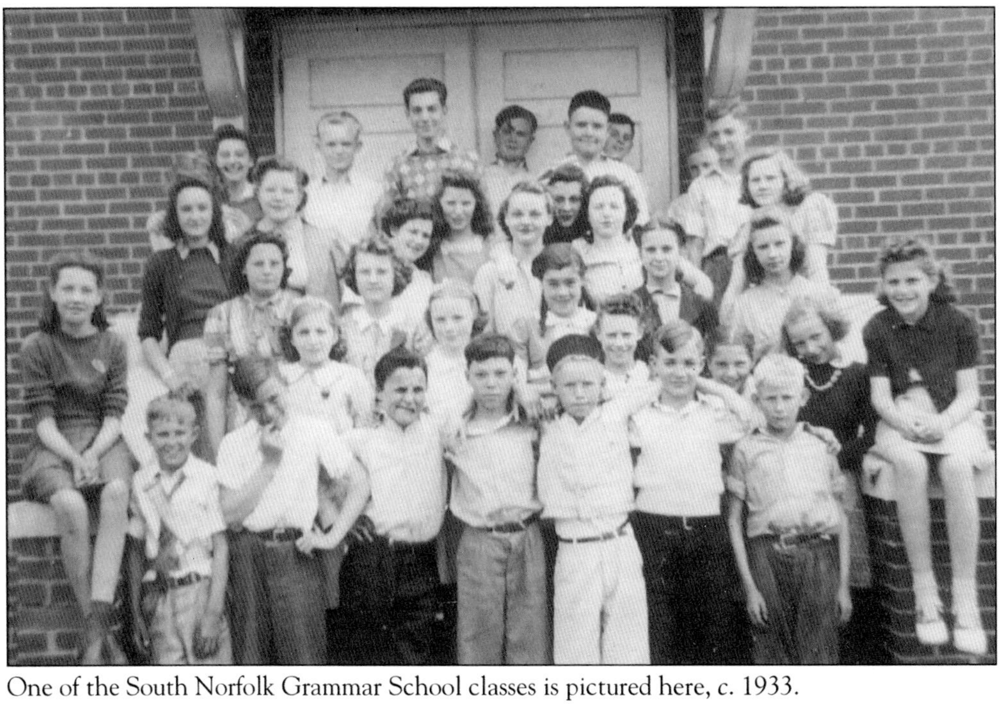

One of the South Norfolk Grammar School classes is pictured here, c. 1933.

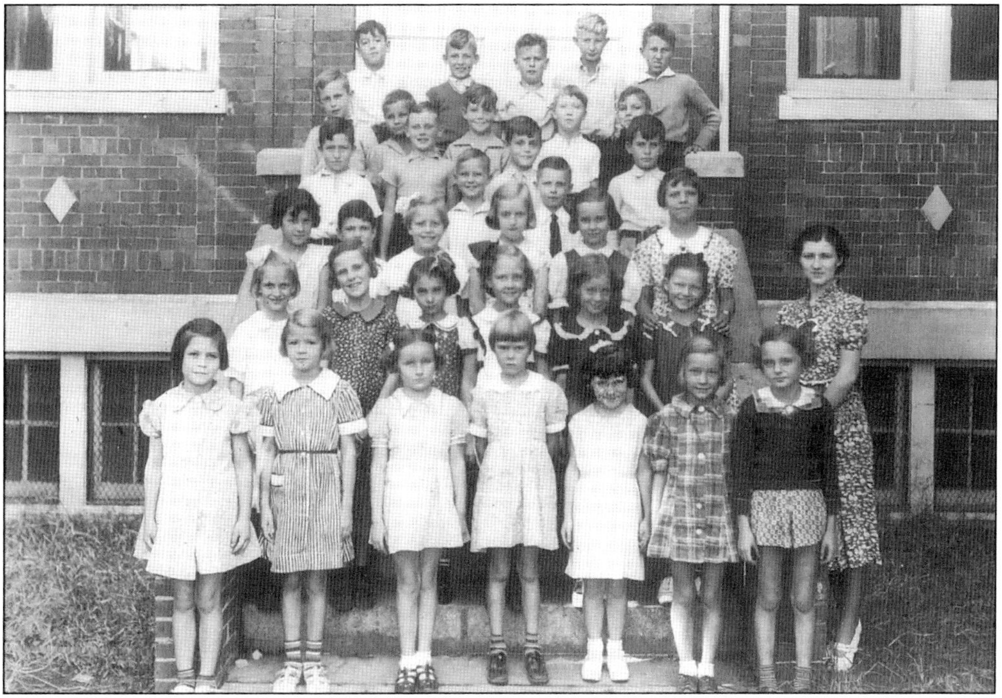

These children are in Miss Spence's third grade class in October 1937. The students are, from left to right, (first row) unidentified, Emily Small, Irene Lassiter, Marian Daily, Erma ?, unidentified, and Mary Earl King; (second row) Delores Hories, Darlene Hubbard, Ann Turlington, Anne Dodson, Shirley Harrell, Doris Williams, and Miss Spence; (third row) Dollie Everton, Gibson Harrell, unidentified, Annie Laurie Griffin, unidentified, and ? White; (fourth row) Marvin Cowand, Ray Henley, Billie Bunch, Jimmy Marshall, and ? Divers; (fifth row) Ellsworth Jernigan, Neil Phelps, Jesse Hardison, David Hundley, unidentified, and unidentified; (back row) unidentified, Joe Hodges, Bruce Pillow, unidentified, and ? Hoyt.

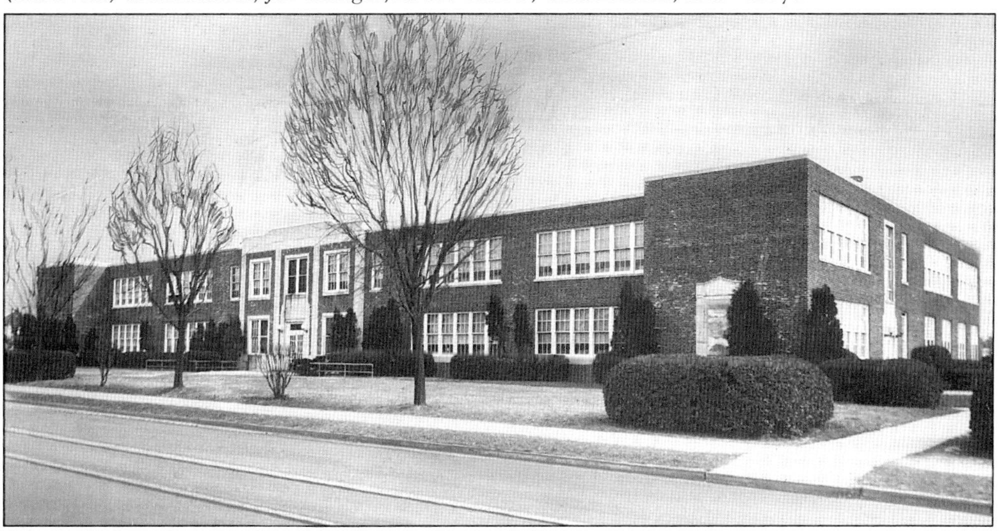

When the school on "B" Street became crowded, a 6-acre site was acquired on Holly Street between Rodgers and Decatur Streets. In 1929, the new high school was built at a cost of $140,430. The first students entered the school on February 3, 1930.

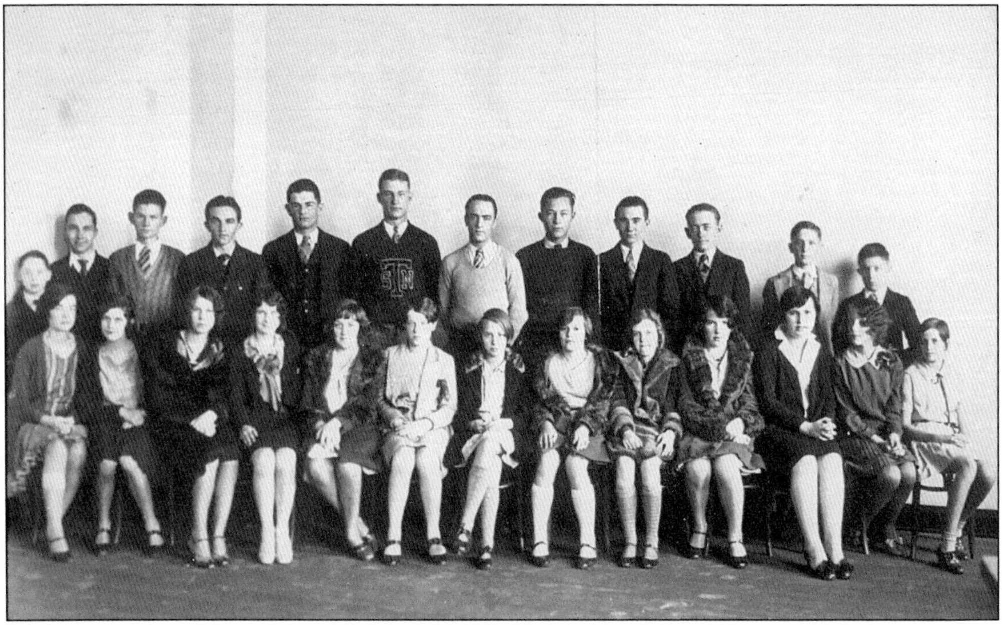

In 1930, these South Norfolk High School students were members of the student council.

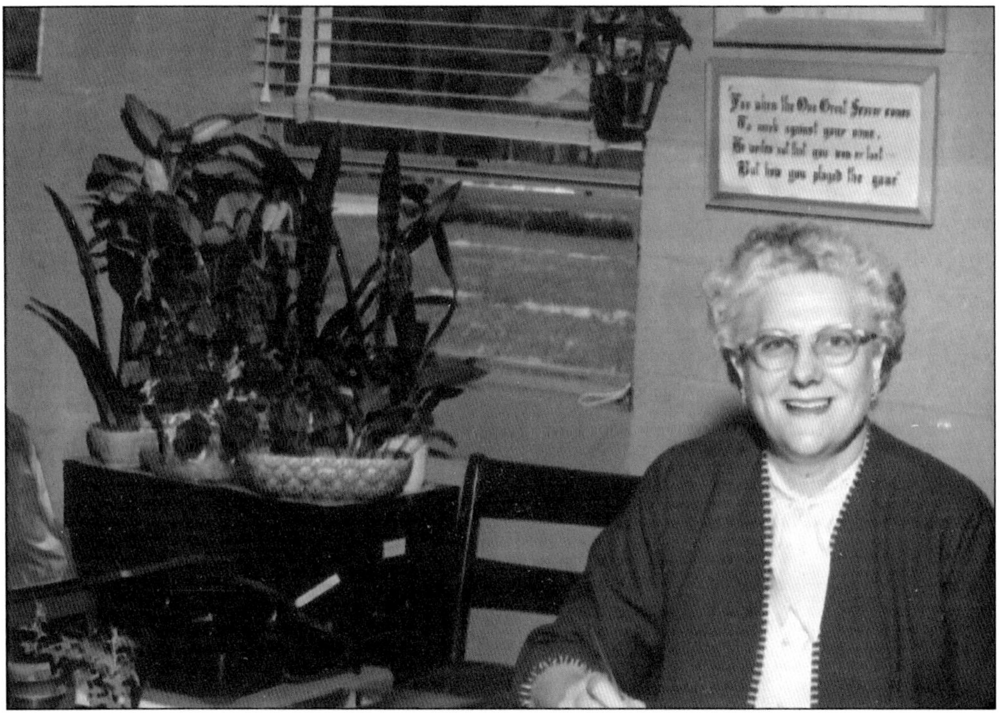

Miss Aurelia Leigh, having just graduated from Mary Washington College, arrived at South Norfolk High School in 1931. During her tenure, she served as teacher of commercial courses, clerk of the school board, assistant principal, and principal. Miss Leigh served both South Norfolk and Oscar Smith High Schools.

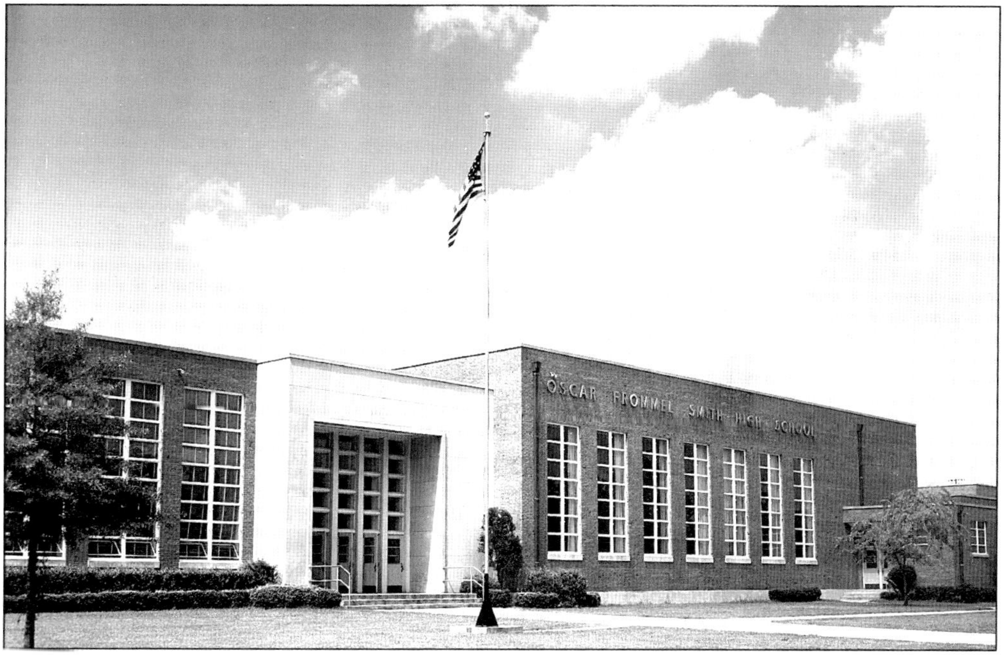

In early 1950, the City of South Norfolk acquired land at the foot of Rodgers Street. It was there that the first Oscar Frommel Smith High School was built at a cost of approximately $1 million. The school received its first students in September 1954.

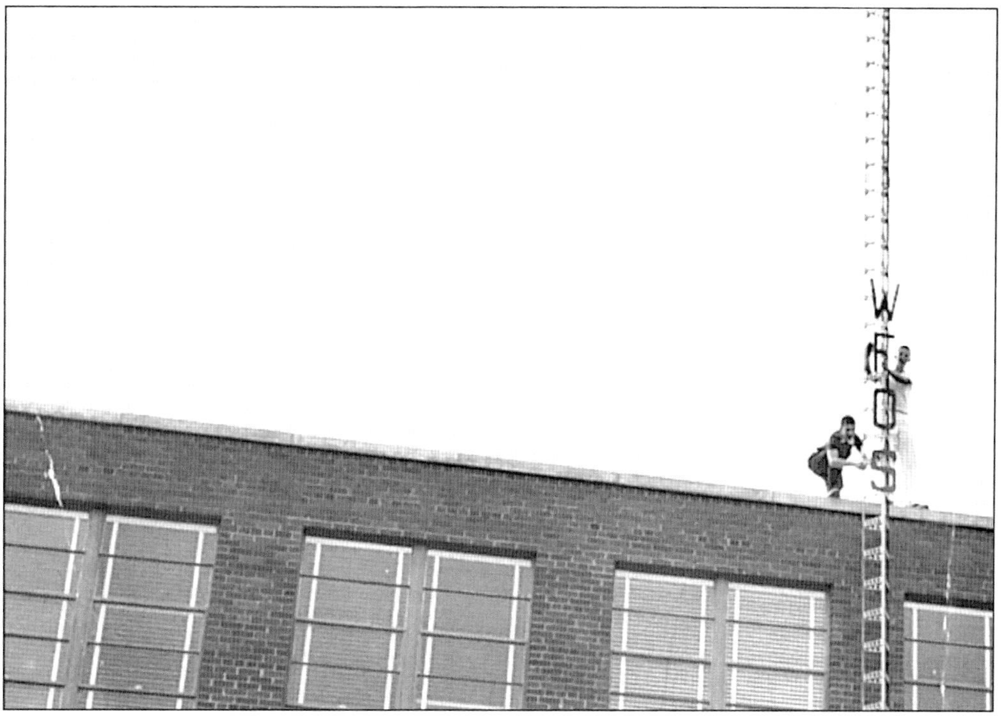

The two students installing station call letters on the radio tower at Oscar F. Smith High School are, from left to right, Stevie Jones and Larry Floyd.

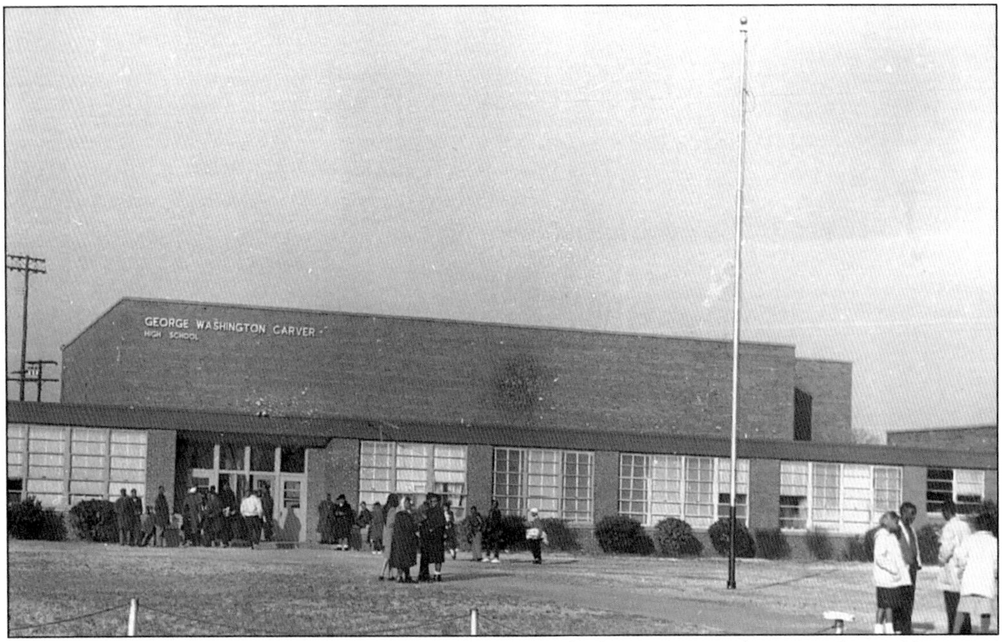

The original George Washington Carver School was built in 1908 and received an addition in 1938. Construction of this school was begun in 1952 on a 28-acre site and was completed in 1953 at a cost of $460,000. Desks and other school furniture cost about $10,000.

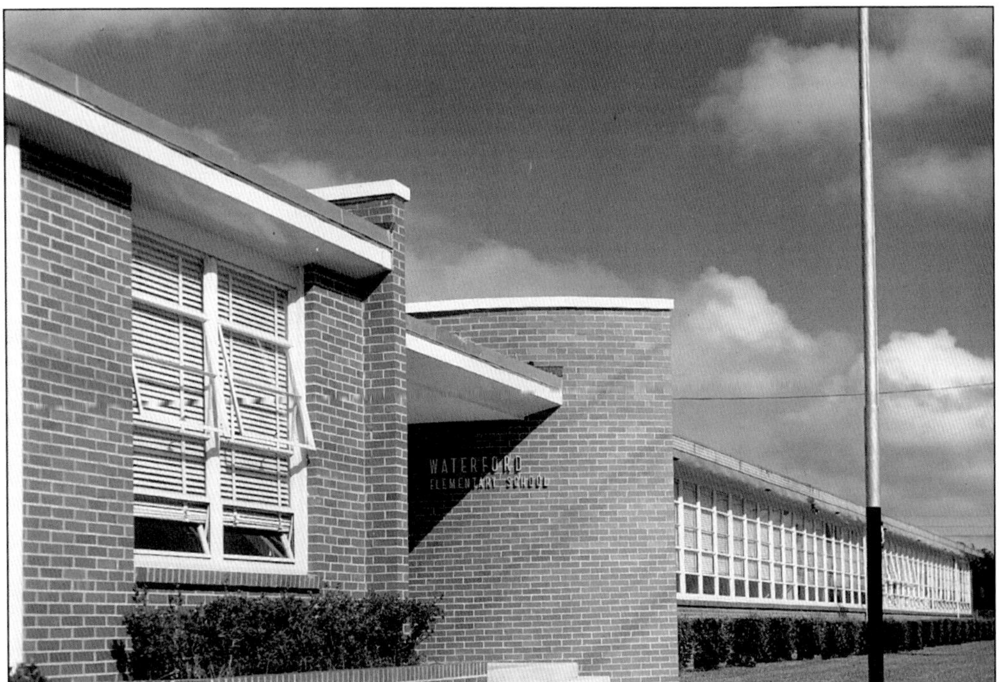

The Waterford Elementary School was built on Liberty Street in 1914 and received an addition in 1959. The school and grounds covered 1.3 acres and had a capacity of 510 students. This photograph was made by Acme Photo Co., Inc. of Norfolk.

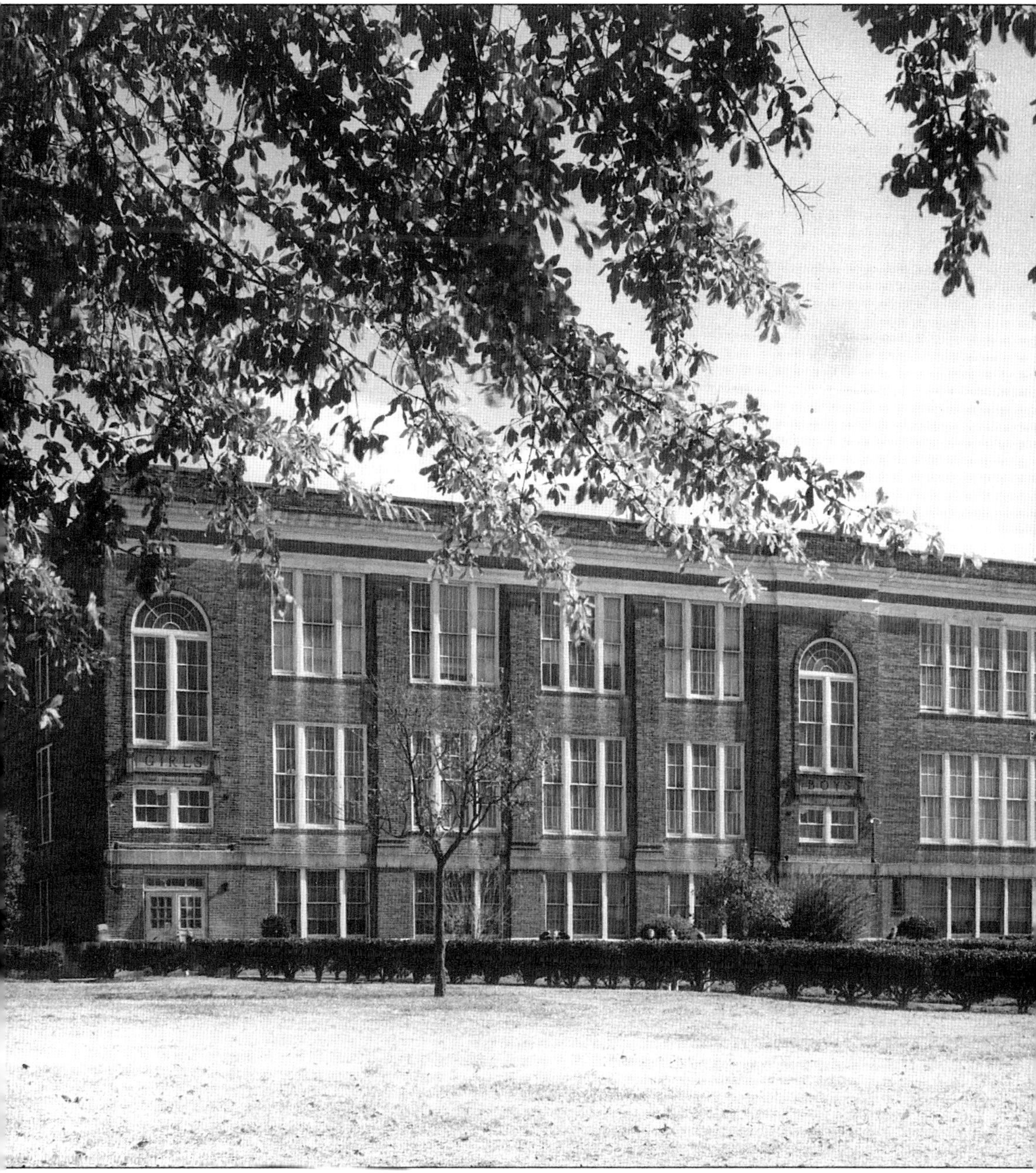

The Portlock High School was one of several three-story schools built in Norfolk County in 1922. Located behind and to the left of the four-room school that was constructed on Bainbridge Boulevard in 1908, this building was demolished in August 1965.

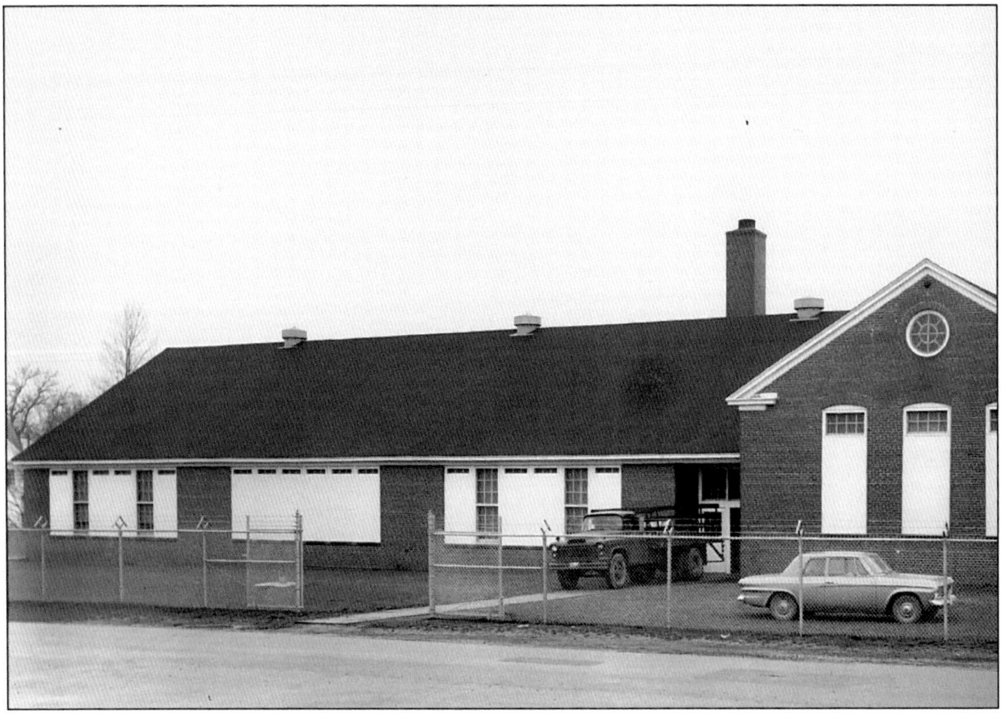

This structure was on Godwin Avenue where the present-day community center is located. It housed the cafeteria and, later, additional classrooms, and was also used for textbook storage.

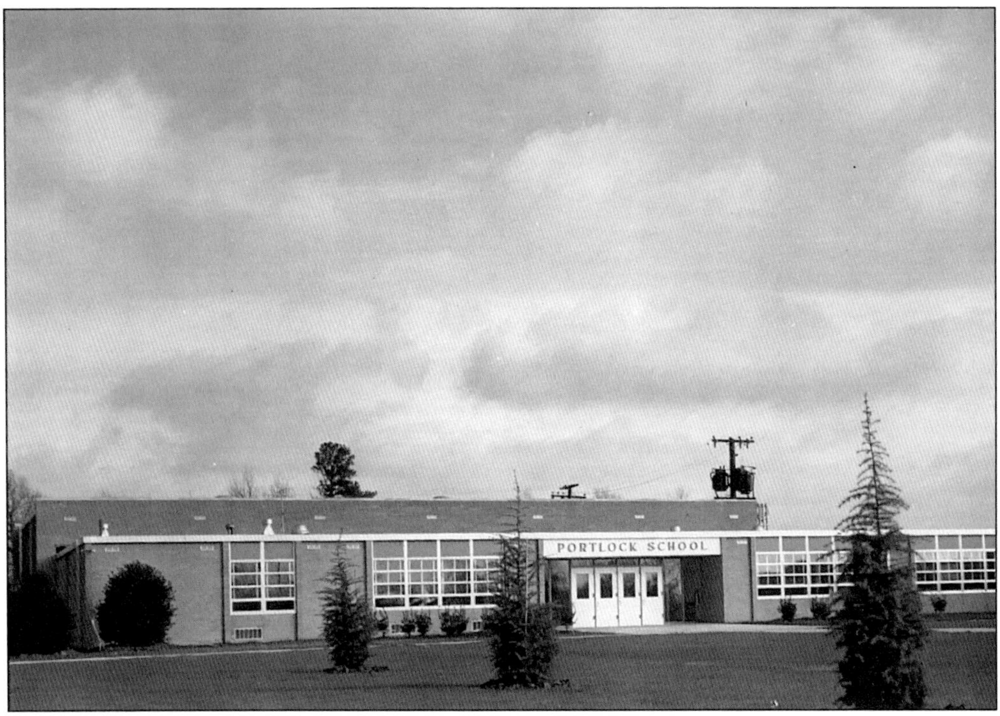

The present-day Portlock Elementary School was constructed on a 23-acre site at 1857 Varsity Drive in 1964.

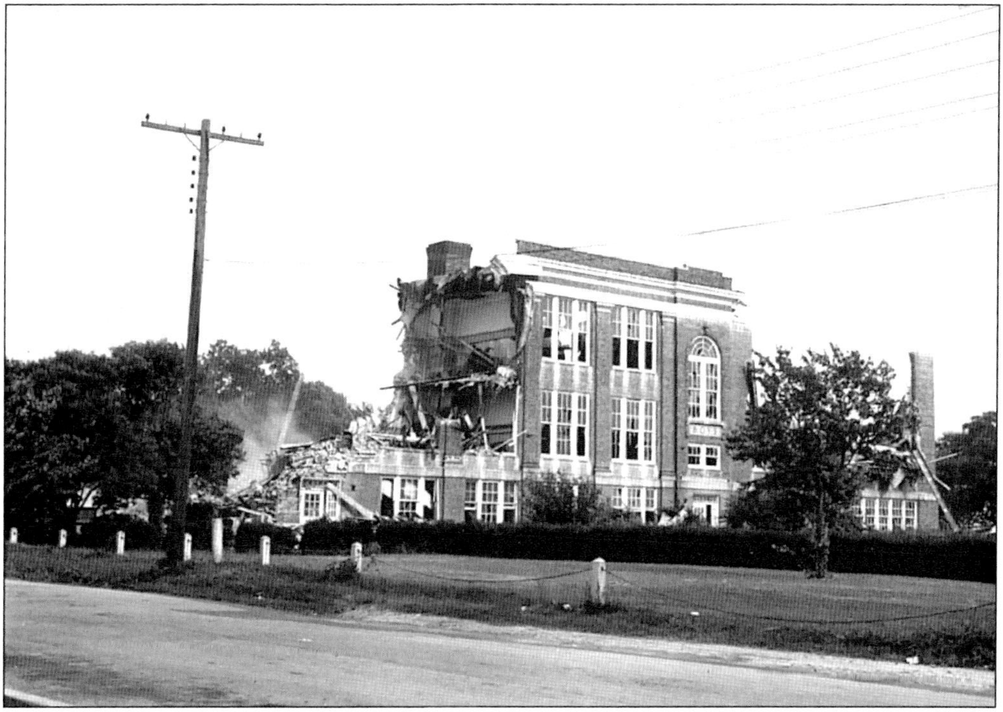

The Portlock High School building, which was built in 1922, was demolished in August 1965.

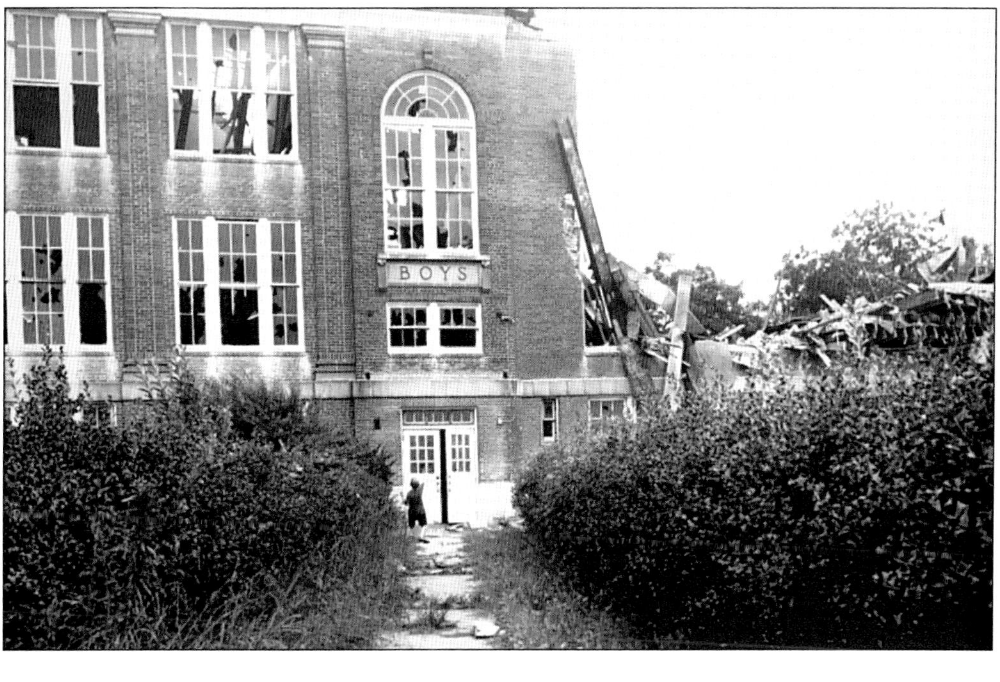

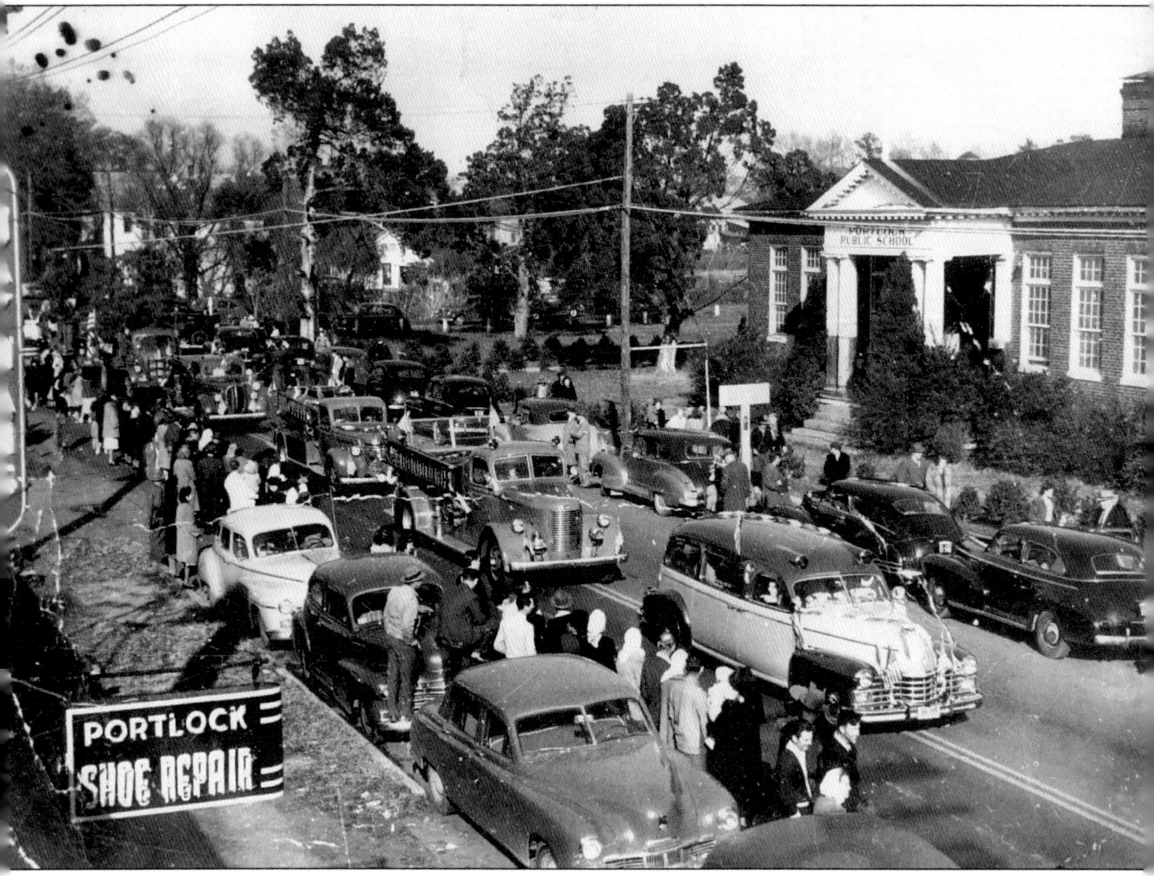

This picture is of the fire prevention parade in October 1948. The Portlock School, shown on the right, was built by Mr. John Jones in 1908. The white sign in front of the building points to the Raleigh Heights Baptist Church. The old school is now the home of Chesapeake's museum.

Seven

Sports Teams

The sports history of South Norfolk is truly one of greatness, and there were many outstanding local athletes who went on to rewarding careers in the pros. But there were also those who could not measure up, not because of ability, for each possessed that in abundance, but strictly because of physical size. Each played for the sheer love of the sport and not for material gain.

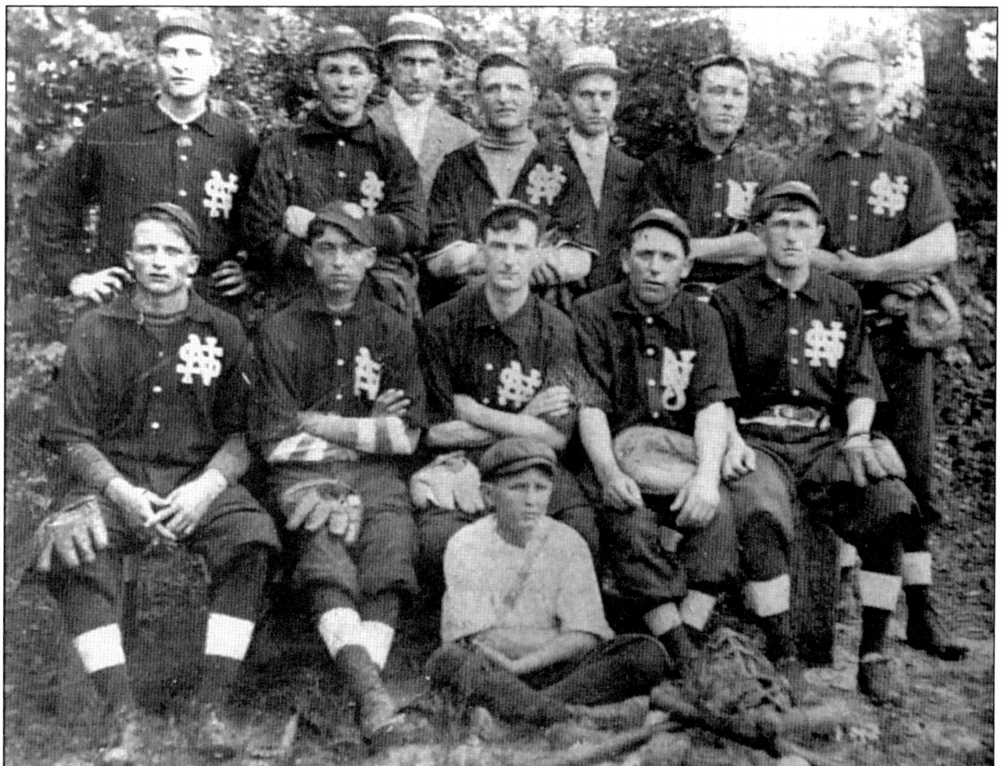

This photograph of a South Norfolk baseball team, probably the Panthers, was taken in 1912. Unfortunately, most of their names have slipped out of memory. The gentleman on the far right end of the first row is Mr. Howell, and the man on the far right end of the second row is Mr. Johnson, father of Jimmy Johnson.

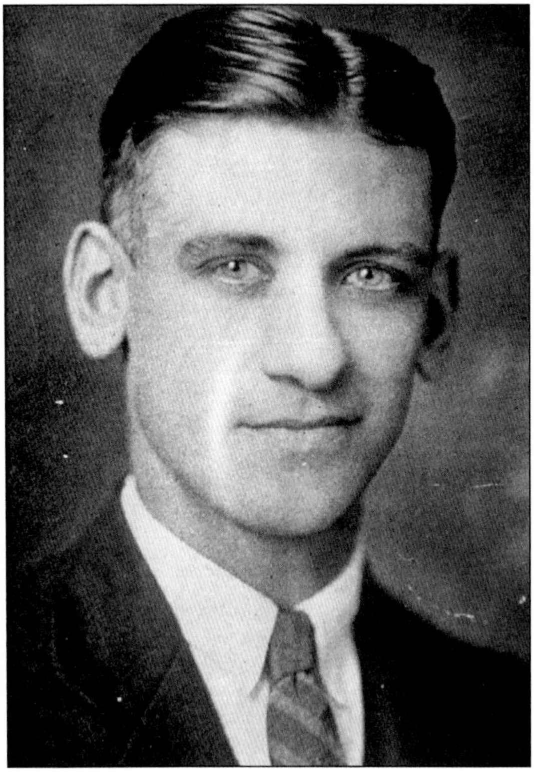

Ted Myers came to South Norfolk High School in 1923 and filled the positions of coach and physical director. Coach Myers had previously served two years with the National Playground Association. He also attended Penn State for two years where he played football and baseball and was a member of the track team. A man of high ideals, Myers believed that the development of his players as respectable persons was just as important as producing good athletes.

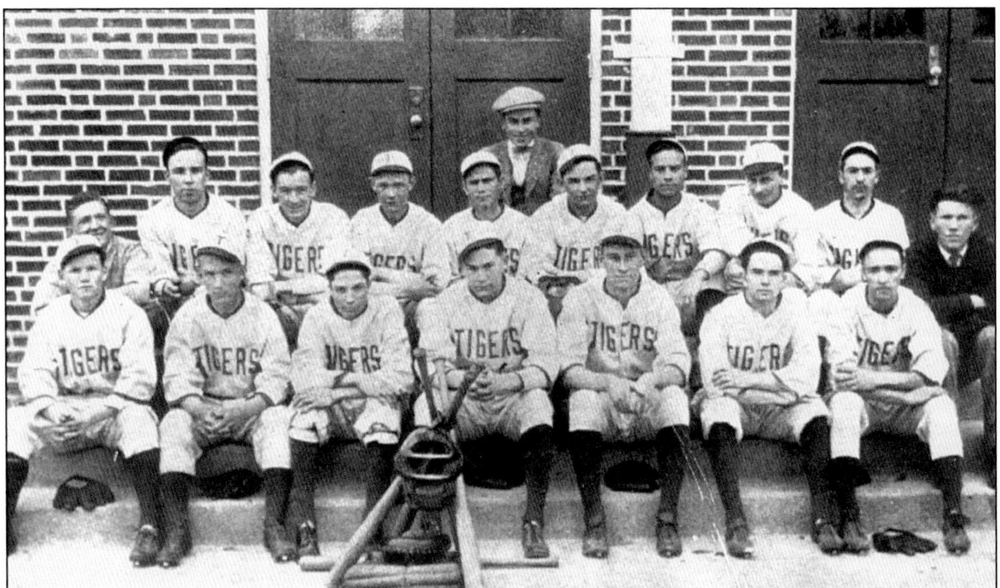

The South Norfolk High School baseball team, *c.* 1930, had some outstanding performers, such as Billy Morgan, Jim Burton, Lee Henley, Sid Harrell, Woody Barnes, and others. Herman Dennis served as the team's manager.

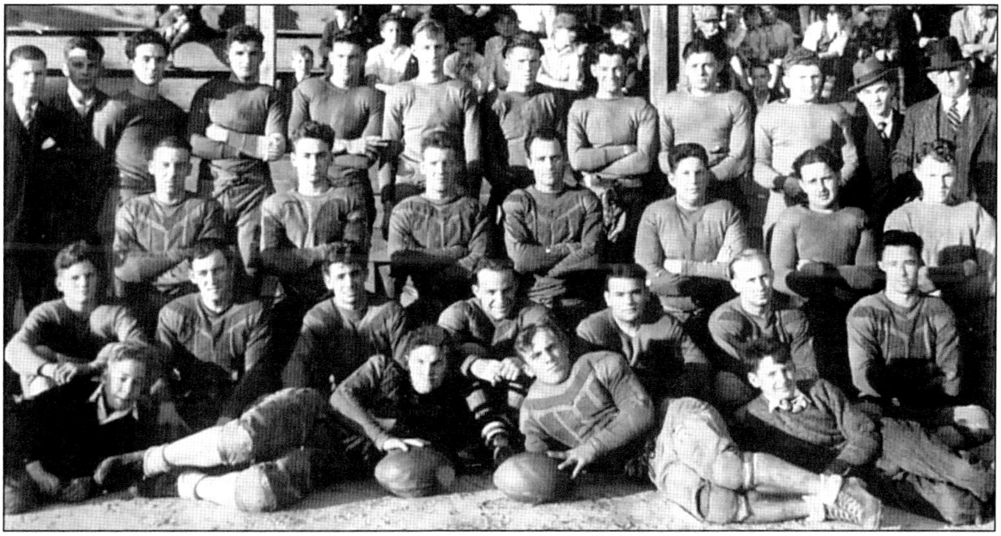

The South Norfolk Athletic Association was formed in 1924. The early history of amateur athletics in South Norfolk is said to have been divided into two parts, the earlier period represented by the Panthers and the latter by the Aces. The Panthers no longer existed after 1929. In the fall of 1931, the Aces were organized, and football and baseball were restored to the sports enthusiast of South Norfolk. This photograph dates back to the early 1930s. The co-captains, each holding a football are, from left to right, Buddy Morgan and Freddie Hodges.

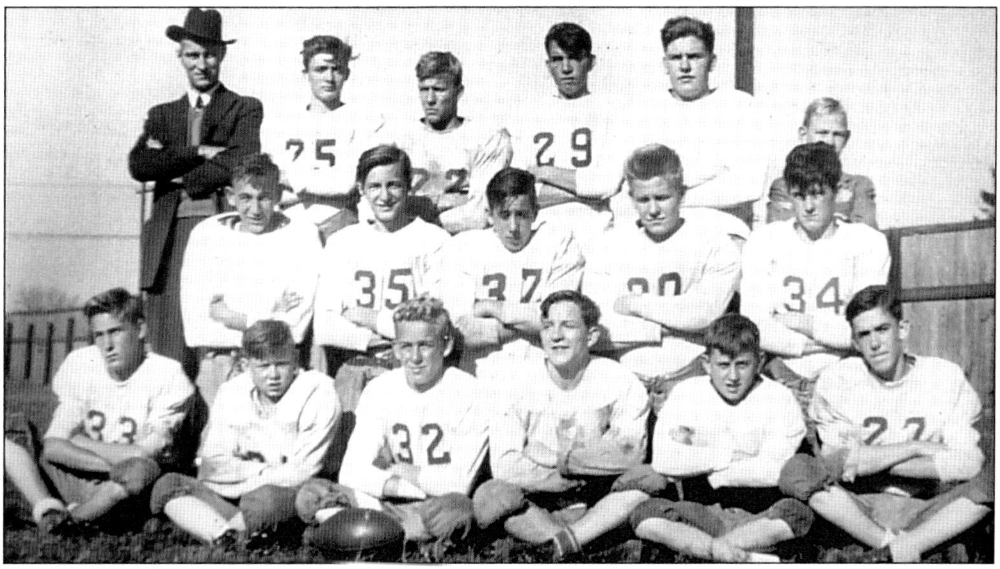

The South Norfolk Community Football League was organized in 1944. There were four teams: the Junior Chamber of Commerce (Jaycees), which was coached by James Benton and Billy Black; the Knights of Pythias, coached by Jim Burton; the American Legion, coached by Mike Smith; and the Odd Fellows, coached by David Pierce. This photograph is of the Knights of Pythias team, and the men are, from left to right, (front row) Paul Wilson, Jimmy Overton, Nick Johnson, Mark Alexander, Henry Casey, and Melvin Creef; (middle row) Otis Baker, Charles Lawrence, Bobby Hornbuckle, Pete Johnson, and Lenville Wilson; (back row) Jim Burton (coach), Eugene Wood, James Maples, Bobby Greenlee, Jack Munden, and Norman "Doc" Jones.

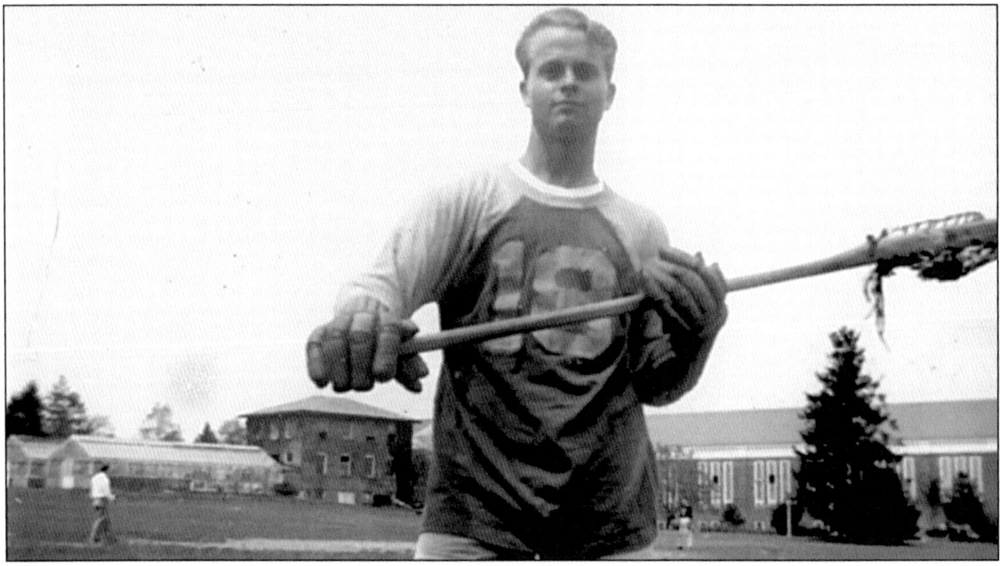

Pictured here is Raymond L. Harper, a member of the College of William & Mary lacrosse team, at the University of Maryland College Park in the spring of 1949.

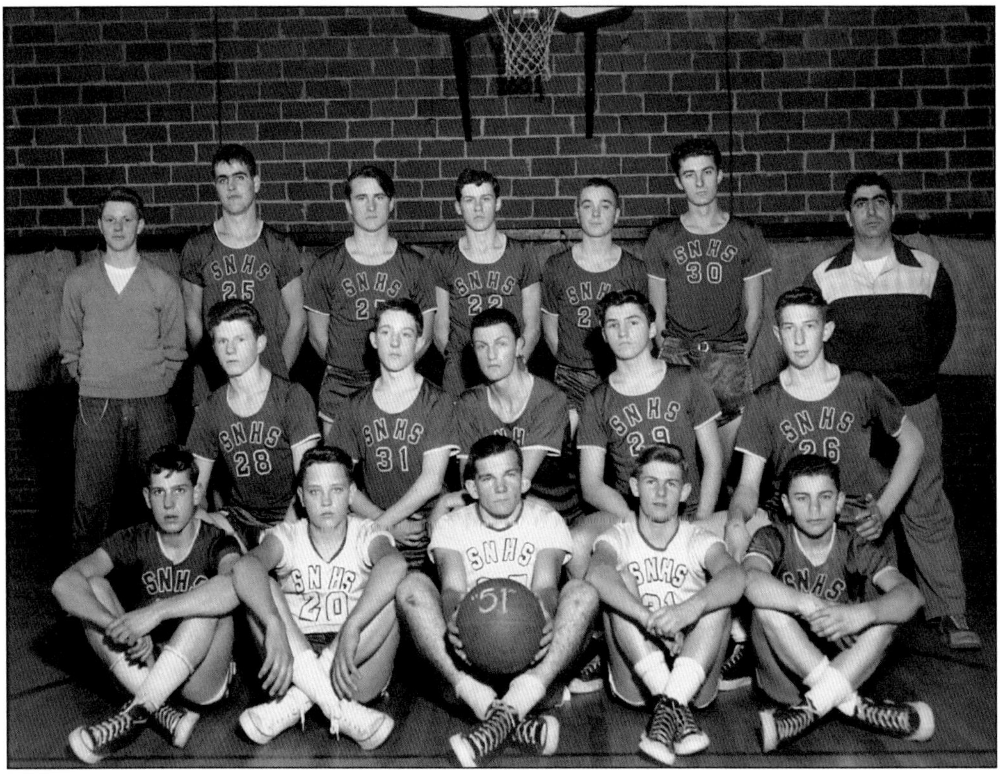

In 1951, members of the South Norfolk High School junior varsity basketball team are, from left to right, as follows: (first row) Herbert Ansell, Garnett Moore, William Wright, Herman Powers, and Edward Griffin; (middle row) Ronnie Seichrist, Ray Koon, Albert Griffin, Preston Grissom, and Buford Hanbury; (back row) Johnny Jackson (team manager), Dallas Coffield, Luther Casper, Darvin Pierce, Lowell Chappell, Tony Burgess, and coach Abe Ferris.

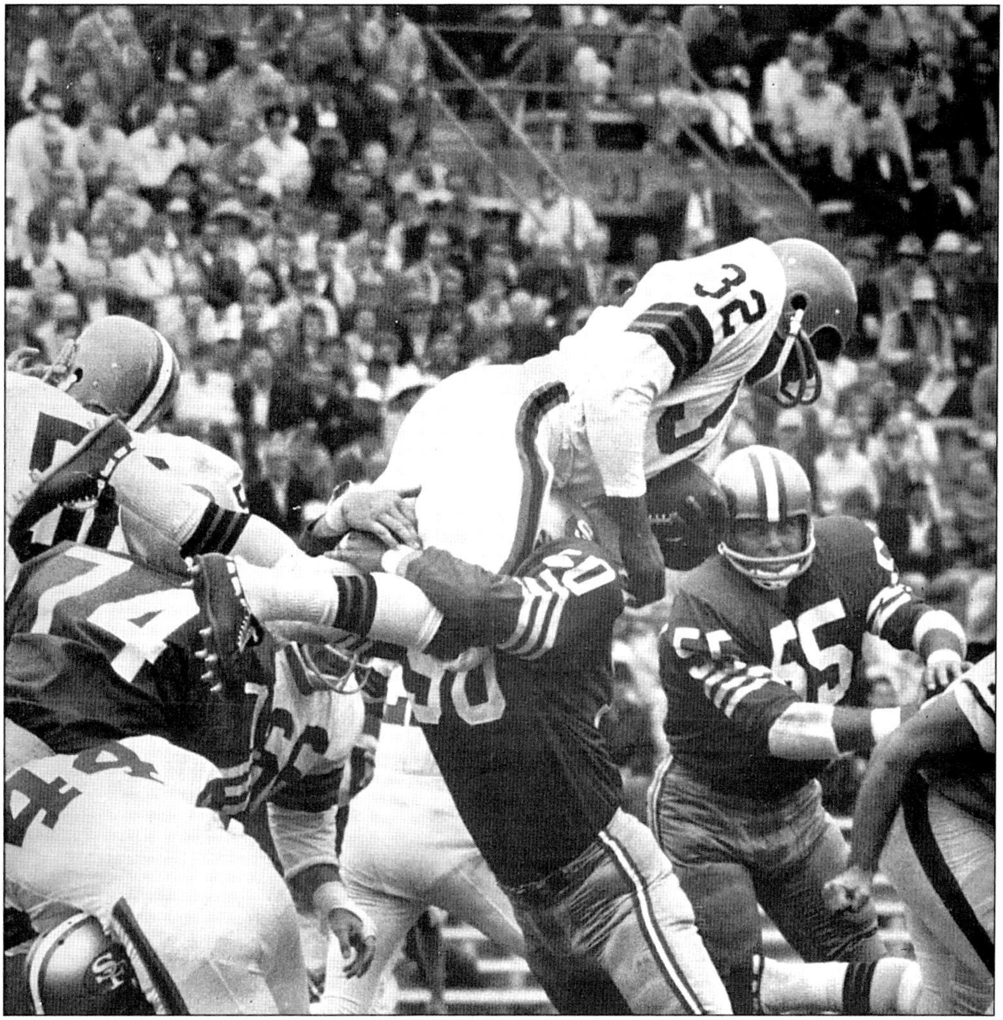

This was the thrill of a lifetime for rookie Ed Beard when he made this fantastic tackle on Jim Brown of the Cleveland Browns in 1965. Ed Beard played for the San Francisco 49ers.

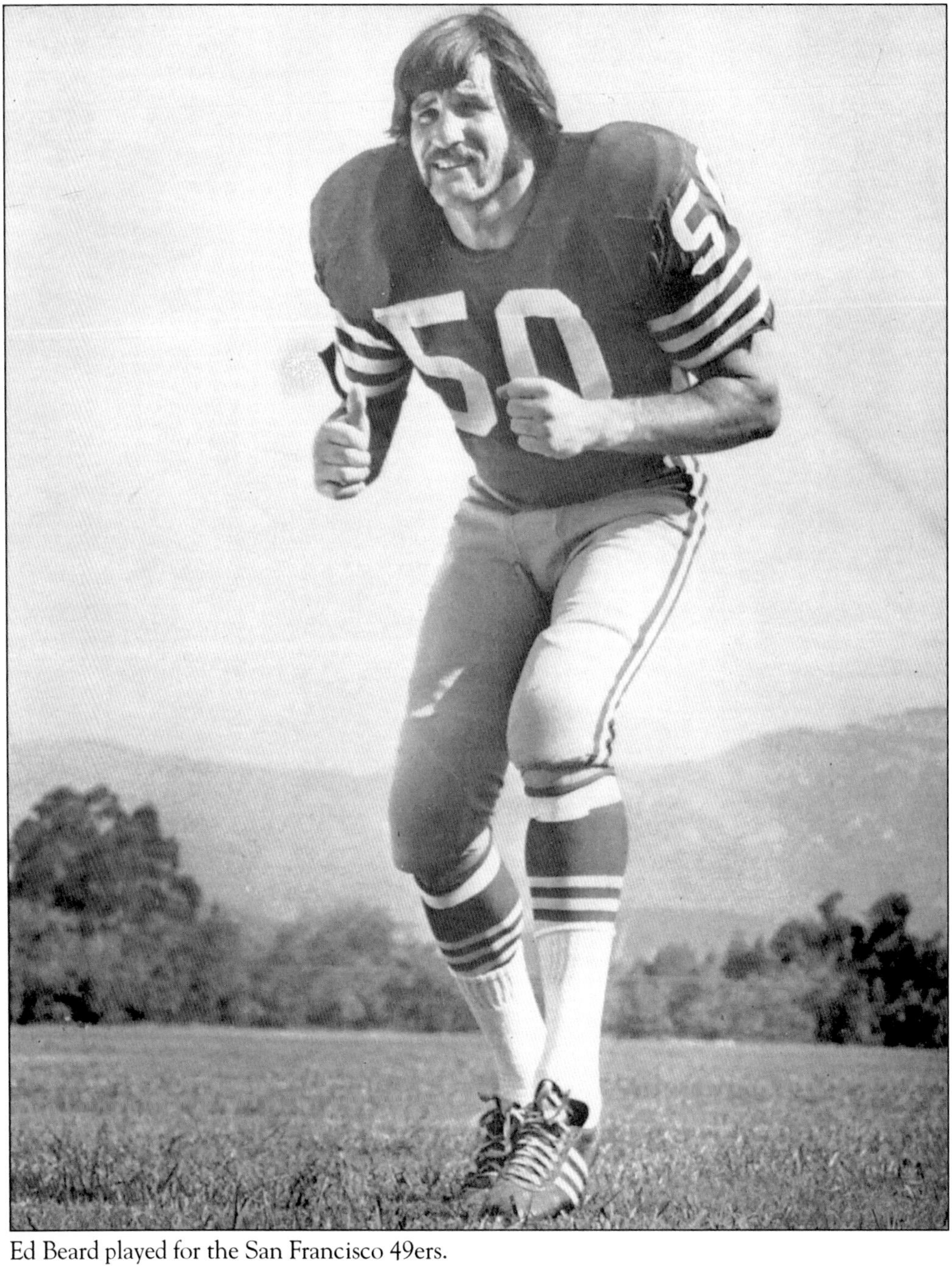
Ed Beard played for the San Francisco 49ers.

Eight

Portlock and the Portlocks

It is quite possible that there were members of the Portlock family in the South Norfolk area as early as 1634. However, the earliest records show that John Portlock first visited the colony in 1685 and returned to England shortly thereafter. His next trip to Virginia was in 1687, and, at that time, he brought several families with him. Those families were his responsibility until they were well settled in the colony. In return for this, he was rewarded with a land grant from the crown of England. The size of the land grant was based on the number of people being sponsored, usually the sponsor received 50 acres for each person that he brought to the colony. John Portlock's property extended from what would become Ferry Point (later Berkley) to Great Bridge along the Southern Branch of the Elizabeth River. Portlock would eventually build his home on part of the land he received from King James II of England. This home is believed to have been in the vicinity of Freeman Avenue and the Belt Line Railroad, near where Money Point is today. There were no roads at that time so travel to and from the home was by way of water.

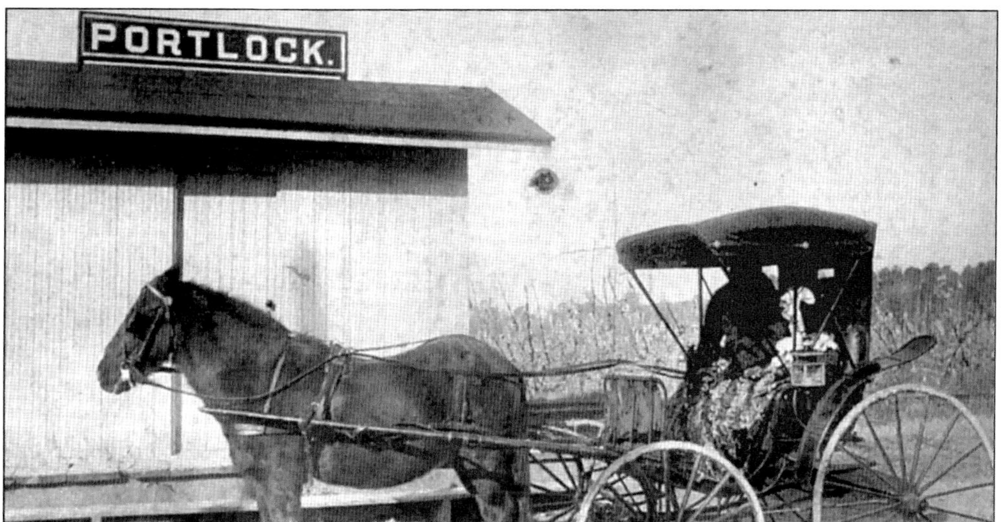

Portlock Station was located at what is now the corner of Freeman Avenue and Bainbridge Boulevard. This structure served as the waiting room for streetcar passengers. The driver of the carriage is Emmie Argyle Portlock, and the young lady with her is Marion Hunter Portlock, age two. This photograph was taken in 1902.

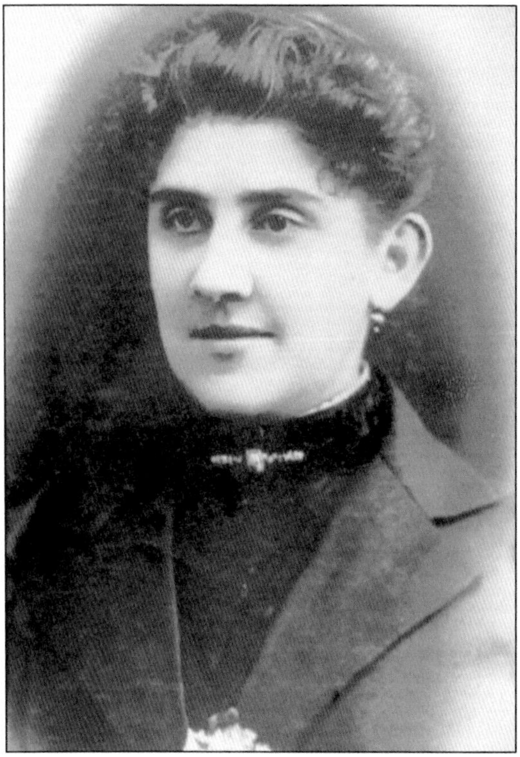

Emma Scarburgh Wise Portlock (1855–1930) was the wife of Tapley Portlock II.

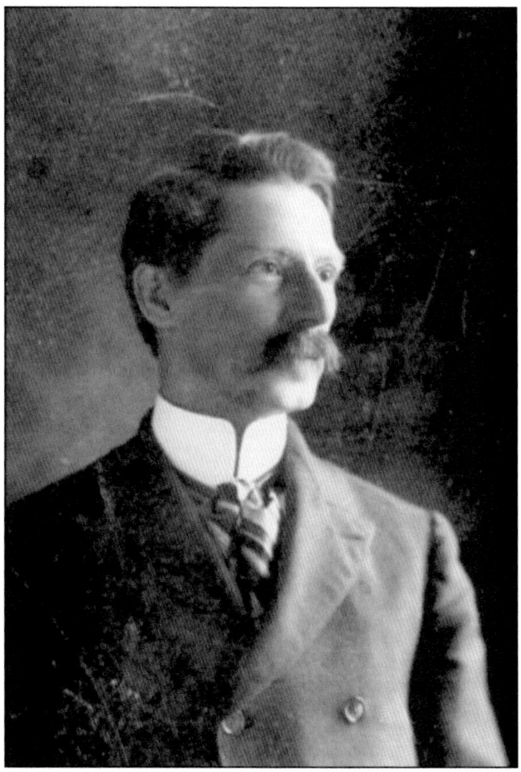

Tapley Portlock II (1849–1933) is pictured here.

Emmie Argyle Portlock (1855–1925) was the daughter of Franklin Portlock.

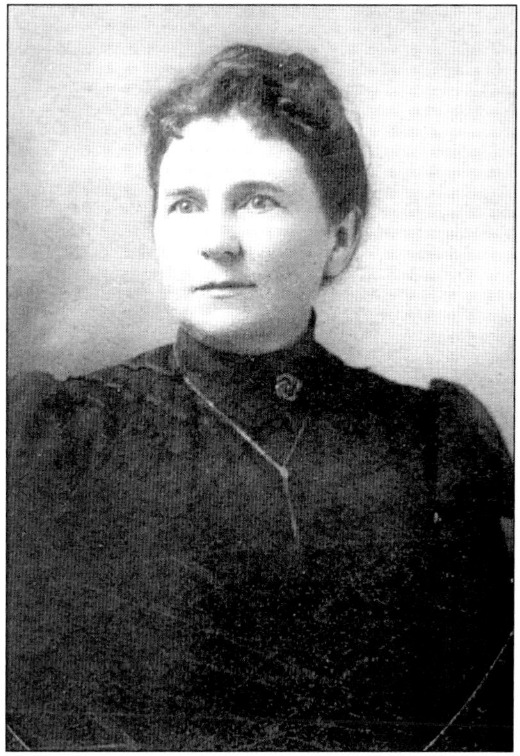

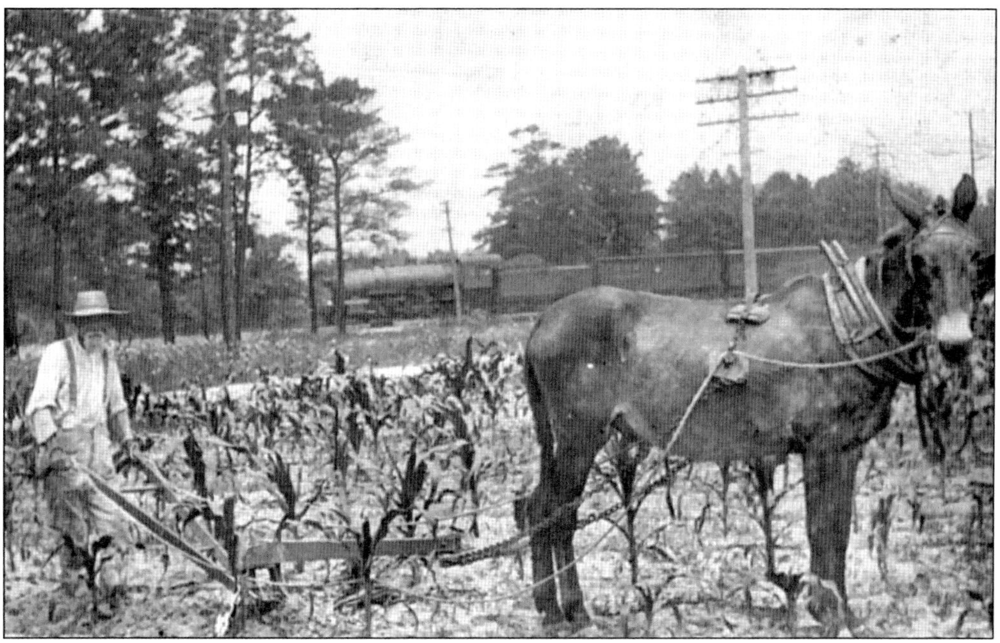

Mr. Liverman farmed the land that is now the site of the Southgate Plaza shopping center. He is shown here, c. 1890, tending a crop of corn that does not appear to be doing very well. The dirt path in the middle of the picture is the present-day Bainbridge Boulevard, and the Virginian Railroad crossing is now the location of the Portlock overpass.

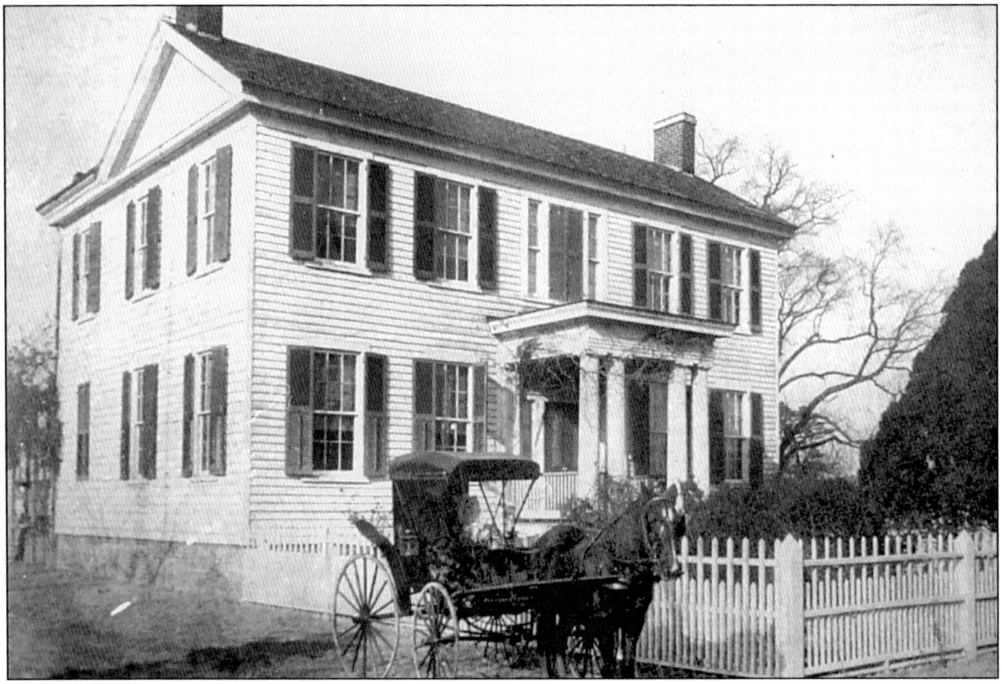

This farmhouse, which has undergone a few changes during the years, was once located near the intersection of Portlock Road and Franklin Street. In 1939, the building was moved a short distance away to Mill Dam Creek. Sometimes referred to as the "Oaks," the surrounding 100 acres constituted a strawberry farm.

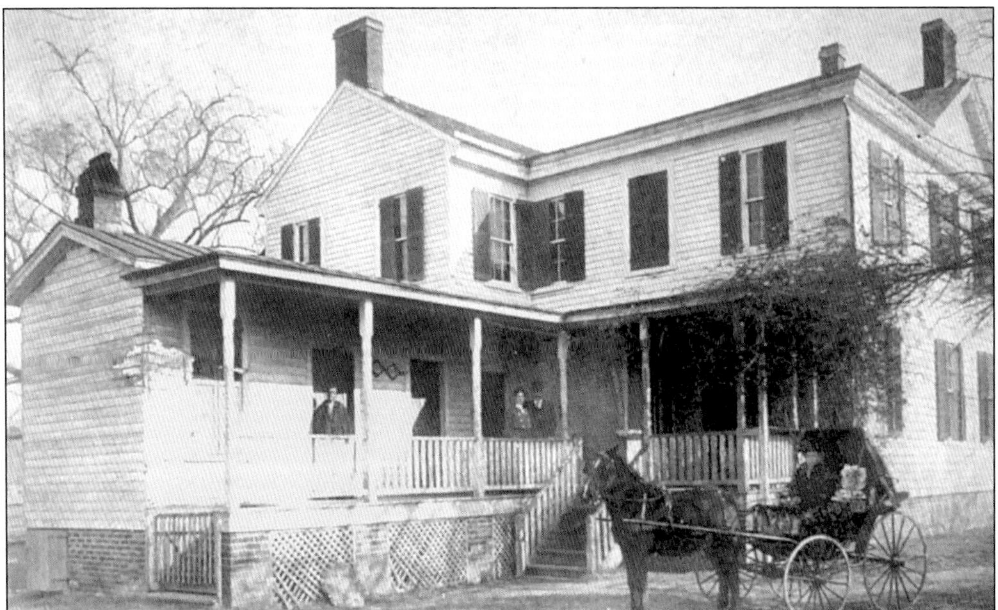

This photograph shows the back porch of the farmhouse as it looked in 1902, and standing on the porch are, from left to right, Bet Towns, the maid; Mrs. Marion West Portlock; and Frank Livingston Portlock Sr. In the buggy are Emmie Argyle Portlock and Marion Hunter Portlock, age two.

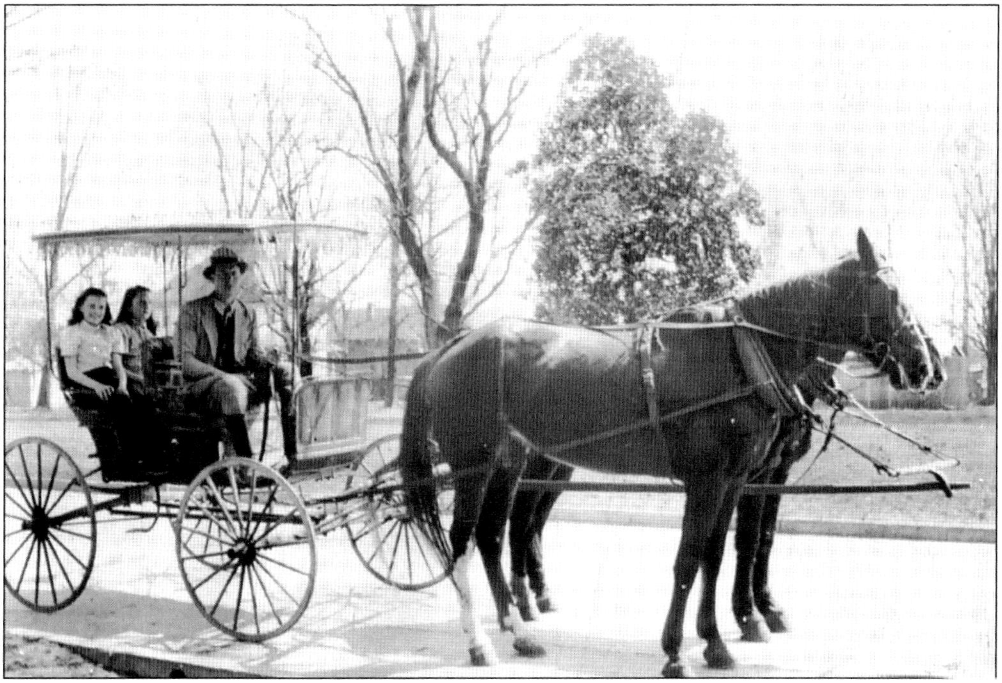

Frank L. Portlock Jr. and friends prepare for a ride in this surrey with the fringe on top. The surrey became popular around 1890 and got its name from Surrey, England. This picture was taken in the 1000 block of Ohio Street near the Portlock home in South Norfolk, c. 1938.

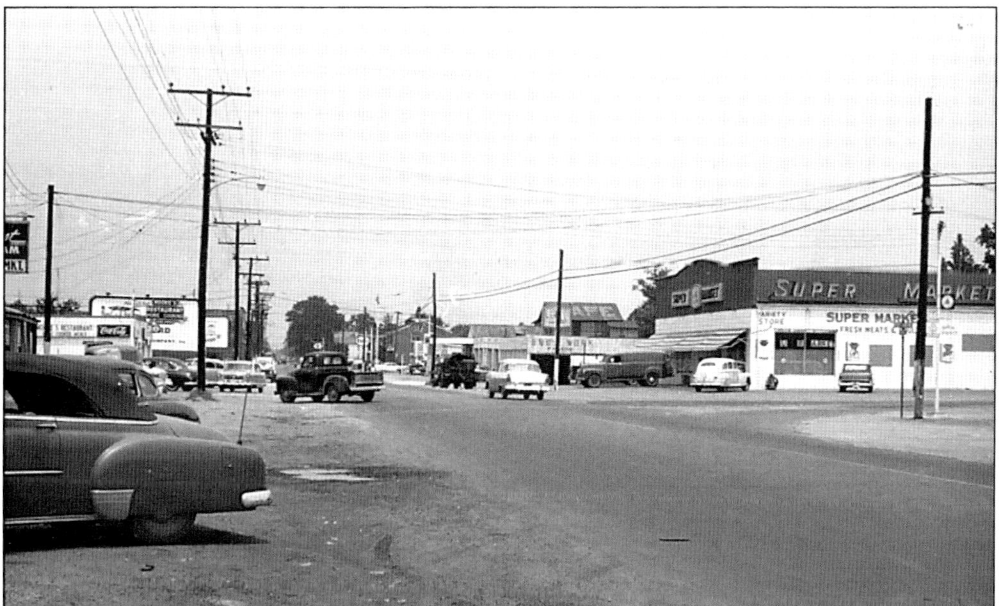

This is the 4000 block of Bainbridge Boulevard as it appeared in July 1955. The supermarket on the right is located at 4027. Other visible businesses on the right are the Body Works, a cafe, a Gulf station, an Esso station, and in the next block is the Portlock fire station. Across from the supermarket is Moore's Restaurant, which later became the Southern Cross.

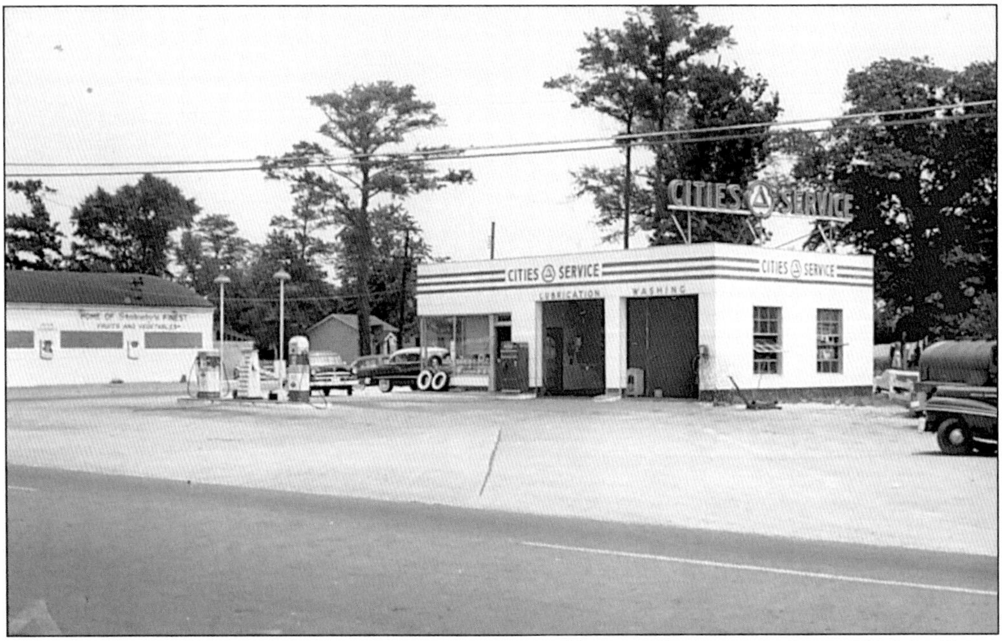

In July 1955, this Cities Service station was operated by Mr. Quinton C. Davis III. Mr. Davis ran a Sunoco station on this corner of Bainbridge Boulevard and Portlock Road prior to it becoming a Cities Service.

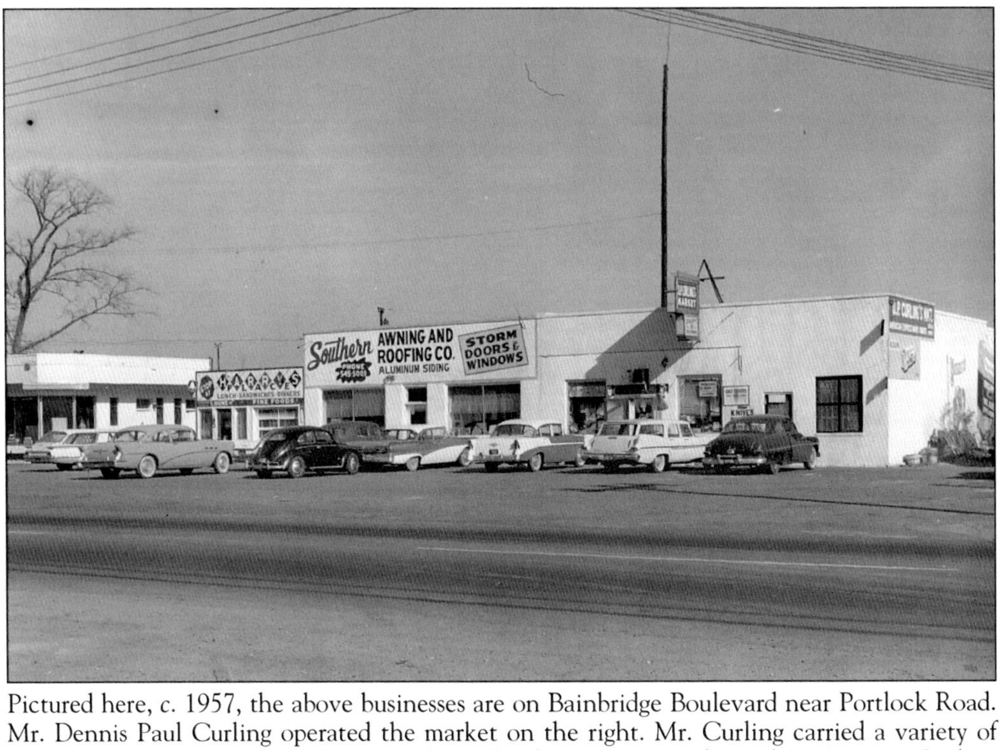

Pictured here, c. 1957, the above businesses are on Bainbridge Boulevard near Portlock Road. Mr. Dennis Paul Curling operated the market on the right. Mr. Curling carried a variety of dry goods, some hardware, groceries, and Birtchard ice cream. In the early 1930s, Mr. Curling delivered milk for Birtchard Dairy, which had its plant in Norfolk.

Nine

People and Points of Interest

There were many individuals and families who figured prominently in the early years of South Norfolk. How very nice it would have been to have known them all. Some were well known and made it big in professional athletics and the business world, while others, whose names were not familiar, contributed much to the world around them and to future generations.

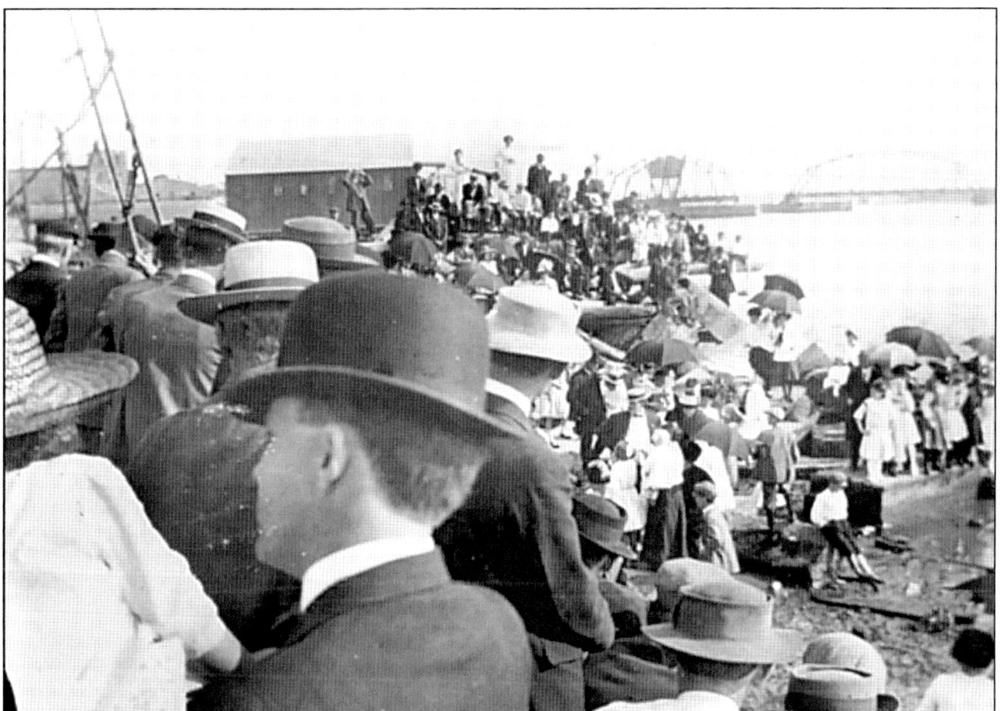

The year was 1909 and this group has gathered along the banks of the Elizabeth River. What was the occasion? No one knows for sure. Was it a service of baptism or did the crowd assemble to watch a fleet of ships? Whatever the reason, it must have been on Sunday afternoon because most of the people are well dressed.

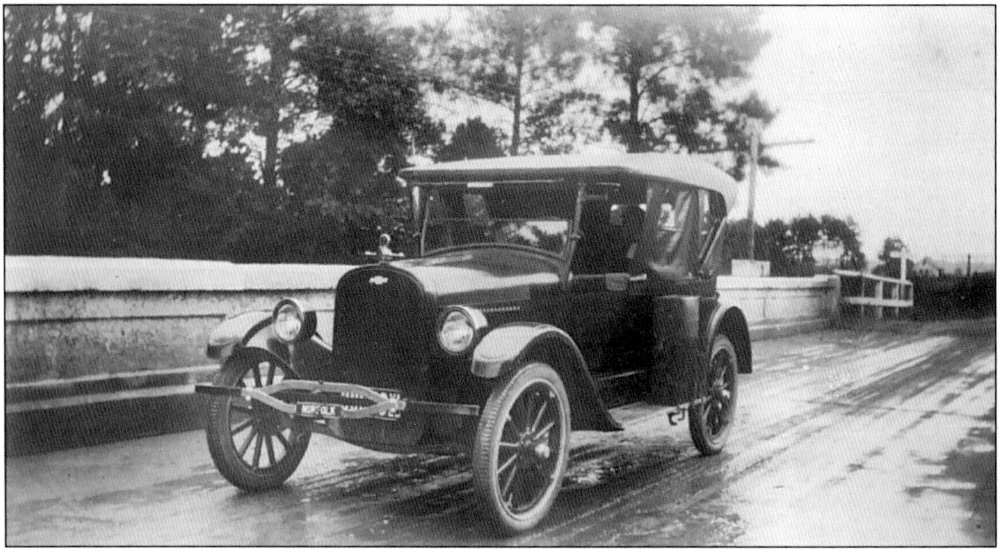

It was August 24, 1923, the street is wet, and there is a passenger in the back seat but no driver. He probably stepped out of the vehicle to take a picture of his new 1923 Chevy.

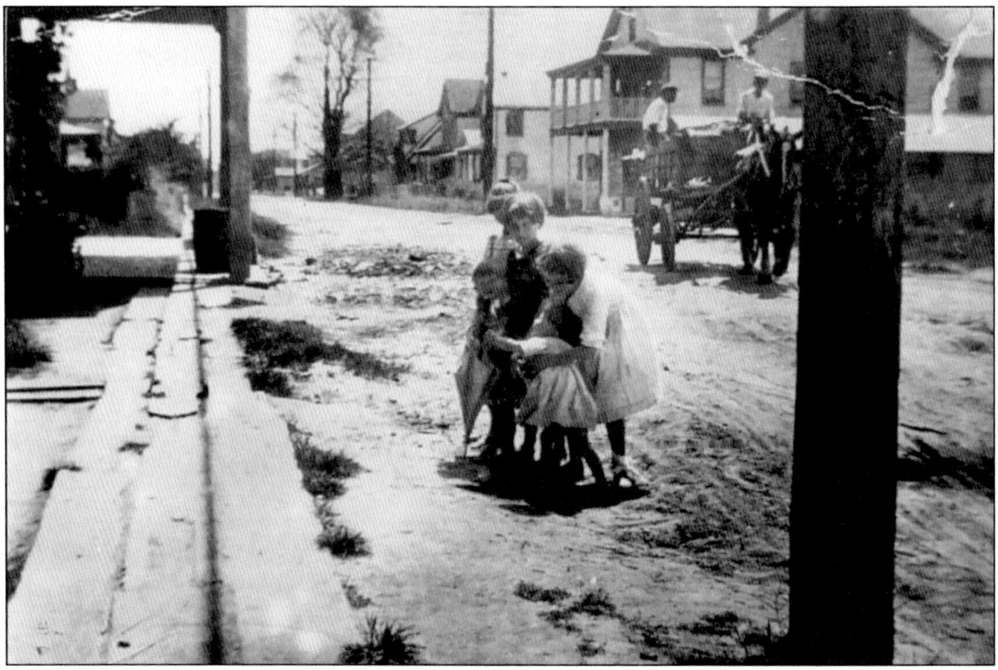

The streets of early South Norfolk were dirt, and some were covered with crushed oyster shells. But there was no curbing and the sidewalks consisted of large boards nailed together. This was the 1200 block of Bainbridge Boulevard prior to 1920. The men with the horse and wagon appear to be delivering ice (the wagon is covered to protect its contents). The large, two-story building behind the delivery wagon was, at one time, Parker's grocery. The people in this photograph have not been identified.

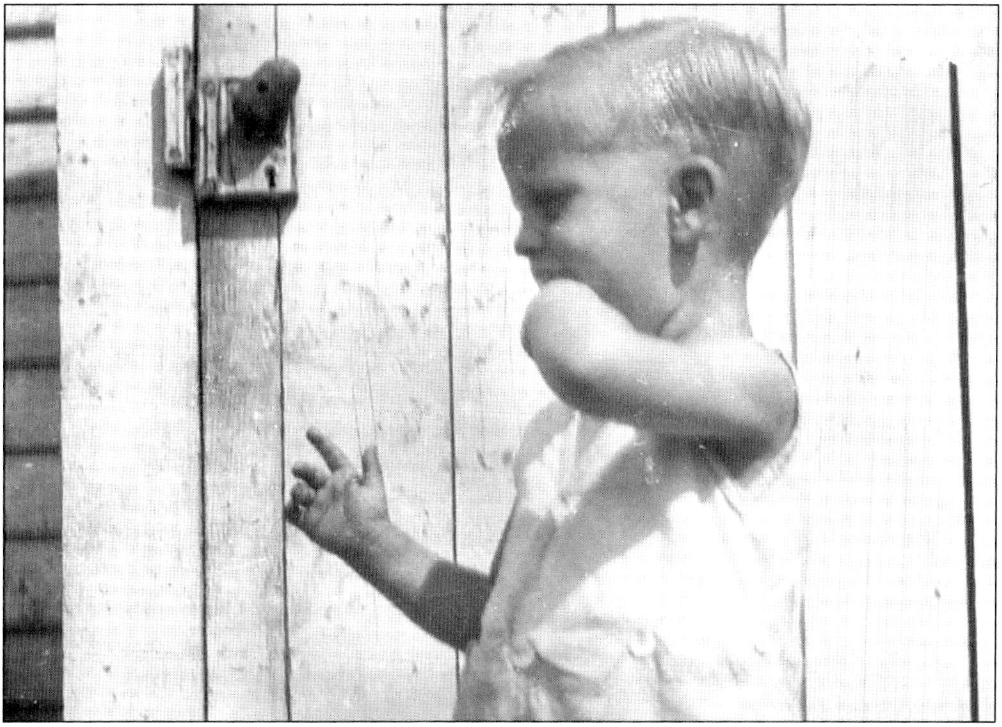

The young man pictured here looks a lot like my grandson, but it's actually me, Raymond L. Harper, standing in front of the outhouse in the back yard of 608 "B" Street in South Norfolk. There was no indoor plumbing or electricity. About two years after this c. 1930 picture was taken, we moved to a more modern neighborhood.

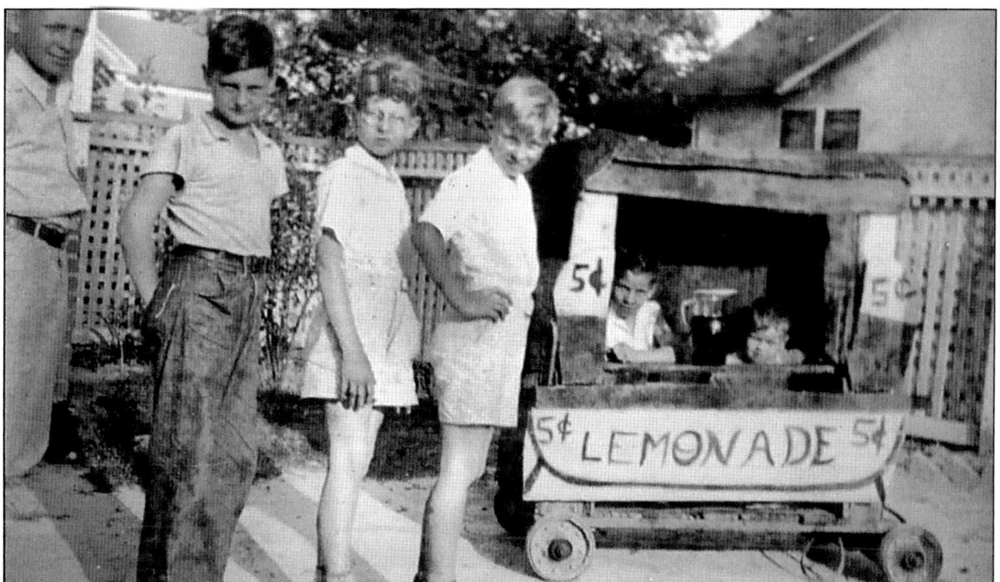

The young entrepreneurs in this photograph are, from left to right, Melvin Newberry, Ray Sykes, Raymond (Dickey) Wallace, Fletcher Hanbury, Durwood Hanbury, and Maywood Wallace. They started their business on a hot summer day in August 1937.

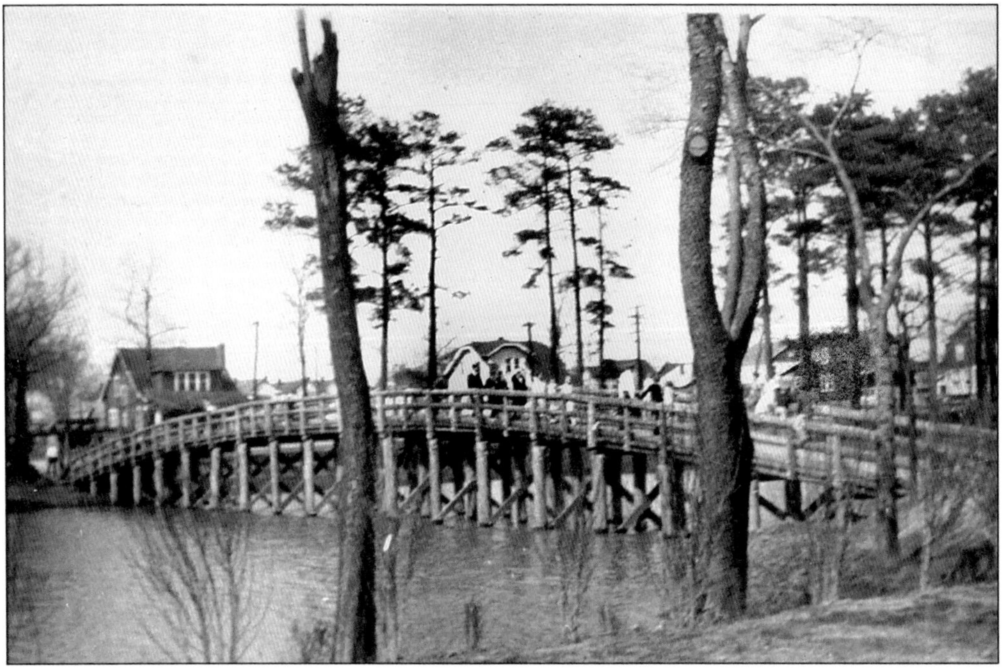

The construction of Lakeside Park was a Work Projects Administration project that was begun in 1933 and completed in the spring of 1934. This first bridge was built of juniper donated by Carl Jordan of Jordan Lumber Company. This rustic structure, built in 1934, has been replaced several times. The existing bridge, which was constructed in 1995, is mostly concrete.

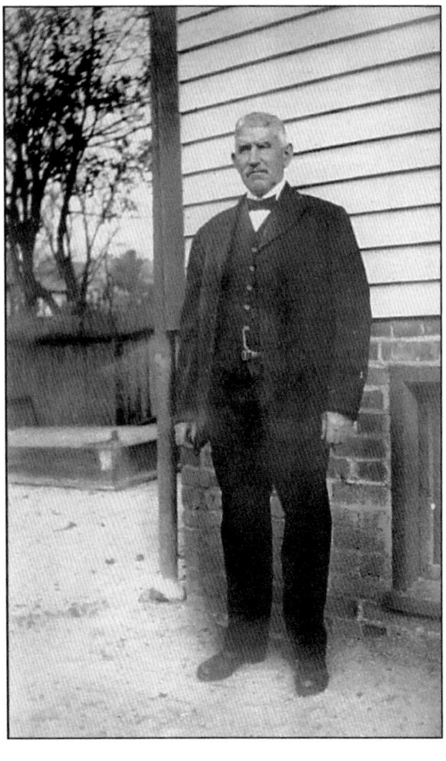

Mr. George Lafayette Grimes was born in Gates County, North Carolina, on June 21, 1860, and died in South Norfolk on February 19, 1948. Mr. Grimes was in the contracting and building business and built his own home on the corner of Chesapeake and Park Avenues in 1910. His was one of 17 houses that he constructed on Chesapeake Avenue. Grimes also built homes on Park Avenue and Jackson Street. Mr. Grimes, along with Mr. John Jones, built most of the houses in early South Norfolk.

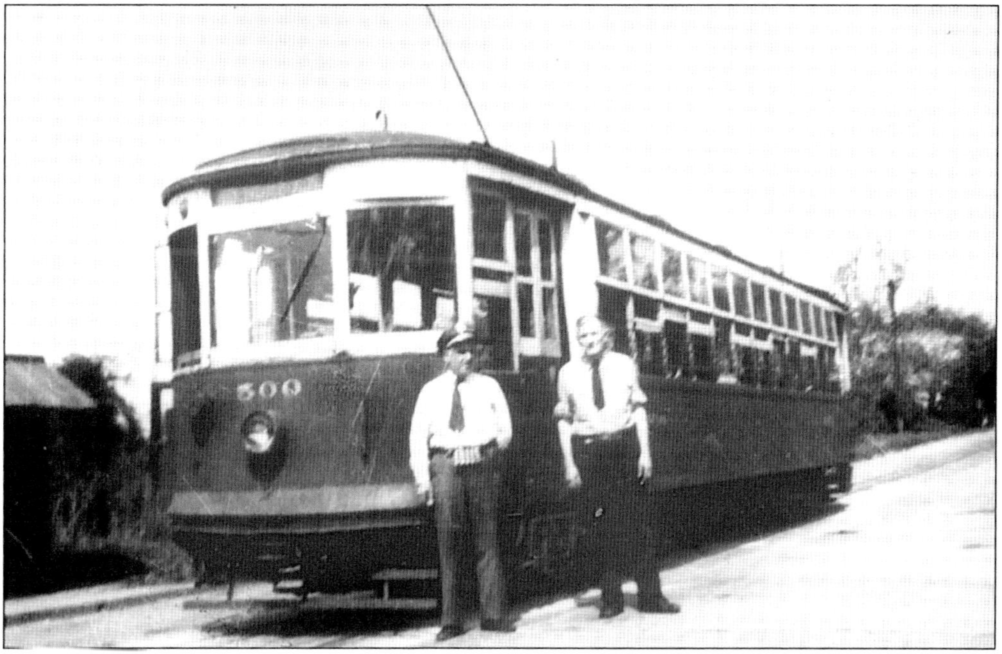

This photograph of motorman J.K. Forbes and Red Hewitt was taken at the end of the line on Holly Street near Bainbridge Boulevard. The position of the trolley indicates that Mr. Forbes was ready to drive the streetcar back to Norfolk.

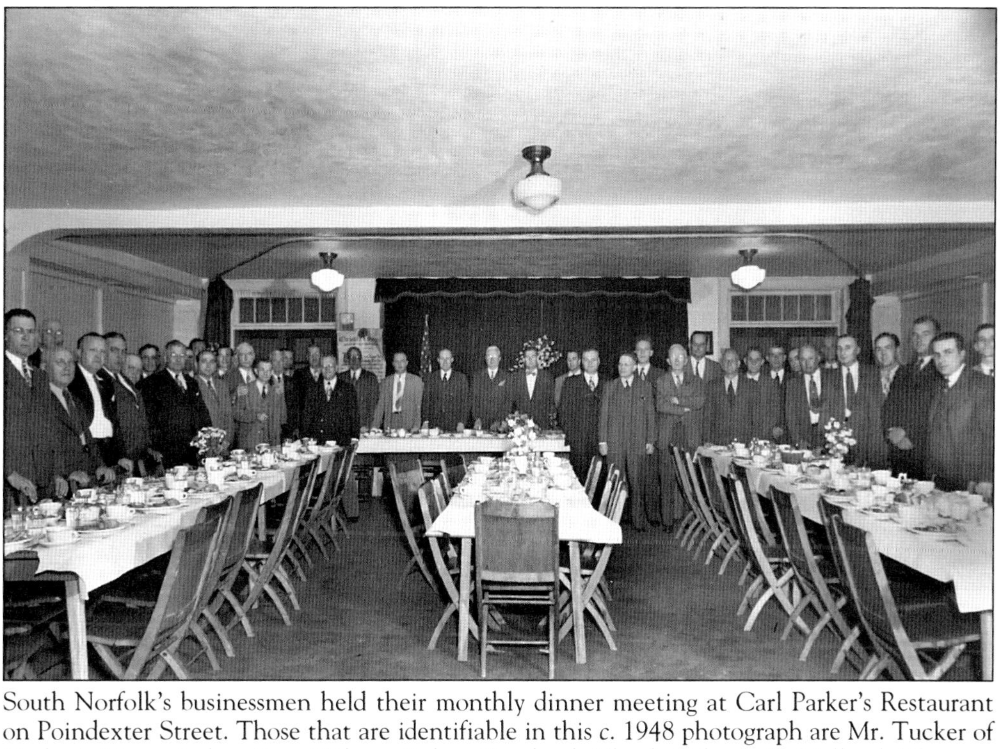

South Norfolk's businessmen held their monthly dinner meeting at Carl Parker's Restaurant on Poindexter Street. Those that are identifiable in this *c.* 1948 photograph are Mr. Tucker of Tucker's Meat Market, Sam Wilson, Robert Rowland, Claude Baker, J.K. Holland, Clarence Forehand, Mr. Winston, Mr. Badeaux, Phil Davis, and Herman Dennis.

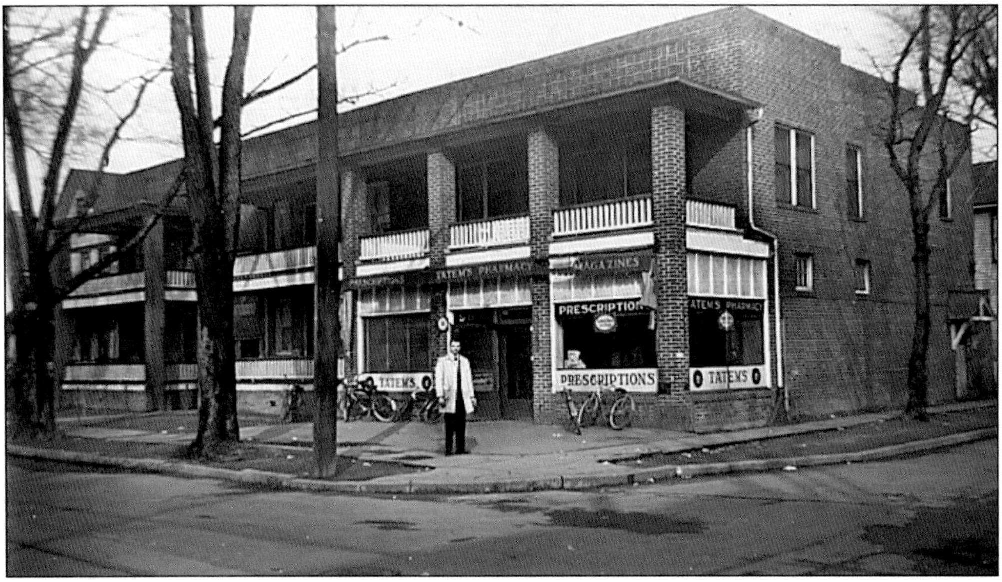

This picture of Jack Hughes was taken in front of Tatem's Pharmacy in the afternoon of Sunday, January 31, 1943. The store and the apartments were built on the corner of Chesapeake Avenue and Ohio Street in 1919. The store's original owner was Mr. Gilliam, who operated the drugstore under the name of Chesapeake Pharmacy.

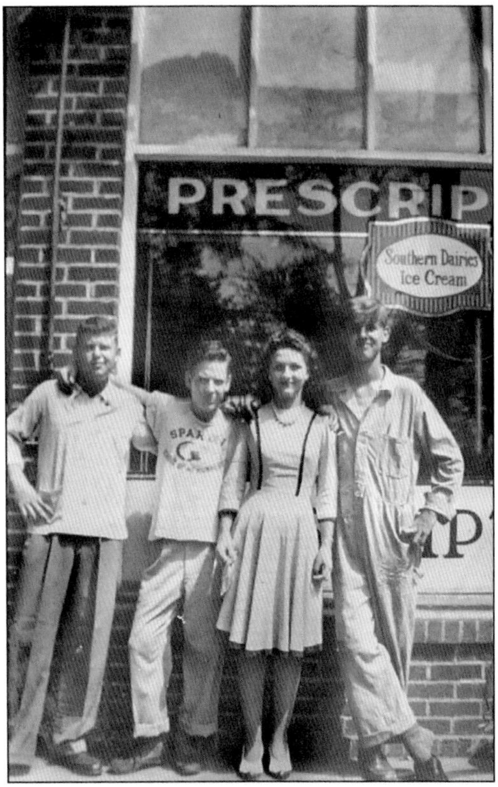

Tatem's Pharmacy was one of several hangouts for high school students. This picture was taken on an afternoon in September 1943, when, from left to right, Bugs Dail, Billy Forbes, Anna Alexander, and Harold Christenson were "just hanging out." Bill Forbes later became chief judge of the Chesapeake Circuit Court.

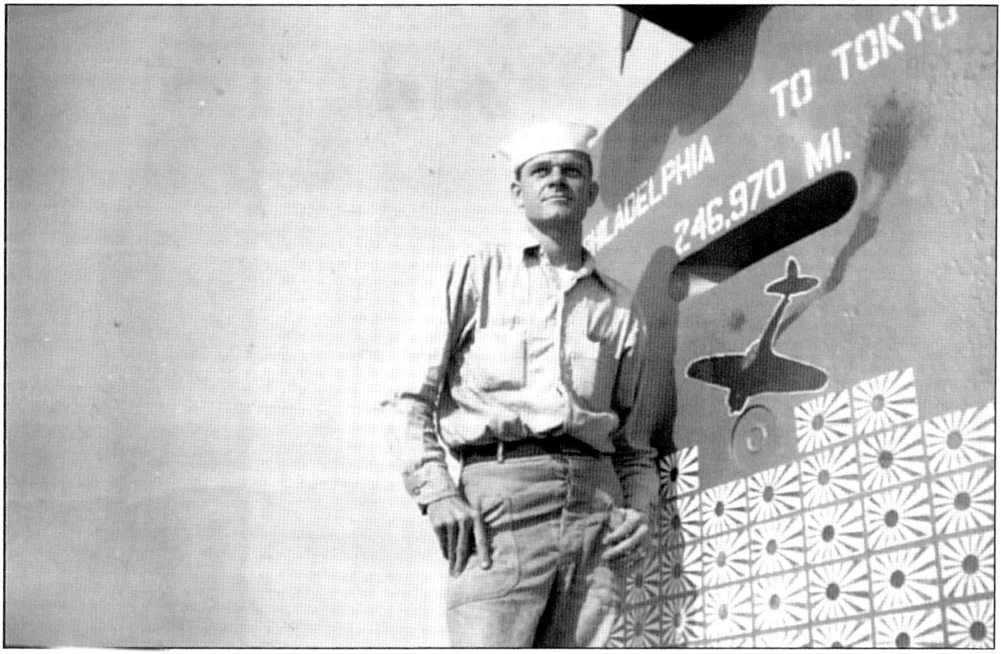

Linwood Briggs stands by the score board on the USS *South Dakota*, which operated in the Pacific during WW II.

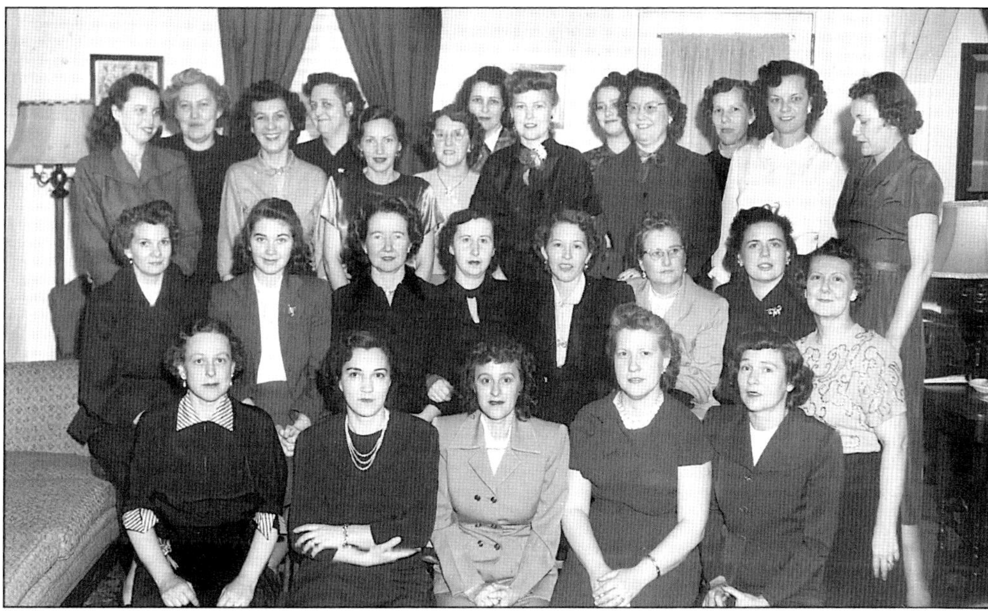

These ladies were members of the South Norfolk Woman's Club in 1951, and are, from left to right, (kneeling) Frances Forehand, Ruth Jolliffe, Virginia Sullivan, Tillie Hogan, and unidentified; (middle row) Mildred Small, unidentified, Mildred Whitney, Virginia Cahoon, Annie Borum, Claudia Robbins, Edith Goodwin, and Mildred Gay; (back row) Thelma Lee Taylor, Mrs. Todd, ? Dowdy, Ada Harper, Ruth Jones, Lillian Rice, Josie Henley, Edna Lassiter, unidentified, unidentified, Mary Evans, Laura Capps, and unidentified. (H.A. Stewart Jr., photographer.)

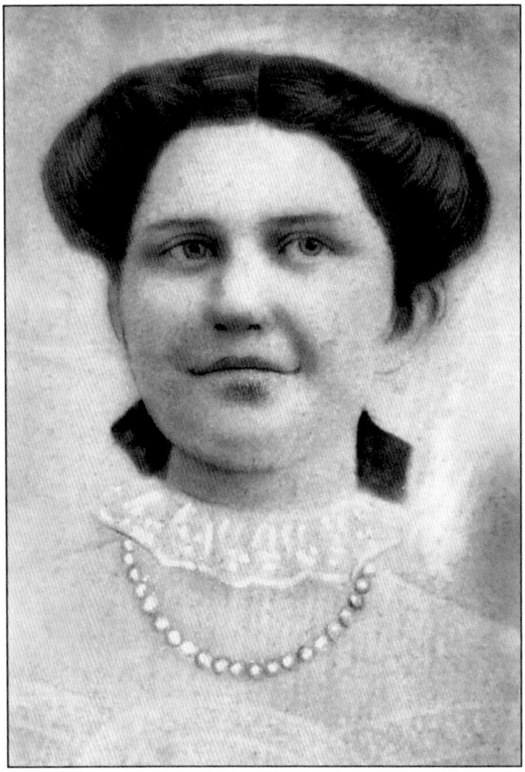

This photograph is of Ella M. Simpson Harper. She was born on October 21, 1891, and died in the summer of 1910 at the age of 18 years, leaving behind a husband and a two-year-old son. In her short lifetime, Harper collected postcards from the Jamestown Exposition and wrote beautiful poetry.

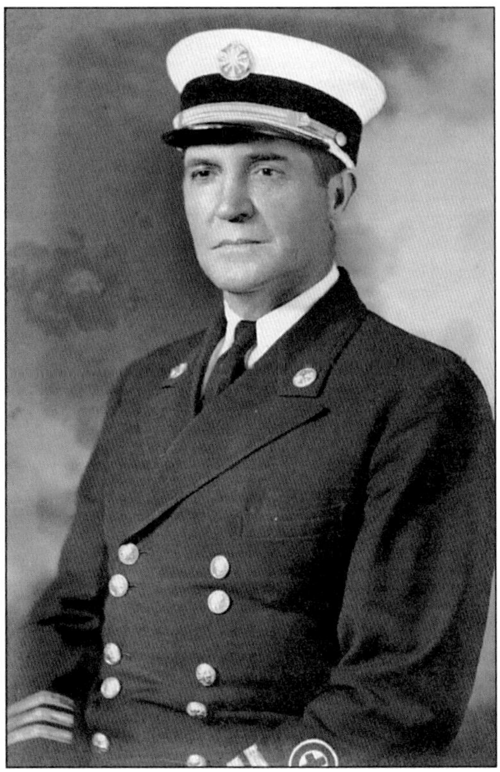

Lennon H. Newberry was an early member of the South Norfolk Volunteer Fire Department and he was elected chief in 1935. Chief Newberry was a very effective leader and his accomplishments were many. A ladies auxiliary was formed to help the department with its social affair, and to promote fire department morale. A chemical hose wagon was purchased in 1935, and the firefighters received new uniforms that same year.

Dr. I.L. Chapman lived at 1446 Chesapeake Avenue and had his office in the basement. Steve Hollowell worked for Dr. Chapman as his full-time driver, taking the doctor to make house calls and hospital rounds. This picture of Hollowell was taken across the street from the Portlock home at 1007 Ohio Street in 1943.

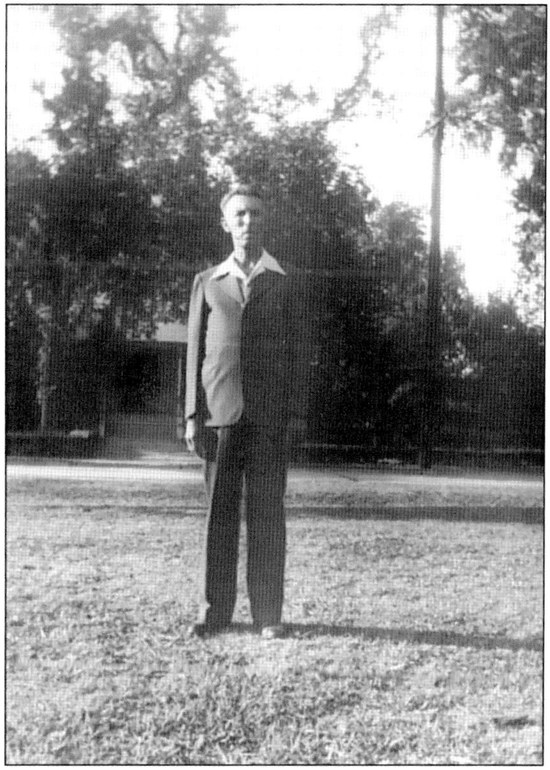

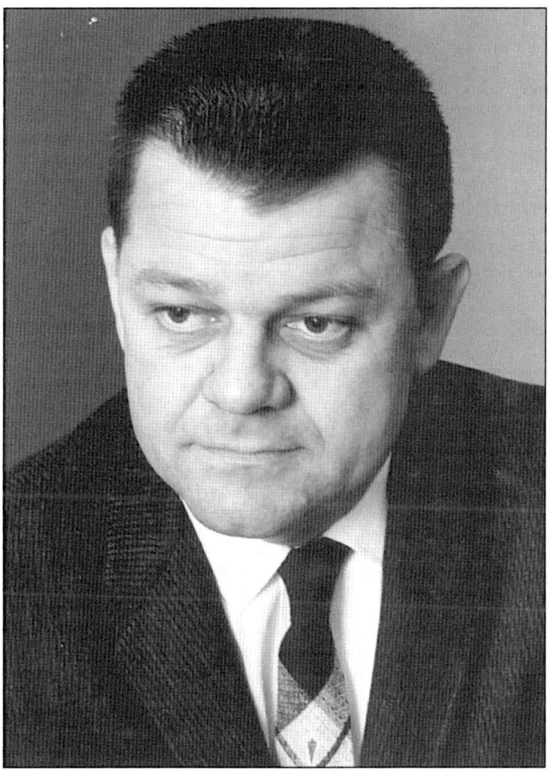

Linwood L. Briggs Jr., pictured here on November 12, 1959, served on the South Norfolk City Council for four years and was then elected mayor for four years. Mr. Briggs served as mayor from 1957 to 1961. (Orby G. Kelley Jr., photographer.)

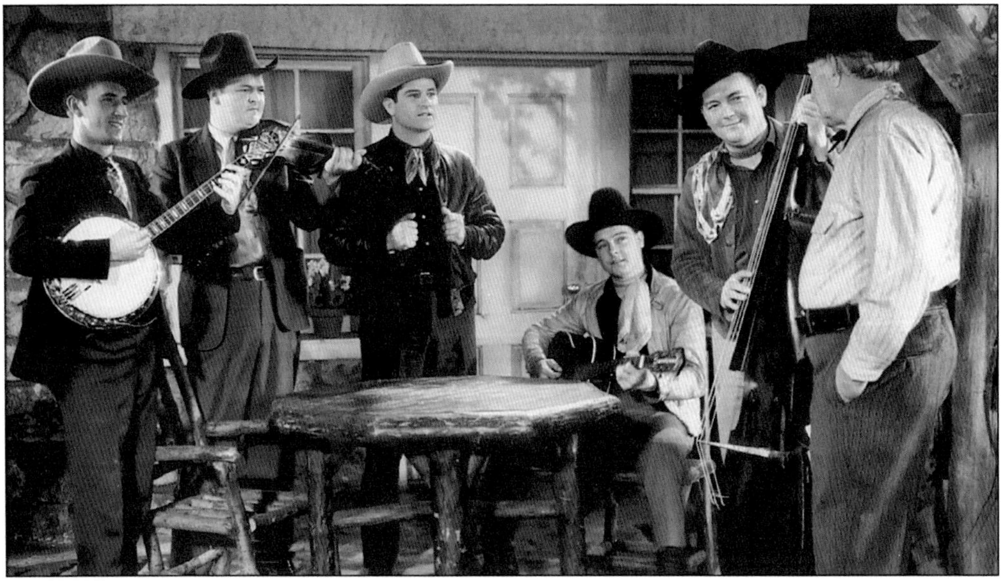

The Phelps brothers, Norman, Earl, and Willie, along with Ray Whitley and Ken Card, made up the western musical group known as Ray Whitley and the Six-Bar Cowboys. The group performed on the rodeo circuit for a while and then, in 1936, headed for Hollywood, appearing in several westerns as singing cowboys. In 1938, they decided to return to Virginia where they continued to play country-western music, billed as Norman Phelps and the Virginia Rounders. This scene is from *Rhythm Wranglers*, which was made in 1937. The members of the group are, from left to right, Ken Card, Earl Phelps, Ray Whitley, Willie Phelps, Norman Phelps, and unidentified.

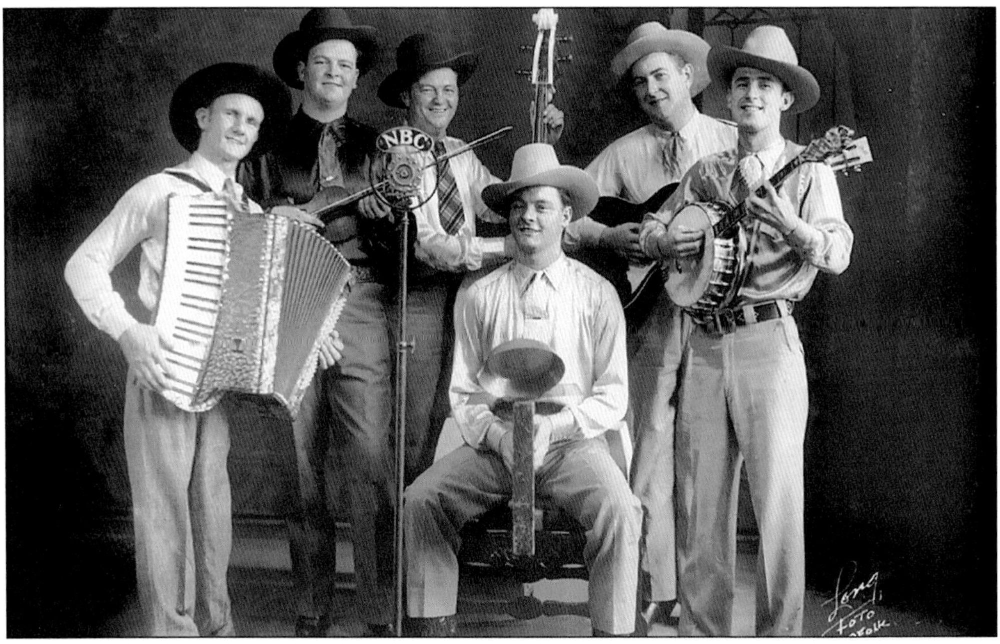

Norman Phelps and the Virginia Rounders were photographed doing their noon-time radio show by Long Studio of Norfolk. The country-western musicians are, from left to right, Happy Daws, Earl Phelps, Norman Phelps, Willie Phelps, William Lloyd Stubbs, and Ken Card.

Ten

WINTER MEMORIES

September has arrived, and the time has come for another school year to begin. The days of summer are just recent memories, but there are a few hot days still ahead. Soon, there is a chill in the air and everyone reaches for a sweater; it is fall, and winter will soon make its debut. At first there are just a few flurries, but, as December approaches, the flurries turn to heavy snow. The annual trip to Norfolk and Christmas shopping have been delayed because of the large accumulation of the white stuff. Eventually, the condition of the streets improve, the streetcars resume their regular schedule, shopping is accomplished, and Christmas comes right on time, as it has always done before.

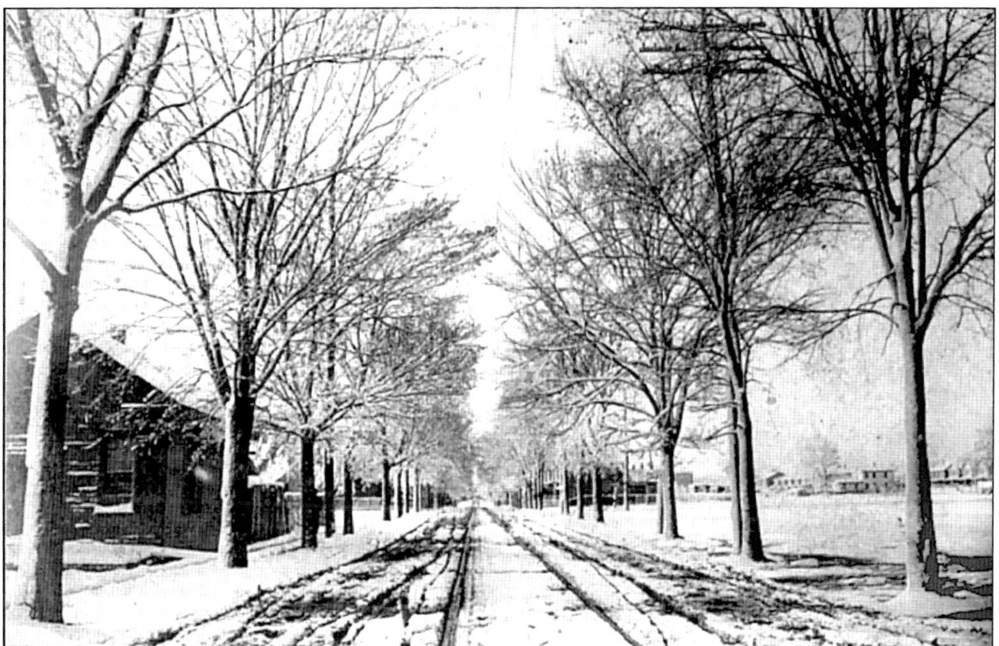

On March 21, 1908, the remains of a late winter storm lay along Liberty Street in South Norfolk. Somewhere in the middle of this vacant land was the beginning of what would become the 500 block. (L.H. Newberry, photographer.)

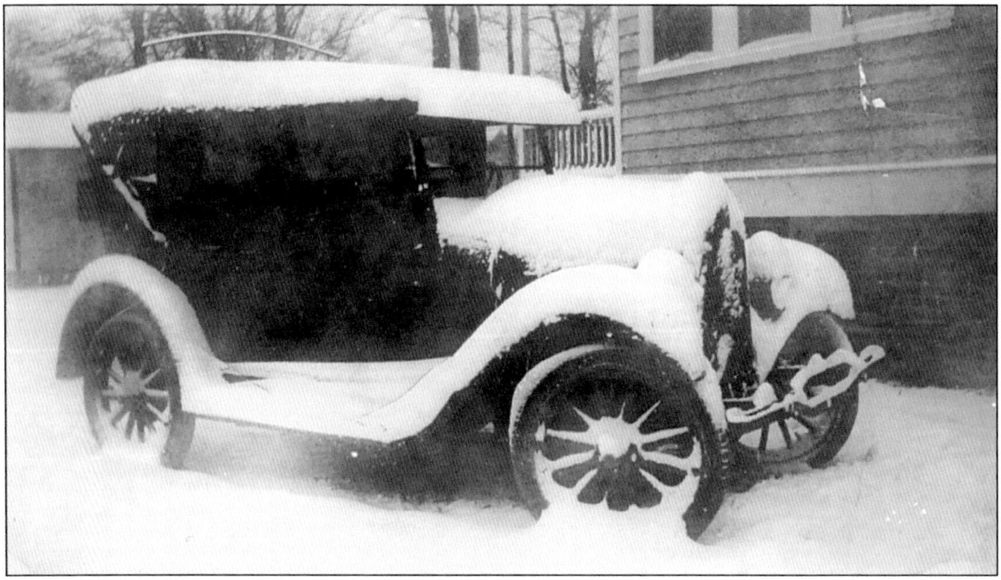

On January 25, 1926, 6 inches of snow blanketed the area. This snow-covered Chevy is parked in the side yard of 1214 Rodgers Street. The old rag top and canvas windows did not provide much protection from the elements.

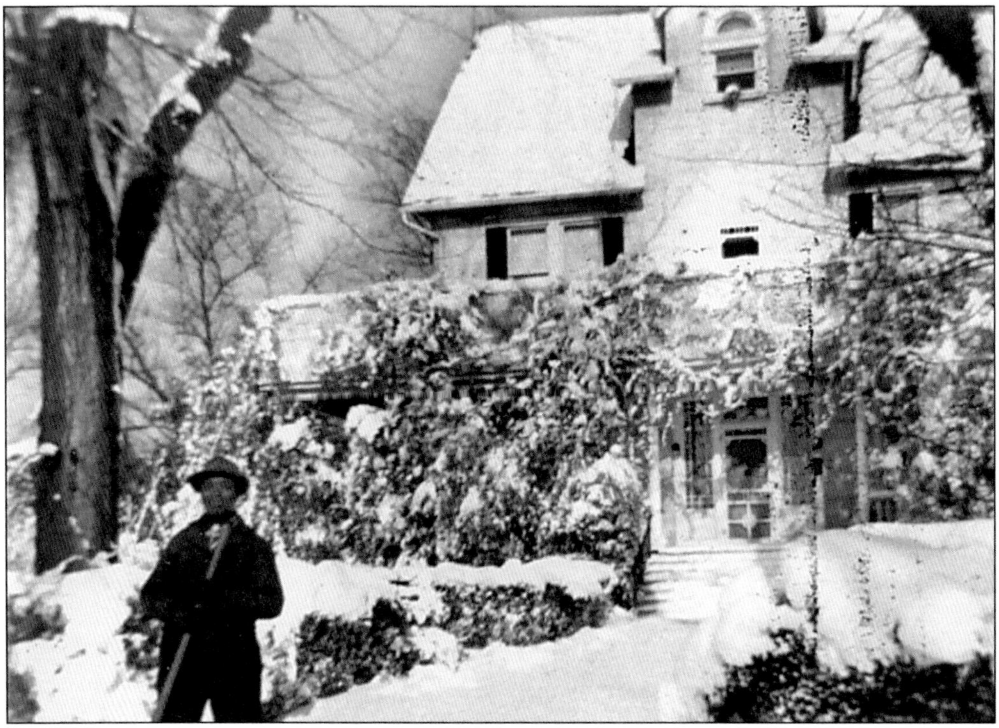

In this winter of 1963 photograph, Vance Smith begins the laborious task of clearing snow from the walks around the Portlock home at 1007 Ohio Street.

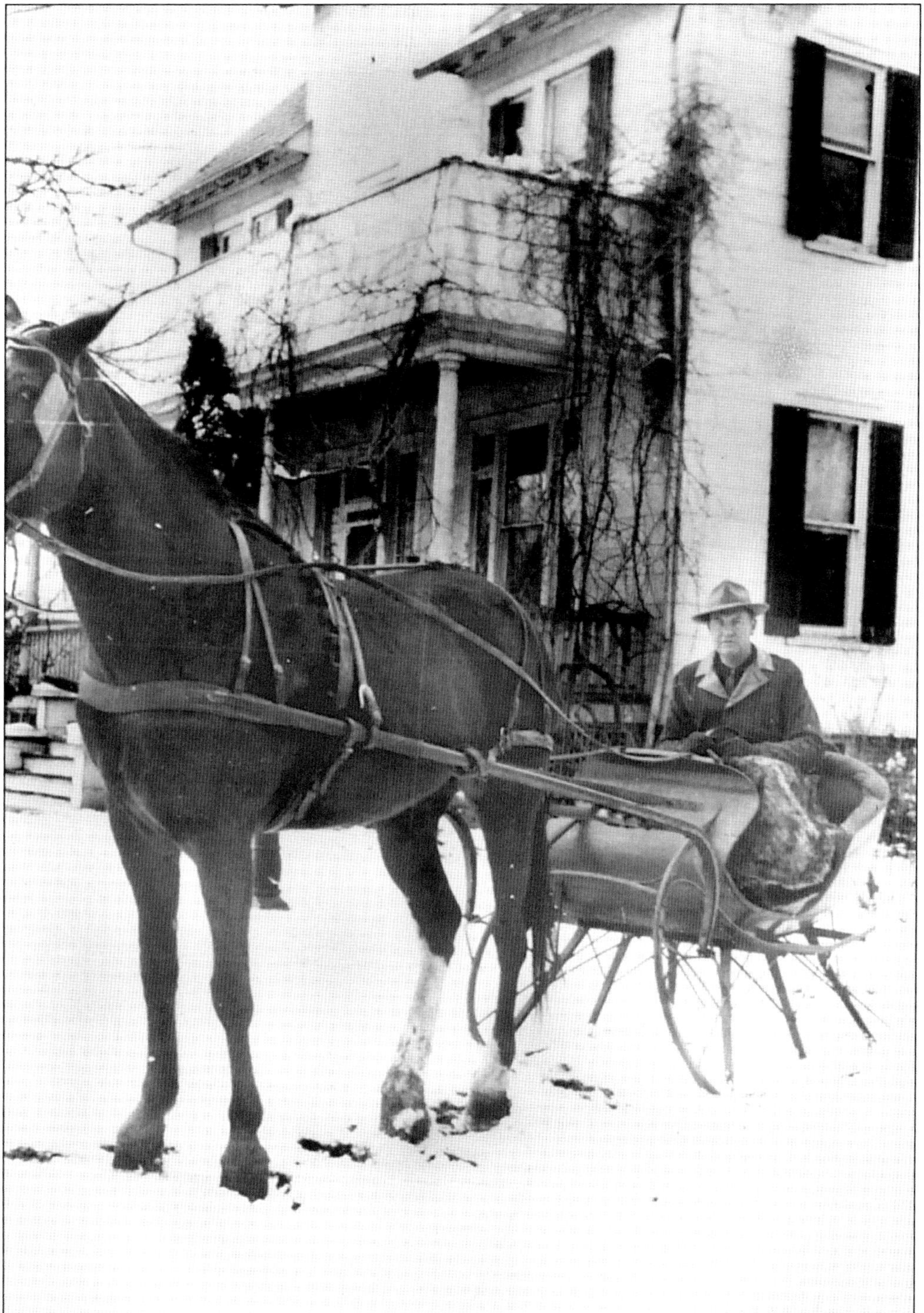

A familiar c. 1940 site after a snowfall was that of Frank L. Portlock and his sleigh. Mr. Portlock enjoyed hitching up the horse to his sleigh and giving the children of South Norfolk a ride through the streets and fields.

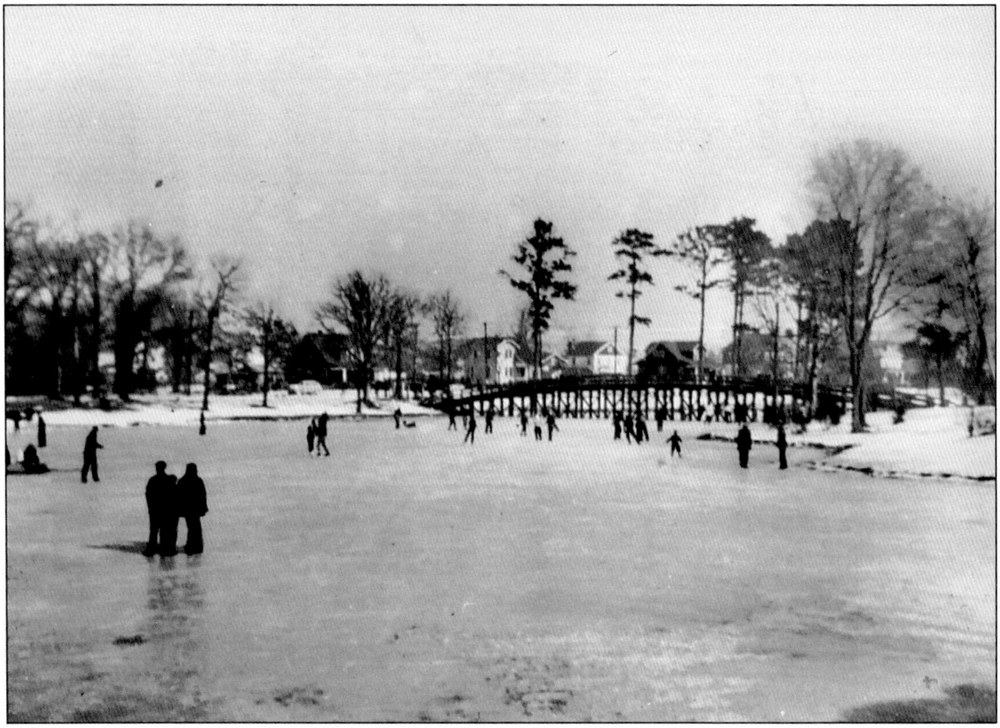

In January 1936, both children and adults enjoy an afternoon of ice skating at Lakeside Park.

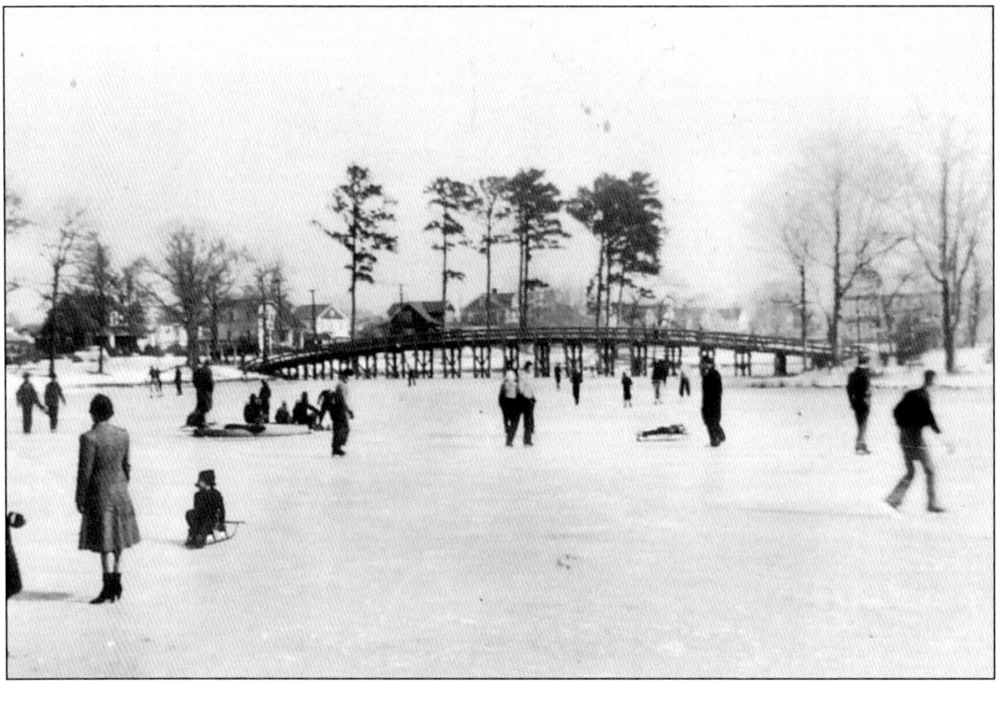

Mr. Portlock and a friend enjoy a sleigh ride in the field across from his home on Ohio Street. The home of Mr. and Mrs. D.W. Lindsey Jr. can be seen in the background, facing Decatur Street.

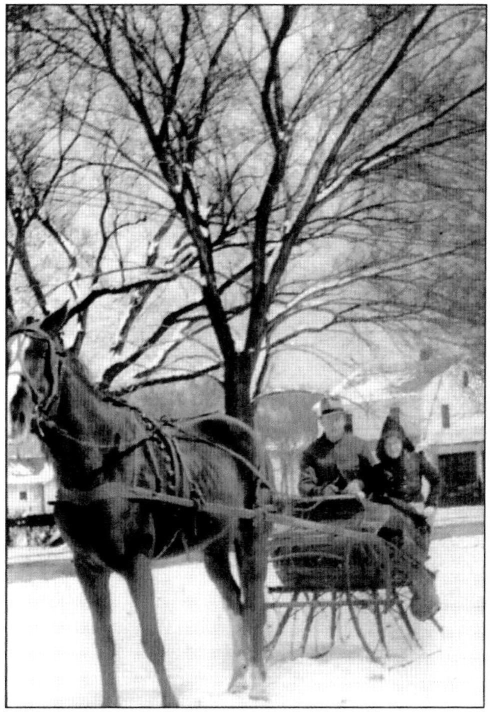

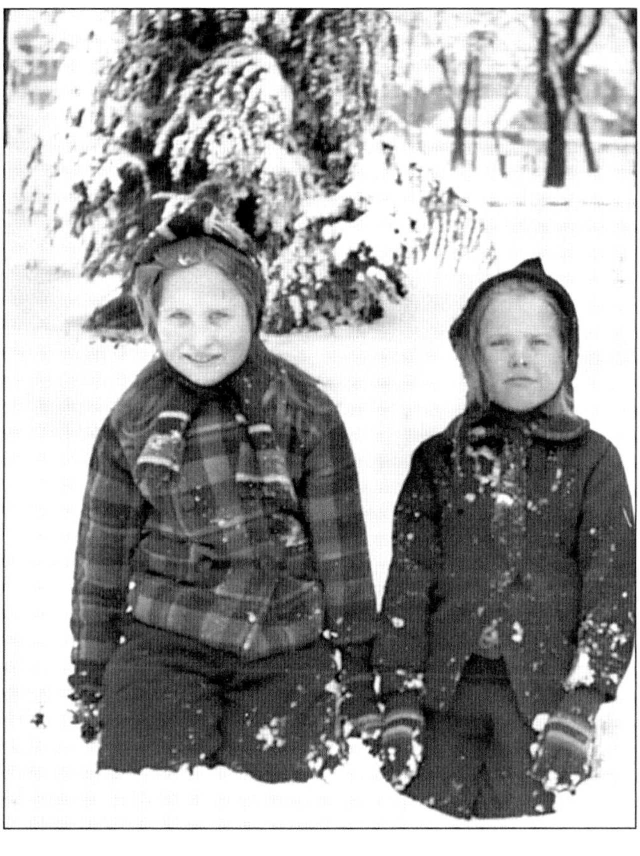

This photograph was taken after a heavy snowfall in 1941. The young ladies are, from left to right, Virginia Harper, age 10, and Marjorie Harper, age 8.

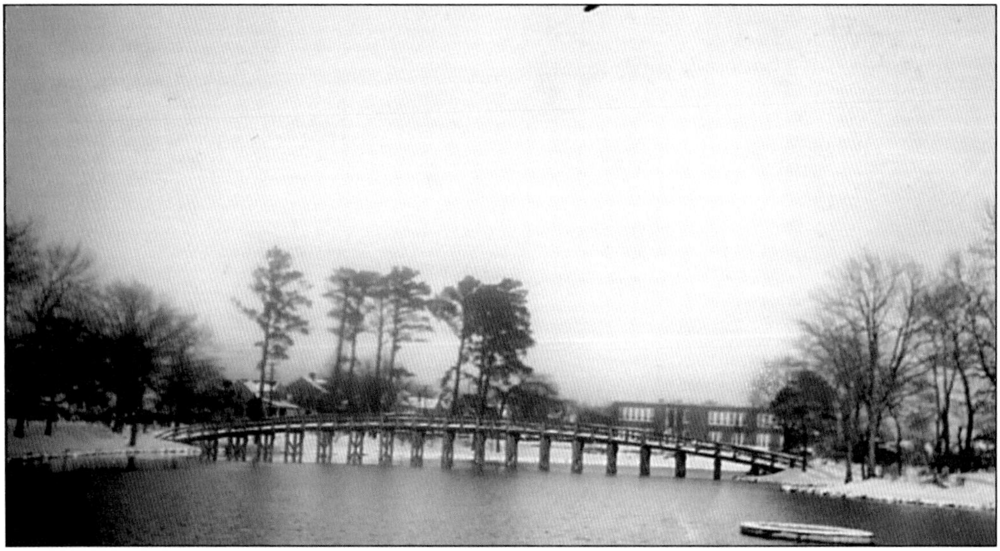

Lakeside Park on Holly Street, at the corner of Bainbridge Boulevard, provides beautiful scenery during all seasons, especially in winter. This picture of the old rustic bridge with the South Norfolk High School in the background was taken in the early 1930s.

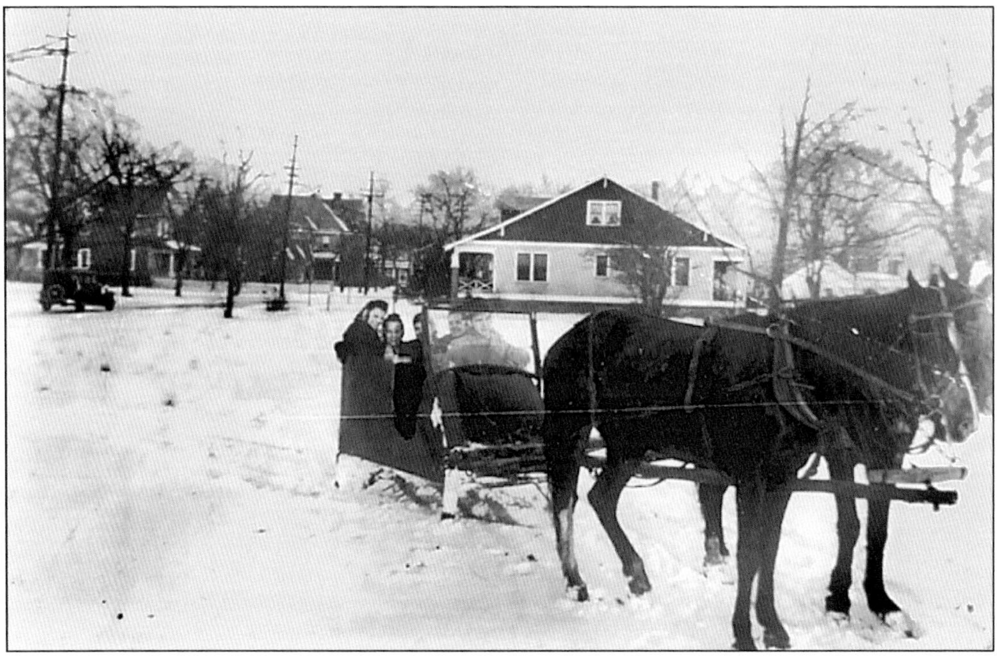

This picture was taken in the 1000 block of Ohio Street across from the Portlock home. The sleigh was built from scrap parts; the front was an old automobile windshield. The large house in the background was built by Mr. Linwood Sawyer shortly after WW II, *c.* 1947.

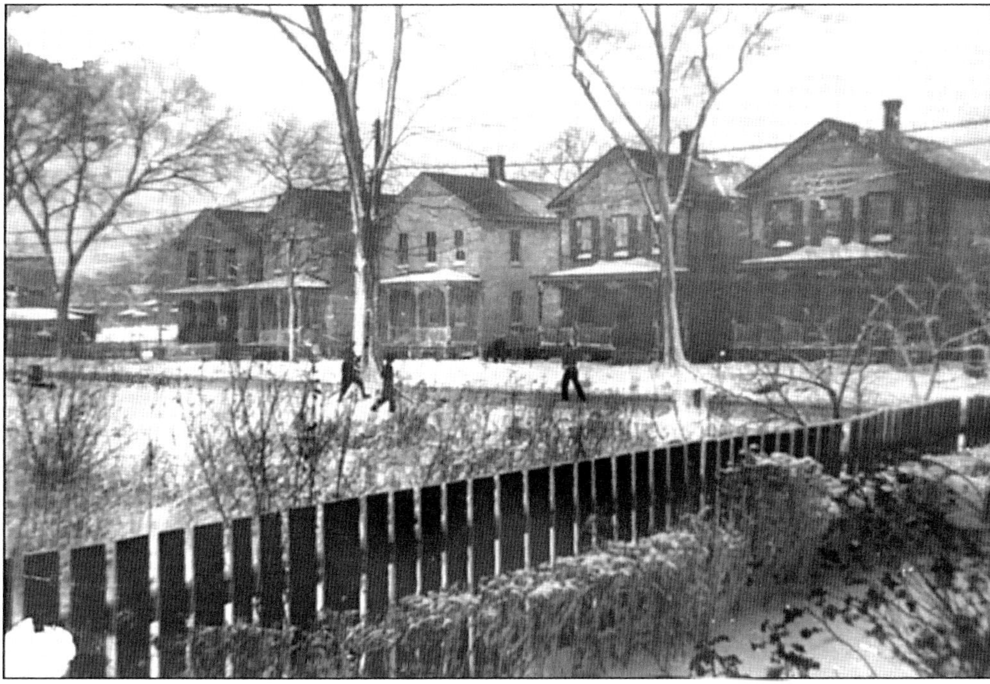

This snowball battle took place on Liberty Street near Eighteenth Street.

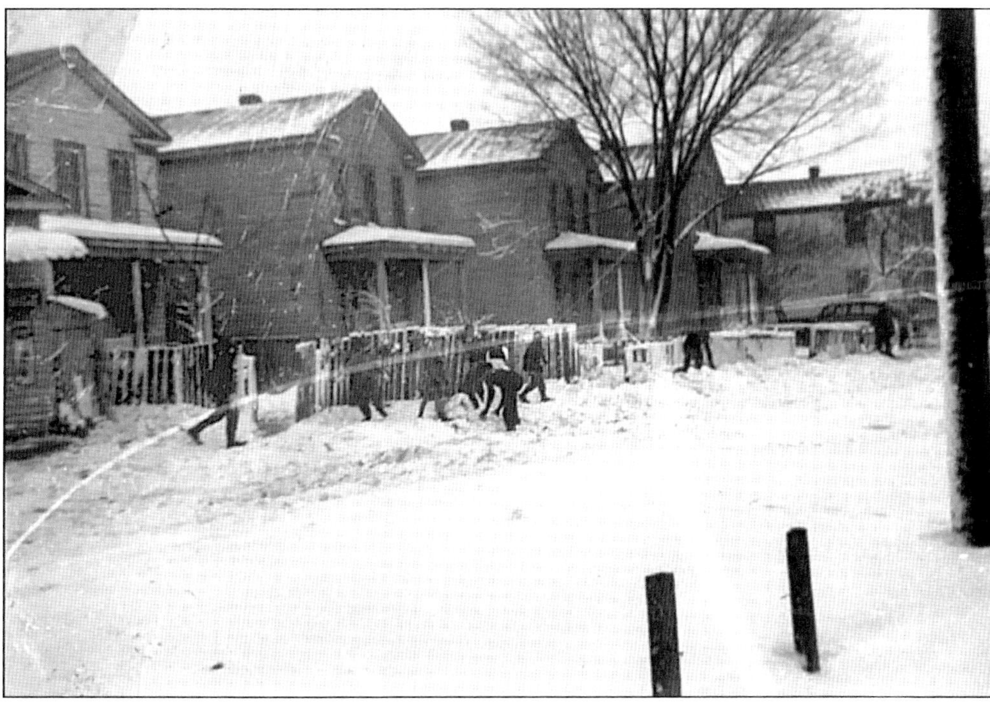

While the battle was happening on Liberty Street, the neighborhood gang back on St. James Street was having a snowball fight of their own.

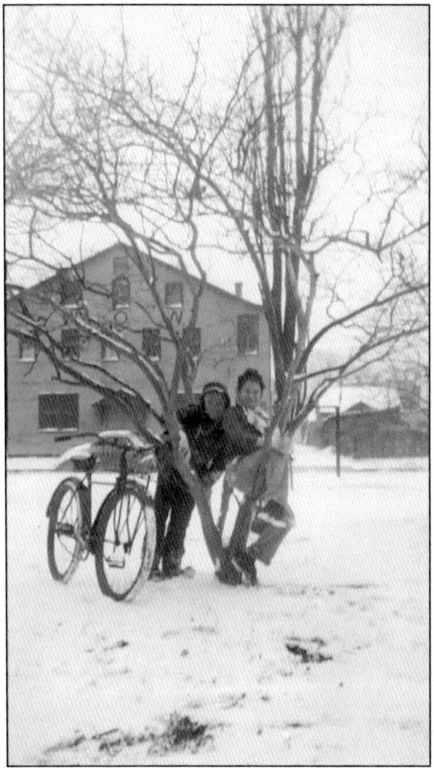

The old W.O.W. Hall on Twenty-second Street is the background for this picture of Hardy Forbes and his friend. The two boys are on the grounds of the South Norfolk Grammar School.

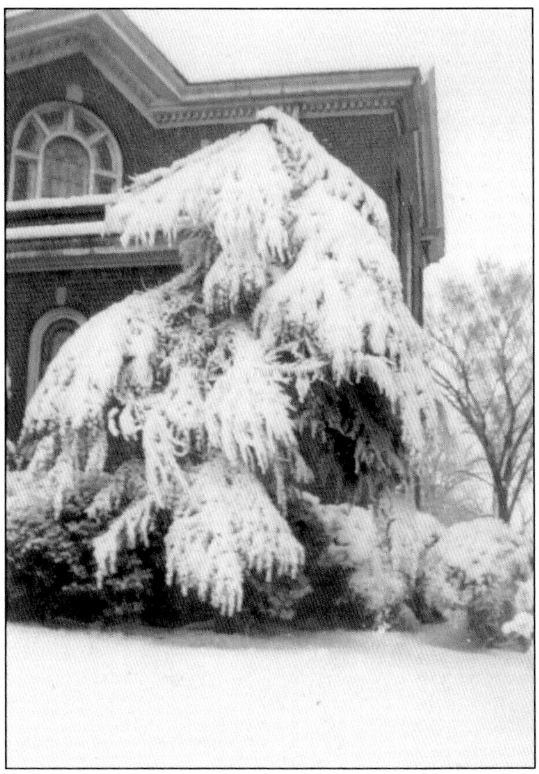

The shrubbery around the South Norfolk Baptist Church was almost at the breaking point after this heavy snowfall.

This spruce was planted in the front yard of 1119 Seaboard Avenue in 1932, and it was used for many years as the background for family pictures. This photograph shows the tree after a light snow in early 1947. The house to the left is the home of Roy and Myrtle Dozier, and the double garage in the right background belongs to the Robert Rowland family.

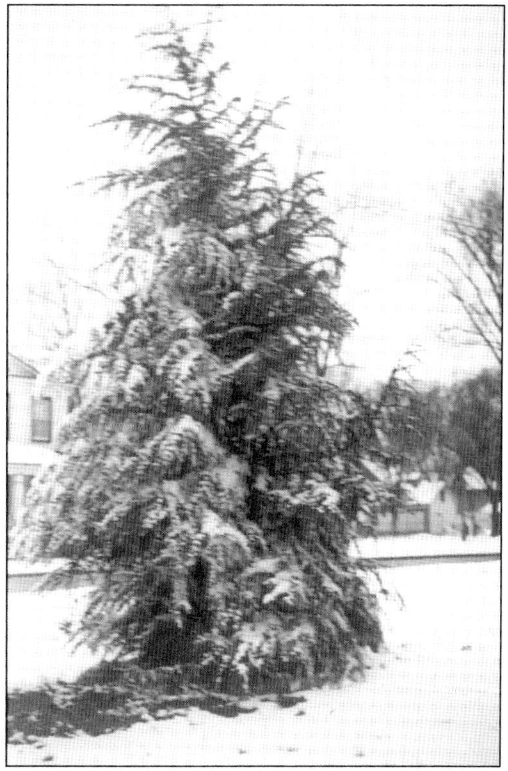

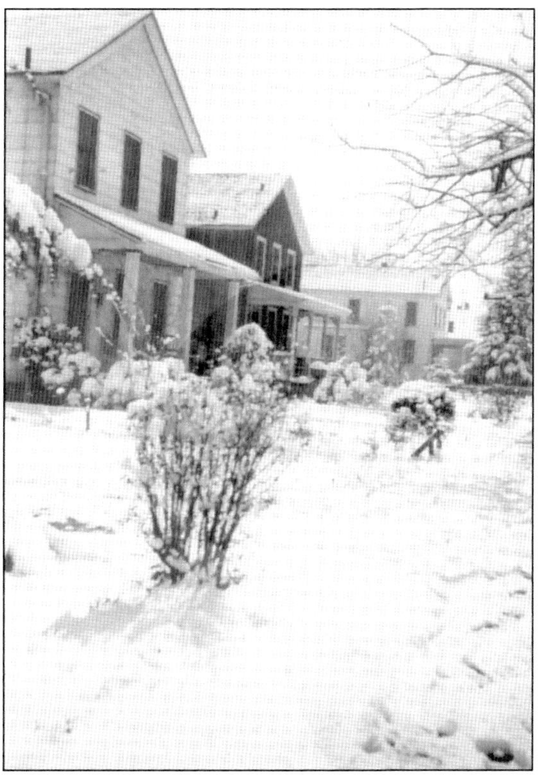

This was the old neighborhood in February 1947. The homes belong to, from left to right, the Dennis Curling family, the Lindsey family, and the Sam Taylor family.

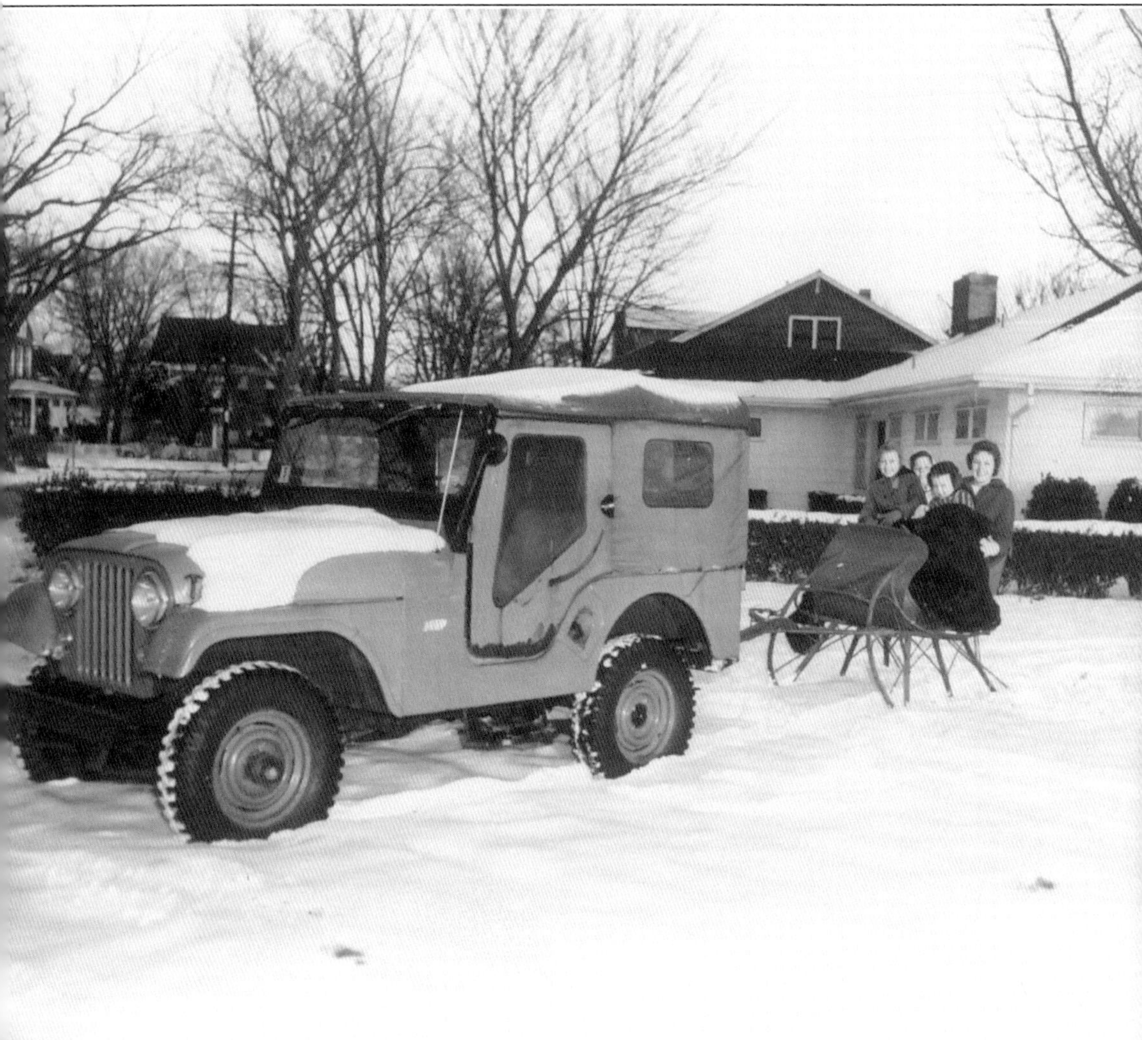

When the horse was no longer available, power for pulling the sleigh was relegated to the Jeep. In this c. 1960s picture, the children waiting for a ride in the sleigh are Beth, unidentified, Daniel Lindsey III, and Martha. The white house behind the sleigh is the home of Judge and Mrs. Jerry G. Bray.

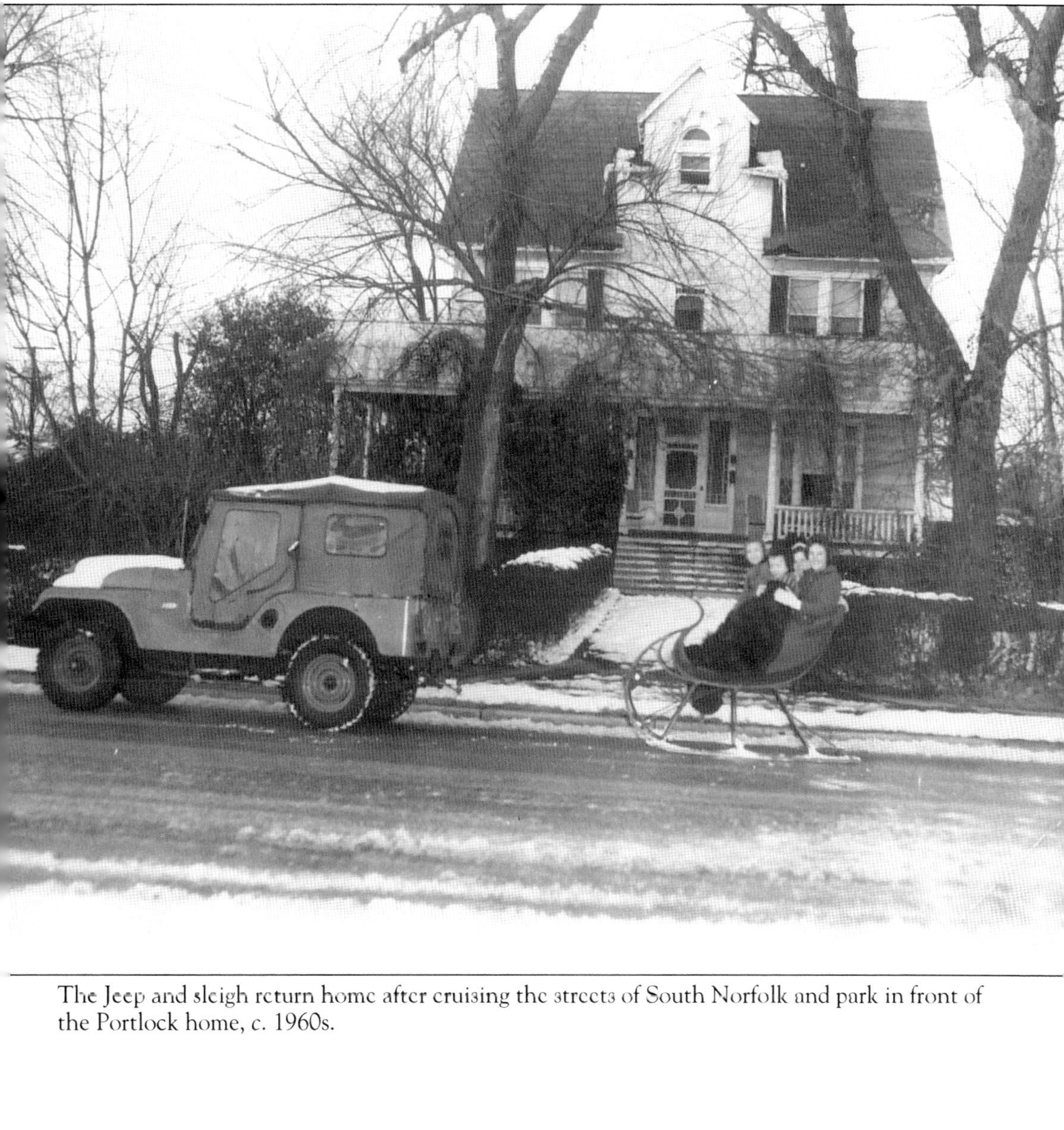

The Jeep and sleigh return home after cruising the streets of South Norfolk and park in front of the Portlock home, c. 1960s.

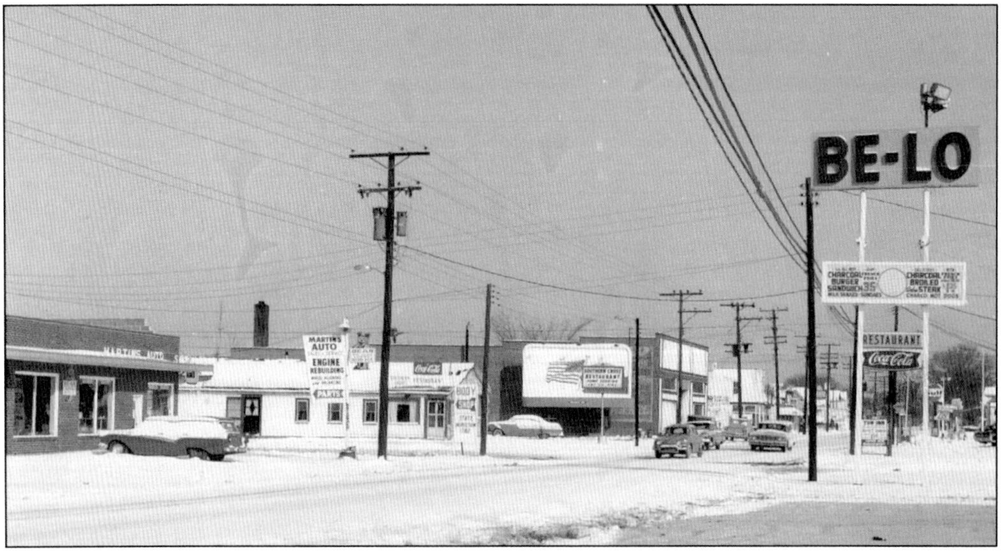

Bainbridge Boulevard in Portlock, looking north, is seen here as it appeared in February 1965, a few days after a snowstorm. It is interesting to note that one could purchase a charcoal burger for 35¢ and a charcoal-broiled steak for $1.35 at the Tum Inn. Also, gasoline was selling for 28¢ per gallon.

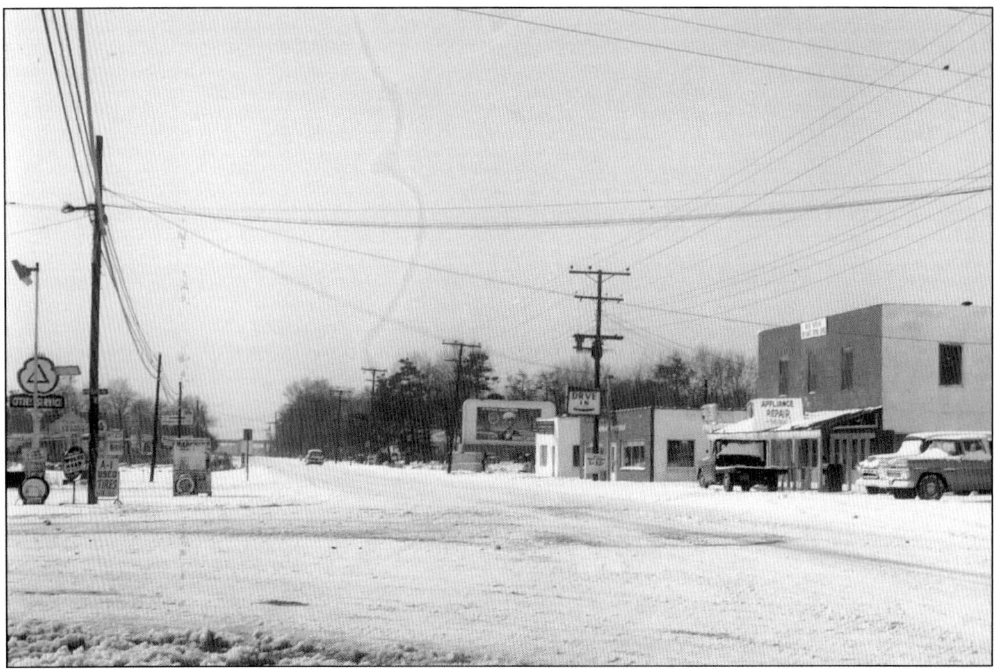

Bainbridge Boulevard, looking south towards the triple-decker overpass, was heavily covered and in need of snow removal in this February 1965 image.